10,000
GERMAN
WORDS

ALSO IN OXFORD MINIREFERENCE

10,000
GERMAN
WORDS

William Rowlinson

Oxford   New York

OXFORD UNIVERSITY PRESS

Oxford University Press, Walton Street, Oxford OX2 6DP

Oxford New York Toronto
Delhi Bombay Calcutta Madras Karachi
Kuala Lumpur Singapore Hong Kong Tokyo
Nairobi Dar es Salaam Cape Town
Melbourne Auckland Madrid

and associated companies in
Berlin Ibadan

Oxford is a trade mark of Oxford University Press

British Library Cataloguing in Publication Data

Data available

Library of Congress Cataloging in Publication Data

Rowlinson, W.
10,000 German words / William Rowlinson.
p. cm.—(Oxford minireference)
1. German language—Conversation and phrase books—English.
2. German language—Vocabulary. 3. German language—Dictionaries—
English. I. Title. II. Series.
438.2'421—dc20   PF3121.R66   93–45641
ISBN 0–19–211686–X

3 5 7 9 10 8 6 4 2

Printed in Great Britain by
Charles Letts (Scotland) Ltd.
Dalkeith, Scotland

CONTENTS

INTRODUCTION

This book contains more than 10,000 German words, phrases, and structures arranged by topic and function. They are collected under fifty-six headings ordered alphabetically, and are then further split into appropriate sub-areas.

The aim has been to make the vocabulary of a topic easily accessible and to provide the most comprehensive information possible about it. So most sub-areas are themselves divided into noun, verb, adjective, and structure sections, with items arranged alphabetically within each section. For many items, closely associated words are given in round brackets immediately after the headword.

- Genders of all head-nouns are indicated by **der/die/das**, bracketed where the noun is usually used without its article. The gender of an element in a noun phrase is shown by *m* or *f*.
- Irregular genitive singulars and all plurals of nouns that commonly take a plural are given, in square brackets after the noun.
- Feminine forms of masculine nouns (e.g. professions, occupations) are given, where they exist.
- Cases taken by prepositions are given in all prepositional constructions.
- Irregular verbs are asterisked, separable prefixes are marked off by |, inseparable ones by '.
- Main sections end with a comprehensive set of cross-references to related topics.

ABBREVIATIONS

abb	abbreviation
A	accusative
adj	adjective
adj n	adjective used as noun
colloq	colloquial
D	dative
jm	**jemandem** (somebody, *dative*)
jn	**jemanden** (somebody, *accusative*)
et	**etwas** (something)
f	feminine
G	genitive
inf	infinitive
inv	invariable
m	masculine
n	neuter
℗	proprietary term
pl	plural
sb	somebody
sing	singular
sth	something

PLURALS

If a diphthong is umlauted in the plural, the umlaut goes on the first of the two vowels (**Baum, Bäume**).

Final **ß** changes to **ss** when a plural ending is added, unless the previous vowel is long (**Biß, Bisse**; **Fuß, Füße**). A change in the plural from **ß** to **ss** is indicated thus: **Biß [-sse]**.

1. Accidents Unfälle

der Aufprall [-e] impact
die Explosion [-en] explosion
der Flugzeugabsturz [≈e]; **das Flugzeugunglück** [-e] aircraft crash
die Gehirnerschütterung concussion
das Mißgeschick [-e] mishap
das Pech bad luck (**Pech *haben bei/mit** + D have bad luck with;
  vom Pech verfolgt *sein be dogged by bad luck)
die Rücksichtslosigkeit heedlessness
der Schaden [≈] *often pl* damage (**der Schaden(s)ersatz**
  compensation; **Schaden(s)ersatz leisten für** + A compensate for)
der Schock [-s] shock
die Seenot distress at sea (**jn aus Seenot retten** rescue sb in
  distress)
der/die Tote *adj n* dead person
der Unfall [≈e] accident (**der Arbeits-/Verkehrsunfall** industrial/
  traffic accident)
die Verbrennung [-en] burn
die Vergeßlichkeit forgetfulness
die Verletzung [-en] injury (**der/die Verletzte** *adj n* injured
  person)
der Zeuge [-n]/**die Zeugin** [-nen] witness (**der Augenzeuge/die
  Augenzeugin** eye-witness; **der Augenzeugenbericht** [-e] eye-
  witness report)
der Zufall [≈e] chance; coincidence
der Zusammenstoß [≈e]; **der Zusammenprall** [-e] collision

be'schädigen damage
das Bewußtsein *ver'lieren lose consciousness
*davon|kommen (**mit** + D) escape (with)
demolieren demolish
er'sticken suffocate
explodieren explode
kaputt|machen destroy

*sterben die (seinen Verletzungen *f* D *pl* *er'liegen die of one's injuries)
töten; *um|bringen kill
*um|kommen get killed
ums Leben *kommen lose one's life
*ver'gessen forget
*ver'lieren lose
ver'ursachen cause
*zer'brechen break
zer'stören smash up; destroy
*zusammen|stoßen; zusammen|prallen collide

betrunken drunk
eingeschlossen [person]; eingeklemmt [part of body] trapped
gedankenlos thoughtless
leichtsinnig reckless
sicher und wohlbehalten safe and sound
tot dead
unaufmerksam inattentive
ungeschickt clumsy
unversehrt unscathed
unvorsichtig careless
verletzt injured (leicht slightly; schwer seriously)
zerstreut absent-minded

Verkehrsunfälle und Eisenbahnunglücke
Road and rail accidents

Alkohol *m* am Steuer drunken driving (das Steuer [-] steering-wheel; unter Alkoholeinfluß *m* under the influence of alcohol; die Alkoholkontrolle [-n] breath test; der Führerscheinentzug [≈e] disqualification; driving ban)
das Eisenbahnunglück [-e] rail accident
die Entgleisung [-en] derailment
die Geldstrafe [-n] fine
das Glatteis black ice

die **Massenkarambolage** [-n] pile-up

die **Müdigkeit** fatigue (***leiden an** + D suffer from)

der **Nebel** fog (**die schlechte Sicht** poor visibility)

der **Prellblock** [railway] buffers

das **Rasen** speeding (**die Geschwindigkeitsüberschreitung** [-en] [legal term] (case of) speeding)

die **Reifenpanne** [-n]; **der Platte** *adj n* puncture

der **Straßenzustand** state of the road

der **Totalschaden** write off (**Totalschaden *ent'steht an** + D . . . is a write-off)

das **Überholen** overtaking (**beim Überholen** when overtaking)

der **Verkehrsrowdy** [-s] road-hog

der **Verkehrsunfall** [ˉe] traffic accident

das **Versagen** failure (**die Bremsen ver'sagen** the brakes fail)

der **Zusammenstoß** [ˉe] crash (**der Frontalzusammenstoß** head-on crash)

be'schleunigen accelerate

ent'gleisen be derailed

*fahren gegen + A run into

die **Kontrolle *ver'lieren** lose control

die **näheren Umstände *auf|schreiben** take the particulars

platzen burst

riskieren risk (**sein Leben in Gefahr *bringen** risk one's life)

das **Rotlicht** [-er]/**das Signal** [-e] ***über'fahren** go through the red light/signal

schlittern; [more serious] **schleudern** skid (**ins Schleudern *ge'raten** go into a skid)

*über'fahren run over

über'holen overtake (**in der Kurve** on the bend)

sich ***über'schlagen** turn over

die **Vorfahrt nicht be'achten** ignore priority; not give way

Unfälle auf See Accidents at sea

das **Ertrinken** drowning

der/die **Ertrunkene** *adj n* drowned person

die Kollision [-en] collision [between ships] (**auf Kollisionskurs** *m* on a collision course)

die Mannschaft [-en] crew

das Rettungsboot [-e] lifeboat (**das Rettungsfloß** [ӫe] life-raft; **der Rettungsring** [-e] lifebelt)

der Schiffbruch shipwreck (**Schiffbruch *er'leiden** be shipwrecked)

die Schwimmweste [-n] life-jacket

*er'trinken drown

gegen einen Felsen/eine Mine/einen Eisberg *laufen hit a rock/ mine/iceberg

kollidieren collide [of ships]

retten rescue

*schwimmen to swim (**schwimmen *können** be able to swim)

*sinken sink

unter der Wasserlinie leckgeschlagen *sein be holed under the waterline

Flugzeugunglücke Aircraft accidents

der Absturz [ӫe] crash

die Bruchlandung [-en] crash-landing

der Fallschirm [-e] parachute

der Irrtum [ӫer] **des Piloten** pilot error

das Luftloch [ӫer] air pocket

die Metallermüdung metal fatigue

der Motorschaden engine trouble

der Notausgang [ӫe] emergency exit

die Notlandung [-en] forced landing

der Steward [-s] steward (**die Stewardeß** [-ssen] stewardess)

die Turbulenz turbulence

aus|setzen fail [engine]

bruch|landen *inf and past part. only* crash-land

landen land (**im Bach landen** *colloq* ditch)

notlanden *inf and past part.*(**notgelandet**) *only* do an emergency landing

Unfälle im Haushalt Accidents in the home

das Feuer [-] fire (**der Rauchmelder** [-] smoke alarm; **die Feuertreppe** [-n] fire-escape)

der Stromschlag [≈e] electric shock (**einen Stromschlag *be'kommen** get an electric shock; **durch Stromschlag getötet *werden** be electrocuted)

der Sturz [≈e] (**aus/von** + D) fall (from)

*fallen fall (***fallen|lassen** drop)

sich [D] **den Knöchel** [etc.] **ver'stauchen/*brechen** sprain/break one's ankle [etc.]

sich *schneiden an + D cut oneself on (**sich** [D or A] **in den Finger** [etc.] **schneiden** cut one's finger [etc.])

*um|stoßen knock over

sich *ver'brennen burn oneself

sich ver'brühen scald oneself

ver'schütten spill

Die Notdienste Emergency services

der Abschleppwagen [-] breakdown truck (**der Abbschleppdienst** recovery service)

der Arzt [≈e]/**die Ärztin** [-nen] doctor

die Erste Hilfe first aid

der Feuerlöscher [-] fire extinguisher

die Feuerwehr fire brigade (**der Feuerwehrmann** [pl ≈er or -leute] fireman; **die Leiter** [-n] ladder; **der Schlauch** [≈e] hose)

die Hilfe help

der Krankenwagen [-] ambulance

die Mund-zu-Mund-Beatmung kiss of life (**der Mund** [≈er] mouth)

der Notfall [≈e] emergency

der Pannendienst breakdown service

die Polizei police

der Rettungsdienst ambulance service (**der Seerettungsdienst** lifeboat service)

der/die Sanitäter/in [-/-nen] ambulance man/woman

6 ACCIDENTS

die Trage [-n] stretcher
der Verbandskasten [¨]; **die Erste-Hilfe-Ausrüstung** first-aid kit
die Versicherung [-en] insurance

ab|schleppen tow away
Bereitschaftsdienst *m* ***haben** be on call
einen Bericht er'statten make a report
einen Krankenwagen kommen *lassen call an ambulance
die Polizei *an|rufen call the police (**110** [eins eins null] **wählen**
  dial 999)

SEE ALSO: **Birth, Marriage, and Death; Disasters; Health and
  Sickness; The Human Body**

2. Adornment Verschönerung

Make-up Make-up

der Augenbrauenstift [-e] eyebrow pencil (**die Augenbraue [-n]** eyebrow)

der Entferner [-] remover

der Eyeliner [-] eye-liner

die Feuchtigkeitscreme [-s] moisturizer

die Gesichtscreme [-s] face cream (**das Gesicht [-er]** face)

der Gesichtspuder face-powder (**die Puderdose [-n]** compact; **die Puderquaste [-n]** powder-puff)

die Grundierungscreme [-s] foundation cream

der Körperpuder talcum powder (**der Körper [-]** body)

die Kosmetik beauty culture

der Lidschatten eye-shadow (**das Lid [-er]** eyelid)

die Lippenpomade [-n] lipsalve

der Lippenstift [-e] lipstick (**die Lippe [-n]** lip)

der Lockenwickler [-] curler

das Make-up make-up

das Mascara; die Wimperntusche mascara

die Nagelfeile [-n] nail-file (**der Nagel [¨]** nail; **die Sandpapierfeile** emery board)

der Nagellack nail varnish (**der Nagellackentferner** nail-varnish remover)

die Nagelschere [-n] (pair of) nail scissors

die Nagelzange [-n] (pair of) nail clippers

das Papiertuch [¨er] paper tissue

die Pinzette [-n] (pair of) tweezers

das Rouge blusher

die Schönheit beauty (**der Schönheits-/Kosmetiksalon [-s]** beauty salon; **die Schönheitsprodukte** *n pl*; **die Kosmetika** *n pl* cosmetics)

der Spiegel [-] mirror

sich ab|schminken take off one's make-up
*auf|tragen auf + A put on [lipstick etc.]
sich [D] **die Fingernägel lackieren** varnish one's nails
sich schminken make up (one's face)
sich zurecht|machen put on one's make-up

Schmuck Jewellery

der Anhänger [-] pendant
die Anstecknadel [-n] pin
das Armband [ˀer] bracelet (**das Glieder-/Amulettarmband** chain/
charm bracelet)
die Armbanduhr [-en] (wrist-)watch
der Armreif(en) [-e/-] bangle
die Brosche [-n] brooch
das Diadem [-e] tiara
das Halsband [ˀer] choker
das/der Juwel [-en]; [more valuable] **der Edelstein** [-e] jewel
[= precious stone] (**das Schmuckstück** [-e] jewel [= ornament];
der Halbedelstein semi-precious stone; **künstlich**; **Kunst-**
imitation)
die Kette/Halskette [-n]; **das Kollier** [-s] necklace
das Kettchen [-] (neck-)chain; chain-bracelet
der Klipp [-s]/**der Clip** [-s] clip (**der Ohr(en)klipp** ear-clip)
der Krawattenhalter [-] tie-clip
die Krawattennadel [-n] tie-pin
das Kreuz [-e] cross
die Krone [-n] crown
der Manschettenknopf [ˀe] cuff-link
der Ohrring [-e] ear-ring (**das Ohrgehänge** [-] drop ear-ring)
der Ring [-e] ring (**der Trau-/Ehering** wedding-ring; **der
Verlobungs-/Siegelring** engagement/signet ring)
der Schmuck jewellery (**der Modeschmuck** costume jewellery)
der Schmuckkasten [ˀ] jewel box
die Tiara [pl Tiaren] tiara
die Uhr [-en] watch (**die Quarz/Digitaluhr** quartz/digital watch)

Edelsteine und Metalle Jewels and Metals

der Amethyst [-e] amethyst

der Bernstein amber

das Chrom chromium (**verchromt** chrome-plated)

der Diamant [-en] diamond

das Elfenbein [substance] ivory (**eine Elfenbeinschnitzerei [-en]** an ivory [object]; **elfenbeinern** ivory adj)

die Emaille/das Email enamel (**emailliert** enamel adj)

das Gold gold (**golden** gold(en); **vergoldet** gold-plated; gilt)

der/die Jade jade

die Koralle [-n] coral (**korallen** coral adj)

das Kristall crystal [glass] (**der Kristall [-e]** crystal [formation])

das Kupfer copper (**kupfern** copper adj)

der Onyx [-e] onyx

die Perle [-n] pearl; bead (**die Perlenkette [-n]** pearl necklace; string of beads)

der Pewter pewter

das Platin platinum

der Rubin [-e] ruby

der Saphir [-e] sapphire

das Silber silver (**silbern** silver adj; **versilbert** silver-plated)

der Smaragd [-e] emerald

der Stahl steel (**rostfrei** stainless; **der Edelstahl** stainless steel)

der Straß [-sse]; der Similistein [-e] imitation gem

der Topas [-e] topaz

der Türkis [-e] turquoise

das Zinn tin; pewter

Parfüm Perfume

das Badesalz bath salts (**das Schaumbad** bubble bath)

das Deodorant [pl -s or -e] deodorant

das Eau de Cologne; das Kölnisch Wasser eau-de-Cologne

das Parfüm/Parfum [-s] perfume; scent

das/der Spray [-s] spray (**das/der Deospray** deodorant spray)

10 ADORNMENT

das Toilettenwasser; das Eau de Toilette toilet water

sich parfümieren put on perfume
***riechen; [pleasanter] duften nach** + D smell of

SEE ALSO: **Clothing; Describing People; Hair; The Human Body**

3. Animals Tiere

die Amphibie [-n] amphibian
das Beuteltier [-e] marsupial
der Fisch [-e] fish
das Insekt [-en] insect
das Reptil [-ien] reptile
das Säugetier [-e] mammal
das Tier [-e] animal (**das Haustier** pet)
der Vogel [ː] bird (**der Raubvogel** bird of prey; **das Geflügel** poultry)
das Weichtier [-e]; die Molluske [-n] mollusc
das Wirbeltier [-e] vertebrate (**der Evertebrat [-en]** invertebrate)
der Wurm [ːer] worm

Säugetiere Mammals

der Affe [-n] monkey
die Antilope [-n] antelope
der Bär [-en] bear (**der Eisbär** polar bear)
der Biber [-] beaver
der Bock [ːe] buck; ram; billy-goat
der Büffel [-] buffalo
der Dachs [-e] badger (**der Bau [-e]** sett)
der Delphin [-e] dolphin
das Eichhörnchen [-] squirrel
der Elefant [-en] elephant
der Esel [-] donkey
die Feld-/Wühlmaus [ːe] vole
die Fledermaus [ːe] bat
das Frettchen [-] ferret
der Fuchs [ːe] fox (**die Füchsin [-nen]** vixen)
die Gazelle [-n] gazelle
die Gemse [-n] chamois
die Giraffe [-n] giraffe

der Gorilla [-s] gorilla

der Hamster [-] hamster

der Hase [-n] hare **(die Häsin [-nen]** doe-hare)

der Hirsch [-e] deer; stag

der Hund [-e] dog **(die Hündin [-nen]** bitch; **der junge Hund** puppy; **der Schäfer-/Windhund** Alsatian/greyhound; **die Hundehütte [-n]** kennel; **wau, wau!** bow-wow!)

die Hyäne [-n] hyena

der Igel [-] hedgehog

der Iltis [-se] polecat

das Kamel [-e] camel **(das Dromedar [-e]** dromedary)

das Kaninchen [-] rabbit **(der Stall [ːe]** hutch)

die Katze [-n] cat **(der Kater [-]** tom-cat; **das Kätzchen [-]** kitten; **miau!** miaow!)

die Kuh [ːe] cow **(der Stier [-e];** **der Bulle [-n]** bull; **das Kalb [ːer]** calf; **das Rind [-er]** cow/bull; *pl* cattle; **das Vieh** cattle; **der Kuhstall [ːe]** cowshed; **muh!** moo!)

der Leopard [-en] leopard

der Löwe [-n] lion **(die Löwin [-nen]** lioness)

der Luchs [-e] lynx

das Maultier [-e] mule

der Maulwurf [ːe] mole

die Maus [ːe] mouse **(die Brand-/Haselmaus** field-mouse/dormouse)

das Meerschweinchen [-] guinea-pig

das Nashorn [ːer] rhinoceros

das Nil-/Flußpferd [-e] hippopotamus

der Ochse [-n] ox

der Otter/Fischotter [-] otter

der Panther [-] panther

das Pferd [-e] horse **(die Stute [-n]** mare; **das Fohlen [-]** foal; **das Hengstfohlen** colt; **das Arbeitspferd** cart-horse; **das Pony [-s]** pony; **der Pferdestall [ːe]** stable)

der Pudel [-] poodle

die Ratte [-n] rat

das Reh [-e] roe-deer **(das (Reh)kitz [-e]** fawn)

das Renntier [-e] reindeer

die Robbe [-n]; **der Seehund** [-e] seal
das Schaf [-e] sheep (**das Mutterschaf** ewe; **der Schafbock** [ᵆe];
  der Widder [-] ram; **das Lamm** [ᵆer] lamb; **der Schafstall** [ᵆe]
  sheep-fold; **mäh! bäh!** baa!)
das Schwein [-e] pig (**die Sau** [ᵆe] sow; **der Eber** [-] boar; **das
  Wildschwein** [-e] wild boar; **das Ferkel** [-] piglet; **der
  Schweinestall** [ᵆe] pigsty)
der Schweinswal [-e] porpoise
der Seelöwe [-n] sea-lion
das Stachelschwein [-e] porcupine
der Tiger [-] tiger (**die Tigerin** [-nen] tigress)
der Wal [-e]; **der Walfisch** [-e] whale
das Wiesel [-] weasel
der Wolf [ᵆe] wolf (**die Wölfin** [-nen] she-wolf)
das Zebra [-s] zebra
die Ziege [-n] goat (**der Ziegenbock** [ᵆe] billy-goat; **die Zicke** [-n]
  nanny-goat; **das Kitz** [-e]; **das Zicklein** [-] kid)

Vögel Birds

der Adler [-] eagle (**der Horst** [-e] eyrie)
der Alk [G -s *pl* -en] auk
die Amsel [-n] blackbird
der Beo [-s] mynah bird
der Buchfink [-en] chaffinch
der Bussard [-e] buzzard
die Dohle [-n] jackdaw
die Drossel [-n] thrush
der Eisvogel [ᵆ] kingfisher
die Elster [-n] magpie
die Ente [-n] duck (**der Enterich** [-e]; **der Erpel** [-] drake; **das
  Entenküken** [-] duckling)
die Eule [-n] owl (**der Uhu** [-s] eagle owl; **die Schleiereule** barn
  owl)
der Falke [-n] falcon
der Fink [-en] finch
der Flamingo [-s] flamingo

die Gans [¨e] goose (**der Gänserich** [-e] gander; **das Gänseküken** gosling)

der Geier [-] vulture

der Gimpel [-] bullfinch

der Habicht [-e] hawk

das Huhn [¨er] chicken; hen (**der Hahn** [¨e] cock; **die Henne** [-n] hen; **das Küken** [-] chick; **der Hühnerstall** [¨e] hen-house; **kikeriki!** cock-a-doodle-doo!)

der Ibis [-se] ibis

der Kakadu [-s] cockatoo

der Kanarienvogel [¨] canary

der Kiebitz [-e] lapwing

der Kormoran [-e] cormorant

die Krähe [-n] crow

der Kuckuck [-e] cuckoo

die Lerche [-n] lark

der Mauersegler [-] swift

die Meise [-n] tit (**die Blaumeise** blue tit)

die Möwe [-n] gull

die Nachtigall [-en] nightingale

der Papagei [G -en or -s *pl* -e(n)] parrot

der Papageientaucher [-] puffin

der Pelikan [-e] pelican

der Pfau [-en] peacock (**die Pfauhenne** [-n] peahen)

der Pinguin [-e] penguin

der Rabe [-n] raven

der Raubvogel [¨] bird of prey

das Rauhfußhuhn [¨er] grouse

der Reiher [-] heron

das Rotkehlchen [-] robin

die Saatkrähe [-n] rook

die Schwalbe [-n] swallow

der Schwan [¨e] swan

der Sittich [-e] parakeet (**der Wellensittich** budgerigar)

der Spatz [-en]; **der Sperling** [-e] sparrow

der Specht [-e] woodpecker

der Star [-e] starling

der Stieglitz [-e]; **der Distelfink** [-en] goldfinch

der Storch [ːe] stork

der Strauß [-e] ostrich

die Taube [-n] dove; pigeon (**die Ringel-/Turteltaube** wood-pigeon/turtle-dove)

das Teichhuhn [ːer] moorhen

der Truthahn [ːe]/**die Truthenne** [-n]; [especially food] **der Puter** [-]/**die Pute** [-n]/turkey(-cock)/turkey-hen

Fische und Weichtiere Fish and molluscs

der Goldfisch [-e] goldfish (**das Goldfischglas** [ːer] goldfish-bowl)

der Hai [-e]; **der Haifisch** [-e] shark

der Krake [-n] octopus

die Qualle [-n] jellyfish

der Seeigel [-] sea-urchin

das Seepferdchen [-] sea-horse

der Tintenfisch cuttlefish; octopus; squid

FOR EDIBLE FISH SEE: **Food**

Insekten Insects

die Ameise [-n] ant

die Biene [-n] bee (**die Hummel** [-n] bumble-bee; **der Bienenstock** [ːe] beehive; **der Bienenstich** [-e] bee-sting)

der Falter [-] moth; butterfly (**der Nachtfalter** moth; **die Motte** [-n] clothes moth; **der Schmetterling** [-e] butterfly; **die Raupe** [-n] caterpillar; **die Puppe** [-n] chrysalis)

die Fliege [-n] fly (**die Stuben-/Schmeißfliege** house-fly/blue-bottle)

der Floh [ːe] flea

die Grille [-n] cricket

die Heuschrecke [-n] grasshopper (**die Wanderheuschrecke** locust)

die Hornisse [-n] hornet

der Käfer [-] beetle

die Schabe/Küchenschabe [-n]; der Kakerlak [-en] cockroach
die Larve [-n] grub
die Laus [≃e] louse
die Libelle [-n] dragon-fly
die Made [-n] maggot
der Maikäfer [-] cockchafer
der Marienkäfer [-] ladybird
der Moskito [-s] mosquito
die Mücke/Stechmücke [-n] midge; gnat; mosquito
die Pferdebremse [-n] horse-fly
die Schnake [-n]; der Weberknecht [-e] daddy-long-legs
die Spinne [-n] spider (das Spinnennetz [-e] spider's web)
die Wanze [-n] bug
die Wespe [-n] wasp
die Zikade [-n] cicada

Reptilien, Amphibien und Würmer
Reptiles, amphibians, and worms

der Alligator [G -s *pl* -en] alligator
die Blindschleiche [-n] slow-worm; blindworm
die Boa [-s] boa
der Egel/Blutegel [-] leech
die Eidechse [-n] lizard
der Frosch [≃e] frog (die Kaulquappe [-n] tadpole)
die Kobra [-s] cobra
das Krokodil [-e] crocodile
die Kröte [-n] toad
die Meeres-/Wasserschildkröte [-n] turtle
die Pythonschlange [-n] python
die Ringelnatter [-n] grass snake
die Schildkröte [-n] tortoise
die Schlange [-n] snake (die Klapperschlange rattlesnake)
die Seidenraupe [-n] silkworm
die Viper [-n]; die (Kreuz)otter [-n] viper; adder
der Wurm [≃er] worm (der Regenwurm earthworm)

Beuteltiere Marsupials

das Känguruh [-s] kangaroo
der Koala [-s] koala

Ihre Körper Their bodies

das Bein [-e] leg
der Beutel [-] pouch [of marsupial] (**der Kehlsack [ːe]** pouch [of pelican])
die Feder [-n] feather
das Fell [-e] coat; fur (**der Pelz [-e]** skin; fur [when dead])
der Flecken [-] spot
die Flosse [-n] fin
der Flügel [-] wing
das Geweih [-e] (set of) antlers
das Haar [-e] hair
das Haus [ːer] shell [of snail]
der Höcker [-] hump
das Horn [ːer] horn
der Huf [-e] hoof (**das Hufeisen [-]** horseshoe)
die Kieme [-n] *sing rare* gill
die Kralle [-n]; die Klaue [-n] claw; talon
die Mähne [-n] mane
das Maul [ːer] mouth
der Panzer [-] shell [of tortoise, turtle]
die Pfote [-n]; die Tatze [-n] paw (**die Pranke [-n]** paw [of lion, tiger, bear])
der Rüssel [-] trunk; proboscis; snout [of pig]
der Schnabel [ː] beak; bill
die Schnauze [-n] muzzle; snout [of mouse]
die Schuppe [-n] scale
der Schwanz [ːe] tail
der Stachel [-n] spine
der Stoßzahn [ːe] tusk
der Streifen [-] stripe

das Vlies [-e]; **das Schaffell** [-e] fleece
das Vorderbein [-e] front leg (**das Hinterbein** back leg)

Ihre Rufe Their calls

bellen bark
blöken bleat; low
brüllen bellow; roar
brummen growl [bear]; buzz [insect]
gackern; **glucken** cluck
grunzen grunt
gurren coo
iahen bray
kläffen yap
kollern gobble
knurren growl
krähen caw; crow
meckern bleat
miauen miaow; mew
muhen moo
piepsen cheep
quaken quack
quiek(s)en squeal
schnattern cackle; chatter
schnurren purr
*****schreien** howl; bray; screech; hoot
*****singen** sing
trompeten trumpet
tschilpen [sparrow]; **zirpen** [cricket] chirp
wiehern whinny; neigh
zischen hiss
zwitschern twitter

Was sie tun What they do

der Biß [-sse] bite
der Stich [-e] sting; bite [mosquito]
die Verbrennung [-en] sting [jellyfish]

auf|richten; spitzen prick up [ears]

*beißen bite (**Vorsicht, bissiger Hund!** beware of the dog!)

blecken bare [teeth]

einen Buckel machen arch its back

Eier *n pl* **legen** lay eggs

flattern flutter

*fliegen fly

*fressen eat (**das Hunde-/Katzenfutter** dog/cat food)

sich häuten cast its skin

hüpfen; [hare] hoppeln hop

*kriechen crawl

*laufen run

ein Nest [-er] bauen build a nest

einen Satz machen/*tun leap

sich schlängeln wriggle

*schleichen slink; creep

schwärmen swarm

schweben hover

*schwimmen swim

segeln soar

*springen jump

*stechen sting

*trompeten trumpet

sich ver'wandeln in + A change into

wedeln (mit dem Schwanz *m***)** wag (tail)

Was wir ihnen antun What we do to them

der Blinden(führ)hund [-e] guide-dog

die Jagd [-en] hunting (**die Fuchs-/Hirschjagd** fox/stag-hunting; **jagen** hunt)

der Käfig [-e] cage

das Pferderennen [-] horse-race (**der Pferderennsport** horse-racing)

das Reiten (horse-)riding (**der Ritt [-e]** ride; **der Zügel [-]** rein; **der Sattel [ˇ]** saddle)

der Stierkampf [≃e] bullfight
der Wachhund [-e] guard dog (**be'wachen** guard)

eine Falle legen / (**auf**)**stellen** set a trap (**in einer Falle *fangen** trap)
*frei|lassen set free (**der/die Tierrechtler/in** [-/-**nen**] animal-rights activist)
gehorsam/zahm *sein be obedient/tame
Männchen machen sit up and beg
*melken milk
Nester n pl ***aus|nehmen** rob birds' nests
Pfötchen *geben shake hands; put out a paw
*reiten ride (**zu Pferd** on horseback)
*scheren shear
streicheln stroke

nieder!; **leg dich!** down!
sitz!; **Platz!** sit!

SEE ALSO: **Food**; **Nature**

4. Arguments For and Against
Argumente für und gegen

das Argument [-e] argument
die Debatte [-n] debate
der Dialog [-e] dialogue
die Diskussion [-en] discussion
der Einwand (gegen + A) criticism (of); objection (to)
die Erklärung [-en] statement
das Gespräch [-e]; die Unterhaltung [-en] conversation
die Idee [-n] idea
die Kritik [-en] (an + D) criticism (of)
die Meinung [-en]; die Ansicht [-en] opinion
das Mißverständnis [-se] misunderstanding
der Standpunkt [-e] point of view
der Streit no pl argument (**immer Streit *haben** be always
 arguing)

Argumente für Arguments for

be'einflussen influence
be'tonen emphasize
er'klären state; declare
er'wähnen mention
hinzu|fügen add
informieren inform
recht *haben be right
ver'teidigen defend
*voraus|sehen predict
wahr *sein be true/right
wieder'holen repeat
zu|stimmen agree

als Beispiel by way of example
auf alle Fälle in any case

auf den ersten Blick at first sight
aus gutem Grund with good reason
das hat zur Folgen, daß the consequence of that is
das sind nackte Tatsachen these are hard facts
den Standpunkt vertreten, daß take the view that
den Tatsachen ins Auge sehen face the facts
einfach weil for the simple reason that
ein Grund mehr, zu . . . all the more reason to . . .
es besteht kein Zweifel, daß there's no question that
es geht nur darum, zu . . . it's only a question of . . . ing
es geht um + A it concerns
es hängt davon ab, ob it depends on whether
es ist genau wie it's just the same as
es ist so viel leichter, zu . . . it's so much easier to . . .
es wäre viel besser, wenn it would be much better if
ganz abgesehen davon, daß quite apart from the fact that
große Fortschritte machen make great strides
ich gebe gern zu, daß I'm ready to admit that
im allgemeinen in general
immer besser better and better
in diesem Fall in that case
in diesem Moment at this moment in time
in erster Linie geht es darum, daß/zu the first priority is to
infolgedessen as a result (of this)
laut Meinungsumfragen according to opinion polls
man darf nicht vergesssen, daß one must not forget that
man muß auch damit rechnen, daß one must also take into
  account the fact that
meinerseits; von mir aus for my part; as far as I'm concerned
meines Erachtens; meiner Meinung/Ansicht nach in my view
natürlich; selbstverständlich of course
nicht nur . . . sondern auch not only . . . but also
offen gesagt to be frank
sicher ist, daß what is certain, is that
sowohl . . . als auch both . . . and
sozusagen so to speak; as it were
Tatsache ist, daß the fact is that

um so mehr, weil all the more so because
und außerdem moreover
Ursache davon ist vor allem that is due above all to
von + D ganz zu schweigen not to mention
vor allem above all
was auffällt, ist what strikes one is
was . . . betrifft as far as . . . is concerned
wenn nötig if necessary
wir können es als gegeben annehmen, daß we can take it for
  granted that
zunächst einmal first and foremost
zweifellos undoubtedly

Argumente gegen Arguments against

ab|lehnen decline; reject
antworten answer (**be'antworten** answer sth)
be'haupten claim
*be'streiten contest; deny (**sich *streiten** argue)
be'zweifeln doubt
*ein|wenden object
ent'gegnen (+ D) reply (to); retort
falsch *sein be wrong (fact) (**unrecht *haben** be wrong [person])
kritisieren criticize
täuschen deceive
*über'treiben exaggerate
ver'leumden slander
vor|täuschen pretend; feign
wider'legen refute
*wider'sprechen contradict

aber; jedoch however
andererseits on the other hand
angenommen, (daß) assuming that
auf alle Fälle in any case
auf keinen Fall on no account
aus keinem ersichtlichen Grund for no obvious reason

dagegen läßt sich vieles einwenden there's a lot to be said against that

da liegt das Problem nicht that's not where the problem lies

das glauben Sie selbst nicht you can't be serious

das ist doch kaum zu glauben that's incredible

das ist ein sehr negativer Standpunkt that's a very negative point of view

das ist etwas ganz anderes that's something else again

das ist zu nichts nütze that serves no useful purpose

das wäre der allerschlimmste Ausgang that would be the worst possible outcome

das will nicht sagen, daß that doesn't mean that

eine schwache Stelle in der Argumentation a weak point in the argument

es hat nichts damit zu tun it has nothing to do with that

es ist eigentlich schade, denn it's rather a pity, because

es ist nicht der Fall it isn't the case

es wäre besser, wenn it would be better if

es wird sicher nicht genug sein, zu it certainly won't be enough to

ganz im Gegenteil quite the reverse

ich bin nicht ganz einverstanden (mit + D) I'm not entirely in agreement (with sb/sth)

ich frage mich, ob I wonder whether

im besten Fall at best

immerhin all the same

in gleicher Weise equally; in the same way

in Wirklichkeit in reality

man könnte genausogut sagen one might just as well say

nicht so sehr not as much as all that

ohne . . . zu erwähnen not counting . . .

sicher, aber certainly, but

Sie stellen mich vor vollendete Tatsachen you're presenting me with a *fait accompli*

Sie werden doch zugeben müssen, daß you must admit that

was noch merkwürdiger ist what is even more extraordinary

weit entfernt far from it

wie die Frage, so die Antwort ask a silly question and you'll get a silly answer

wir neigen zu sehr dazu, zu . . . we tend too much to . . .

Zu einem Schluß kommen
Drawing a conclusion

sich auf|regen (über + A) get worked up (about)

kapieren *colloq* understand; follow

über'reden persuade

über'zeugen convince

***ver'stehen** understand (**zu verstehen *geben** give to understand)

auf jeden Fall at all events

das wird keine Probleme aufwerfen that will pose no problems

deshalb therefore

deswegen for that reason; that's why

einerseits . . . andererseits; auf der einen Seite . . . auf der anderen Seite on the one hand . . . on the other hand

ein für allemal once and for all

fest steht jedenfalls: this much is certain:

ich jedenfalls I for one

im allgemeinen in general

im schlimmsten Fall; schlimmstenfalls if the worst comes to the worst

in höherem/geringerem Maße to a greater/lesser extent

klar ist, daß what is clear, is

kurz gesagt in short

letztendlich in the end

letzten Endes in the event

mit anderen Worten in other words

mit einem Wort in a word

mit einer einzigen Ausnahme with a single exception

ohne weiteres (Aufhebens) without more ado

schließlich ultimately

sich grundsätzlich einigen come to a general agreement

stimmt! I agree!

teilweise partly
überzeugt convinced (**überzeugend** convincing)
was ist denn zu tun? what then is to be done?
wenn es nicht anders geht if there's no other way
**wir können nur darin übereinstimmen, daß wir nicht überein-
stimmen** we can only agree to differ
wir sind uns darüber einig we're in agreement about it
wir wollen klare Verhältnisse schaffen we must set things straight
zusammenfassend möchte ich sagen in summing up, I should like
to say

SEE ALSO: **Liking, Dislike, Comparing**

5. Art and Architecture
Kunst und Architektur

Kunst Art

der Abdruck [ᵉe] cast (**der Gipsabdruck** plaster cast)

der Akt [-e] nude [male or female]

das Aquarell [-e] [painting]; **die Wasserfarbe** [-n] [paint] water-colour

das Atelier [-s] studio

die Ausstellung [-en] exhibition

das Bild [-er] picture

der Bildhauer [-] sculptor (**die Bildhauerin** [-nen] sculptress)

die Bildhauerei; **die Plastik** sculpture [the art] (**eine Plastik** [-en]; **eine Skulptur** [-en] a sculpture [the product])

der Bildteppich [-e]; **die Tapisserie** [-n] tapestry

die Büste [-n] bust

die Farbe [-n] colour; paint (**die Ölfarben** oils)

der Firnis [-se] (picture) varnish

das Fresko [*pl* Fresken] fresco

das Gemälde [-] picture; painting

die Gemäldegalerie [-n] picture-gallery

die Glasmalerei [-en] glass-staining; stained glass

die Holzschnitzerei [-en] wood-carving [art and object]

die Karikatur [-en] caricature; cartoon

der Katalog [-e] catalogue

die Keramik [-en]; **die Töpferware** [-n] ceramic(s); pottery

die Kohle charcoal

die Kunst [ᵉe] art (**die schönen Künste** fine arts; **die bildenden Künste** the plastic arts; **das Kunstwerk** [-e] work of art)

die Kunstgalerie [-n] art gallery

der/die Künstler/in [-/-nen] artist

der Kupferstich [-e]; [the art] **die Gravierung** engraving

die Landschaft [-en] landscape (**die Landschaftsmalerei** land-scape painting)

der/die Maler/in [-/-nen] painter
die Malerei painting
die Miniatur [-en] miniature
das Modell [-e] model (**Modell *stehen/*sitzen** + D model for)
das Mosaik [G -s *pl* -en or -e] mosaic (**der Mosaikboden** [ɵ] mosaic [floor])
das Museum [*pl* Museen] museum
die Palette [-n] palette (**das Palettenmesser** [-] palette-knife)
die Pastellkreide [-n] pastel (**die Pastellzeichnung** [-en] pastel [drawing])
der Pinsel [-] brush
das Porträt [*pl* -s or -e]/**das Portrait** [-s]; **das Bildnis** [-se] portrait
der Rahmen [-] frame
die Sammlung [-en] collection (**die Kunstsammlung** art collection)
die Skizze [-n] sketch
der Sockel [-] plinth
die Staffelei [-en] easel
die Statue [-n] statue
das Stilleben [-] still-life
der Ton [-e] clay
das Zeichnen [the activity]; **die Zeichnung** [-en] [the product] drawing

be'arbeiten (**zu** + D) shape (into)
formen (**aus** + D) mould (from)
gravieren engrave
malen paint (**in Öl** in oils)
meißeln [stone]; **schnitzen** [wood] carve
posieren pose
*schaffen; kreieren create
skizzieren sketch
zeichnen draw (**nach dem Leben** *n* from life)

künstlerisch artistic
künstlich artificial
kunstvoll ornate

Architektur Architecture

der/die Architekt/in [-en/-nen] architect (**das Architektenbüro** [-s]
firm of architects)

die Architektur [-en] architecture; edifice

der Baustil [-e] architectural style

der Bogen [≈] arch

der Dom [-e] cathedral

das Gebäude [-]; **der Bau** [*pl* **Bauten**] building [edifice] (**der Bau**
no pl building [the act]; **im Bau** under construction; **bauen**
build)

das Gewölbe [-] vault

das Kapitell [-e] capital

die Kuppel [-n] cupola; dome

die Mauerstrebe [-n] buttress (**der Schwibbogen** [≈] flying
buttress)

der Pfeiler [-] pillar

die Säule [-n] column

der Säulenvorbau [*pl* **-bauten**] portico

das Schmücken [act]; **der Schmuck** [object] decoration

architektonisch architectural

barock baroque (**das Barock** baroque *noun*)

gotisch Gothic (**die Backstein-/Neogotik** Brick Gothic/Gothic
Revival)

klassisch classical

romanisch Romanesque (**die Romanik** the Romanesque)

SEE ALSO: **Cinema and Photography; Colours; Materials**

6. Birth, Marriage, and Death
Geburt, Ehe und Tod

Geburt Birth

das Baby [-s] baby (**die Babynahrung** baby food)

der/die Babysitter/in [-/-nen] baby-sitter (**das Babysitting** baby-sitting; **babysitten** *inf only* baby-sit)

die Empfängnis conception

der Fötus [-se]/der Fetus [*pl* -se *or* Feten] foetus

die Geburt [-en] birth (**feiern** celebrate; **die Geburtsanzeige [-n]** birth announcement)

das Geburtsdatum [*pl* -daten] date of birth

der Geburtstag [-e] birthday (**Geburtstag feiern** celebrate one's birthday; **das Geburtstagsgeschenk [-e]** birthday present)

der Hochstuhl [ː e] high chair

das Kinderbett [-en] cot

der Kinderwagen [-] pram

die Mutter [ː] mother

der Namenstag [-e] saint's day

der Pate/Taufpate [-n]; der Patenonkel [-] godfather (**die Patin/Taufpatin [-nen]; die Patentante [-n]** godmother; **das Patenkind [-er]** godchild; **der Patensohn [ː e]** godson; **die Patentochter [ː]** goddaughter)

die Saugflasche [-n]; das Fläschen [-] feeding-bottle

der Säugling [-e] baby; infant

der Schnuller [-] dummy

die Schwangerschaft [-en] pregnancy

der Sportwagen [-] push-chair

die Taufe [-n] christening; baptism

der Vater [ː] father

die Windel [-n] nappy (**die Wegwerfwindel** disposable nappy)

ab|stillen wean

füttern (mit + D) feed (with)

*gebären bear; give birth to (**geboren *sein** be/have been born)
stillen breast-feed
trocken|legen change [a baby]

Ehe Marriage

die Aussteuer dowry
die Braut [ᵘer] bride (**der Bräutigam** [-e] bridegroom; **das Brautpaar** [-e] bridal couple; **die Brautjungfer** [-n] bridesmaid; **das Brautkleid** [-er] wedding dress)
die Ehe [-n] marriage (**die Vernunftsehe** marriage of convenience; **die (Ehe)frau** [-en] wife; **der (Ehe)gatte** [-n]/**die (Ehe)gattin** [-nen] spouse; **der (Ehe)mann** [ᵘer] husband; **das Ehepaar** [-e] married couple; **der Ehe-/Trauring** [-e] wedding-ring; **das Ehevermittlungsinstitut** [-e] marriage bureau)
der Ehebruch adultery
der Ex-Mann [ᵘer] ex-husband (**die Ex-Frau** [-en] ex-wife; **mein Verflossener/meine Verflossene** adj n, colloq my ex)
der Familienstand marital status
der Freund [-e] boy-friend (**die Freundin** [-nen] girl-friend)
die Heirat [-en] marriage (**die Liebesheirat** love match)
der Heiratsantrag [ᵘe] proposal (**jm einen Heiratsantrag machen** propose to sb; ***an|nehmen** accept; ***ab|weisen** refuse)
die Hochzeit [-en] wedding (**die silberne/goldene Hochzeit** silver/golden wedding)
die Hochzeitseinladung [-en] wedding invitation
das Hochzeitsessen [-] wedding breakfast
das Hochzeitsgeschenk [-e] wedding present
der Hochzeitskuchen [-] wedding-cake
die Hochzeitsnacht [ᵘe] wedding-night
die Hochzeitsreise [-n] honeymoon [trip] (**die Flitterwochen** f pl honeymoon [period])
der Hochzeitstag [-e] wedding day; wedding anniversary
der Junggeselle [-n] bachelor (**die Junggesellin** [-nen] single girl; **die alte Jungfer** [-n] old maid; **der eingefleischte Junggeselle** confirmed bachelor)
die Jungverheirateten adj n, pl newly-weds

die Kirche [-n] church
das Konfetti confetti
die Scheidung [-en] divorce
das Standesamt [ˈ̈er] registry office (**sich standesamtlich trauen
*lassen** be married in a registry office)
der Trauschein [-e] marriage certificate
der Trauzeuge [-n]/die Trauzeugin [-nen] witness
die Trennung separation
der/die Verlobte *adj n* fiancé/fiancée
die Verlobung [-en] engagement (**der Verlobungsring [-e]**
engagement ring; **die Verlobung auf|lösen** break the engage-
ment)
die Zeremonie [-n] ceremony

gratulieren (zu + D) congratulate (on) (**ich gratuliere!** congratulations!)
heiraten + A; sich ver'heiraten mit + D marry (**wieder heiraten**
remarry)
sich scheiden *lassen (von + D) divorce (sb)
sich trennen separate; split up
sich ver'loben get engaged

geschieden divorced
getrennt separated (**getrennt leben** be separated)
ledig single
verheiratet/unverheiratet married/unmarried
verlobt engaged

Tod Death

die Asche *sing* ashes
die Beerdigung [-en]; [more formal] **die Bestattung [-en]** funeral;
burial
das Bestattungsunternehmen [-] funeral firm (**der/die Bestattungs-
unternehmer/in [-/-nen]; der/die Leichenbestatter/in [-/-nen]**
undertaker)
die Einäscherung [-en] cremation
der Erbe [-n] heir (**die Erbin [-nen]** heiress)

die Erbschaft [-en]; das Erbe *no pl* inheritance

der Friedhof [¨e] cemetery; churchyard

der/die Gestorbene *adj n* the deceased

das Grab [¨er] grave (**das Grabmal [¨er]** monument; **der Grabspruch [¨e]** epitaph; **der Grabstein [-e]** gravestone)

der Kranz [¨e] wreath

das Krematorium [*pl* Krematorien] crematorium

das Legat [-e] (an + A) bequest (to)

die Leiche [-n] corpse (**das Leichentuch [¨er]** shroud; **der Leichenwagen [-]** hearse)

der Mord [-e] murder (**der Selbstmord** suicide; **Selbstmord *be'gehen** commit suicide)

der Nachlaß estate

der Sarg [¨e] coffin

der Scheiterhaufen [-] funeral pyre

das Testament [-e] will

der Tod death

der/die Tote *adj n* dead person (**das Toten-/Sterbebett** deathbed; **der Totengräber [-]** grave-digger; **der Totenschein [-e]** death certificate)

die Trauer mourning (**in Trauer *sein; Trauer *tragen** be in mourning)

der Trauerakt [-e]; die Trauerfeier [-n] funeral ceremony

der Trauerfall [¨e] bereavement

der Trauerzug [¨e] funeral procession

die Urne [-n] urn

die Waise [-n] *always f;* **das Waisenkind [-er]** orphan (**er ist Waise** he's an orphan; **verwaist** orphaned)

die Witwe [-n] widow (**der Witwer [-]** widower; **verwitwet** widowed)

be'erdigen bury

ein|äschern cremate

ent'erben disinherit

erben inherit

*er'trinken drown

*hinter'lassen leave [in will]

*sterben die (eines natürlichen/gewaltsamen Todes sterben die a natural/violent death)
töten; ***um|bringen** kill
trauern mourn
*um|kommen perish
ver'machen bequeath

SEE ALSO: **Accidents; Disasters; Health and Sickness; Identity; Relationships; War, Peace, and the Armed Services**

7. Cinema and Photography
Kino und Fotografie

Kino Cinema

die Anzeige [-n] advert
die Aufführung [-en]; **die Vorstellung** [-en] showing; performance
die Dekoration [-en] set
das Drehbuch [¨er] film script
der Dokumentarfilm [-e] documentary
der Film [-e]; *colloq* **der Streifen** [-] film (**der Schwarzweiß-/Farb-/
Stumm-/Kurzfilm** black-and-white/colour/silent/short film; **der
Spiel-/Hauptfilm** feature film)
der Filmausschnitt [-e] film clip
die Filmkamera [-s] cine-camera
der Filmschauspieler [-] film actor (**die Filmschauspielerin** [-nen]
film actress)
der Horrorfilm [-e] horror film
das Kamerateam [-s] film crew
die Karte [-n] ticket (**die Eintrittskarte** [-n] entrance ticket)
die Kasse [-n] box-office (**der Kassenerfolg** [-e] box-office success)
das Kino [-s] cinema
die Kopie [-n] print
der Kriminalfilm [-e]; **der Krimi** [*pl* -s or -] thriller; crime film
die Leinwand [¨e] screen
das Parkett *sing* stalls
die Pause [-n] interval
der Platz [¨e] seat (**die Platzanweiserin** [-nen] usherette)
das Programm [-e] programme
der Projektor [G -s *pl* -en] projector
das Publikum spectators
der Rang [¨e] circle
der/die Regisseur/in [-e/-nen] director
der Saal [*pl* Säle] cinema [the building]

der **Science-fiction-Film** [-e] science-fiction film (die **Science-fiction** science fiction)

der **Star** [-s] star [male or female]

der **Trickfilm/Zeichentrickfilm** [-e] cartoon (film)

der **Untertitel** [-] subtitle (**OmU** [= **Originalfassung mit Unterteln**] subtitled)

das **Video** [-s] video [the medium or the object] (der **Videofilm** [-e] video film)

die **Videoaufzeichnung** [-en] video recording

das **Videoband** [¨er] videotape

der **Videoclip** [-s] videoclip

die **Videokamera** [-s] camcorder

die **Videokassette** [-n] video cassette

der **Videorecorder** [-] video recorder

der **Western** [-] western

die **Zeitlupe** slow motion (**in Zeitlupe** in slow-motion)

drehen shoot; make [film]

filmen film

*****laufen** be running/showing

synchronisieren dub

unter'titeln subtitle

ver'filmen film [a book]

vor|be'stellen; reservieren *lassen book (in advance)

zum Kino/Film *gehen go into films (**ins Kino gehen** go to the cinema)

Fotografie Photography

der **Abzug** [¨e] print (der **Glanz-/Mattabzug** glossy/matt print)

das **Album** [pl Alben] album

die **Batterie** [-n] battery

die **Belichtung**; [shot] die **Aufnahme** [-n] exposure (der **Belichtungsmesser** [-] exposure meter)

das **Blitzlicht** flash (**mit Blitzlicht fotografieren** use flash; die **Blitzlichtaufnahme** [-n] flash photo; das **Blitzbirnchen** [-] flash bulb; der **Blitzwürfel** [-] flash-cube)

das Dia [-s]; das Diapositiv [-e] slide/transparency (**der Dia(positiv)projektor** [G -s *pl* -en] slide projector)

die Dunkelkammer [-n] dark-room

der Entfernungsmesser [-] range-finder

die Entwicklung development

der Film [-e] film (**der Rollfilm** roll film; **die Filmkassette [-n]** cassette/cartridge; **der Filmtransport [-e]** film winder)

der Filter [-] filter

das Foto [-s] photo (**das Schwarzweiß-/Farbfoto** black-and-white/colour photo)

der Fotoapparat [-e]; die Kamera [-s] camera

der/die Fotograf/in [-en/-nen] photographer

die Fotografie [-n] photography; photograph

die Kameratasche [-n] camera case

das Negativ [-e] negative

das Objektiv [-e] lens (**der Objektivdeckel [-]** lens cap; **das Weitwinkel-/Teleobjektiv** wide-angle/telephoto lens)

das Paßbild [-er] passport photo

der Rahmen [-] frame

die Scharfeinstellung focus (**die Schärfentiefe** depth of focus)

der Schnappschuß [⸗sse] snapshot

das Stativ [-e] tripod

der Sucher [-] viewfinder

die Vergrößerung [-en] enlargement

der Verschluß [⸗sse] shutter (**die Verschlußzeit [-en]** shutter speed/setting; **der Auslöser [-]** shutter release)

*ab|ziehen print

be'lichten expose (**zu kurz belichten** underexpose)

ein|legen (in + A) load (into)

ein|rahmen frame

ein|stellen (auf + A) focus (on)

ent'wickeln develop

klemmen; sich ver'klemmen be stuck; jam

machen; *schießen take [photo]

retuschieren retouch

ver'größern enlarge

automatisch automatic
Feinkorn- fine grain
hochempfindlich fast [film]
scharf/unscharf in focus/out of focus

SEE ALSO: **Art and Architecture; Leisure and Hobbies; The Media; Theatre**

8. Clothing Kleidung

Was man auf dem Kopf trägt . . .
What you wear on your head . . .

die Baskenmütze [-n] beret
die Haube [-n] bonnet
der Hut [≈e] hat (**die Krempe** [-n] brim)
das Kopftuch [≈er] headscarf
die Melone [-n] bowler
die Mütze [-n] cap (**die Badekappe** [-n] bathing-cap)
der Schleier [-] veil
der Sonnenhut [≈e] sun-hat
der Strohhut [≈e] straw hat

. . . und an den Füßen . . . on your feet

der Freizeitschuh [-e] casual shoe
der Hausschuh [-e] slipper
der Holzschuh [-e]; [fashionable] **der Clog** [-s] clog
der Mokassin [-s] moccasin
der Pantoffel [-n] (backless) slipper; mule
die Sandale [-n] sandal
der Schuh [-e] shoe (**das Paar** [-e] pair; **der Wander-/Strandschuh**
walking-/beach shoe; **die Schuhcreme** shoe polish)
die Socke [-n] sock
der Stiefel [-] boot (**der Gummistiefel** wellington boot)
der Strumpf [≈e] stocking; long sock (**der Kniestrumpf** knee sock;
die Strumpfhose [-n] (pair of) tights)
der Trainingsschuh [-e] trainer
der Turnschuh [-e] gym shoe; trainer
der Überstrumpf [≈e]; **der Legwarmer** [-s] leg-warmer

. . . und am Körper . . . on your body

die Abendkleidung *no pl* evening dress (**das Abendkleid** [-er] [woman's] evening dress; **der Gesellschaftsanzug** [¨e] [man's] dress-suit)

der Anorak [-s] anorak

der Anzug [¨e] suit (**der Straßen-/Büro-/Maßanzug** lounge/office/made-to-measure suit)

der Arbeitsanzug [¨e] (set of) working clothes

der Badeanzug [¨e] swim-suit

die Badehose [-n] (pair of) swimming-trunks

der Bademantel [¨]; [woman's] **der Morgenrock** [¨e] dressing-gown

der Bikini [-s] bikini (**im Bikini** in a bikini)

das/der Blouson [-s] blouson; bomber jacket

die Bluse [-n] blouse

das Braut-/Hochzeitskleid [-er] wedding dress

die Brille [-n] (pair of) spectacles (**die Sonnenbrille** sun-glasses)

der Büstenhalter [-]/**der BH** [*pl* - or -s] bra

das Dinnerjacket [-s]; **der Smoking** [-s] dinner-jacket

der Dufflecoat [-s] duffle-coat

der Fausthandschuh [-e] mitten

der Frack [¨e] tailcoat (**im Frack** in tails)

die Freizeitkleidung *no pl* casuals; casual clothes

der Gehrock [¨e] frock-coat

der Gürtel [-] belt

der Handschuh [-e] glove

die Handtasche [-n] handbag (**die Umhängetasche** shoulder-bag)

das Hemd [-en] shirt (**das Sporthemd** sports shirt)

das Höschen [-] (pair of) panties (**heiße Höschen** *n pl* hotpants)

die Hose [-n] (pair of) trousers (**die Hosenträger** *m pl* braces)

der Hosenanzug [¨e] trouser-suit

der Hosenrock [¨e] (pair of) culottes

der Hüfthalter [-] girdle

die Jacke [-n]; [of suit] **das Jackett** [-s] jacket (**der/das Sakko** [-s] (sports) jacket)

die Jeans [-] *sing or pl*; **die Jeanshose** [-n] (pair of) jeans

der Jumper [-] jumper

das Kleid [-er] dress (**die Kleider** *pl* dresses; clothes; **tief ausgeschnitten** low-necked; **hochgeschlossen** high-necked)

die Kleidung *sing* clothing; clothes (**die Konfektionskleidung** ready-mades; **die Gesellschaftskleidung** formal dress)

die Kniehose [-n] (pair of) knee-breeches

das Kostüm [-e] [woman's] suit (**das Schneiderkostüm** tailored suit)

die Latzhose [-n] (pair of) dungarees

die Lederhose [-n] (pair of) lederhosen/leather shorts

die Lumpen *m pl* rags

der Mantel [‥] (over)coat (**der Pelzmantel** fur coat)

der Muff [-e] muff

das Nachthemd [-en] night-dress; night-shirt

der Overall [-s] (pair of) overalls

der Pullover [-]/**der Pulli** [-s] pullover; sweater (**mit V-Ausschnitt** V-necked)

der Pullunder [-] slip-over

der Regenmantel [‥] raincoat

der Regenschirm [-e] umbrella (**der Sonnenschirm** parasol)

der Rock [‥e] skirt (**der Minirock** mini-skirt)

der Rollkragenpulli [-s]/**der Rolli** [-s] polo-neck sweater

der Schal [*pl* -s or -e] scarf

der Schlafanzug [‥e]; **der Pyjama** [-s] (pair of) pyjamas

der Schlips [-e]; **die Krawatte** [-n] tie (**die Fliege** [-n] bow-tie)

der Schlüpfer [-] (pair of) panties

die Schürze [-n] apron

die Shorts *pl* shorts

die Skihose [-n] (pair of) ski pants

der Slip [-s] (pair of) briefs

der Spazierstock [‥e] walking-stick

die Stola [*pl* Stolen] stole; shawl

der Stresemann [man's] morning dress (**der Cut(away)** [-s] morning coat)

die Strickjacke [-n] cardigan

die Strumpfbänder *n pl*; **die Strumpfhalter** *m pl* suspenders (**der Strumpfbandgürtel** [-] suspender belt; **die Sockenhalter** *m pl* sock-suspenders)

das Sweatshirt [-s] sweat-shirt

das Taschentuch [ᵘer] handkerchief

die Tracht [-en] costume; uniform (**die Nationaltracht** national costume)

der Trainingsanzug [ᵘe] tracksuit

das T-Shirt [-s] T-shirt

das Umschlagtuch [ᵘer] shawl

die Uniform [-en] uniform

das Unterhemd [-en] vest

die Unterhose [-n] (pair of) (under)pants

der Unterrock [ᵘe] petticoat; underskirt

die Wäsche/die Unterwäsche underwear (**die Damenunterwäsche** lingerie)

die Weste [-n] waistcoat

der Zweireiher [-] double-breasted jacket

Teile eines Kleidungsstücks
Parts of a piece of clothing

der Absatz [ᵘe] heel (**der Stöckelabsatz** stiletto heel; **der Stöckelschuh** [-e] stiletto-heeled shoe; **hochhackig** high-heeled; **flach** low-heeled)

der Ärmel [-] sleeve (**hoch|krempeln** roll up; **in Hemdsärmeln** in shirt-sleeves; **ärmellos** sleeveless)

der Aufschlag [ᵘe] turn-up

das Band [ᵘer] ribbon

der Druckknopf [ᵘe] press-stud

die Falte [-n] pleat

das Futter *no pl*; **die Fütterung** [-en] lining

der Gürtel [-] belt (**das Koppel** [-] uniform belt)

der Haken [-] hook

der Knopf [ᵘe] button (**das Knopfloch** [ᵘer] buttonhole)

der Kragen [-] collar (**der Rollkragen** polo neck; **der Kragenknopf**
[∸e] collar-stud)

die Manschette [-n] cuff (**der Manschettenknopf** [∸e] cuff-link)

die Naht [∸e] seam

der Reißverschluß [∸sse] zip

der Saum [∸e] hem

die Schnalle [-n] buckle

der Schnürsenkel [-] shoe-lace

die Sohle [-n] sole (**die Leder-/Gummi-/Krepp-/Plateausohle**
leather/rubber/crêpe/platform sole; **der Plateauschuh** [-e] platform shoe; **die Einlegesohle** insole)

die Tasche [-n] pocket

die Verzierung [-en] trimming (**der Spitzenbesatz** lace trimmings)

Wie Kleider aussehen What clothes are like

abgetragen threadbare; worn out

altmodisch old-fashioned

auffällig flashy

bauschig bouffant

bedruckt print(ed)

bequem geschnitten loose-fitting

bestickt embroidered

bügelfrei non-iron; drip-dry

dekolletiert low-cut

einfach plain; simple

einreihig single-breasted (**zweireihig** double-breasted)

elegant elegant

eng tight

enganliegend close-fitting

farbecht colour-fast

die Figur betonend figure-hugging

formell formal

geblümt flowered

gefältelt pleated

gepunktet spotted

geschmackvoll in good taste (**geschmacklos** in bad taste)

gestreift striped
in *colloq*; **in Mode** in; in fashion
kariert check
knallig loud; gaudy
knitterfrei crease resistant
kurzärm(e)lig short-sleeved (**langärm(e)lig** long-sleeved)
lässig casual
maßgeschneidert made to measure
modisch fashionable
nagelneu brand-new
passend (**zu** + D) matching
proper trim; neat
rauh rough
schäbig shabby
schick smart
schlampig slovenly; sloppy
schlicht sober
sportlich casually smart
steif stiff
synthetisch synthetic
uni *inv* plain
von der Stange off the peg
zerknittert crumpled
zerrissen torn

Was man damit tut What you do with them

*ab|laufen [shoes]; ***auf|tragen** [clothes] wear out
*ab|nehmen take off [from head]
ändern alter
*an|haben [on body]; ***auf|haben** [on head] have on
an|nähen sew on
an|probieren try on
sich *an|ziehen get dressed (**anziehen** put on [clothes])
auf|knöpfen unbutton
auf|setzen put on [on head]
aus|bessern mend

sich *aus|ziehen get undressed (**ausziehen** take off [clothes])
be'setzen mit + D trim with
be'sohlen sole
*binden tie (***auf|binden** untie)
bügeln iron (**der Hosenbügler** [-] trouser-press)
*ein|laufen shrink
fälteln pleat
flicken patch
knittern crease
kürzer/länger machen shorten/lengthen
öffnen unfasten
passen (+ D) fit (sb) (**passen zu** + D go well with)
säumen hem
schlüpfen in + A slip into
schnallen buckle
schneidern make; tailor (**schneidern *lassen** have made)
*sitzen fit; be straight
*stehen (+ D) suit (sb)
stopfen darn
stricken knit
*tragen wear
sich *um|ziehen get changed (**die Umkleidekabine** [-n] changing-cubicle)
*waschen wash (**in der Waschmaschine waschen** machine-wash; **in die Handwäsche *kommen** be washed by hand)
zu|knöpfen button up
zu|machen fasten

Textilien Textiles

das Acryl acrylic
der Batist cambric
die Baumwolle cotton (**der Baumwollsamt** velveteen)
der Chiffon chiffon
der Cord cord (**der Cordsamt** corduroy; cord velvet)
der Denim®; **der Jeansstoff** denim
der Drillich drill

der Filz felt
der Flanell flannel
das/der Frottee terry
der Gabardine gabardine
das/der Gummi rubber (**das/der Kreppgummi** crêpe)
der Jersey jersey
der Kambrik cambric
das Kamelhaar camel-hair
das Kammgarn worsted
der Kaschmir cashmere
der Krepp crêpe
der Kunststoff [-e] synthetic material; plastic (**die Kunstfaser** [-n] man-made fibre)
das Leder leather (**ledern** leather *adj*)
das Leinen linen
die Leinwand canvas
der Manchester [heavy] corduroy
das Nylon® nylon
der Pelz [-e]; **das** Fell [-e] fur
der Polyester polyester
der Popelin(e) poplin
der Samt velvet (**samten** velvet *adj*; **samtig**; **samtweich** velvety)
der Satin satin
die Seide silk (**seiden** silk *adj*; **die Kunstseide** artificial silk; rayon)
die Spitze lace (**Spitzen-** lace *adj*)
der Stoff [-e] cloth; fabric
das Stroh straw
der Tweed tweed
das Wachstuch oilcloth
das Wildleder; [finer] **das** Veloursleder suede
die Wolle wool (**die Schurwolle** new wool; **wollen** woollen)

Mode Fashion

der Dressman [*pl* -men] male model
die Haute Couture *haute couture*
die Kollektion [-en] (fashion) collection

die Konfektion off-the-peg clothes; the clothing industry (**die Damen-/Herrenkonfektion** ladies'/men's fashions)

das Mannequin [-s]; das Modell [-e] (fashion) model

die Mode [-n] fashion (**die Damen-/Herrenmode** ladies'/men's fashions; **große Mode** all the rage; **in Mode** in fashion)

der Modeartikel [-] fashion accessory

die Modebranche rag trade

das Modegeschäft [-e] fashion boutique

das Modellkleid [-er] model dress

die Modenschau [-en] fashion show

der/die Modeschöpfer/in [-/-nen] fashion designer (**modellieren** design [clothes])

das Muster [-] pattern

die Schattierung [-en] shade

die Schneiderei tailoring; dressmaking

der/die Schneider/in [-/-nen] tailor; dressmaker

die Stange [-n] (clothes) rail (**von der Stange** off the peg)

SEE ALSO: **Adornment; Colours; The Human Body; Numbers and Quantities**

9. Colours
Farben

Welche Farbe hat es? What colour is it?

es ist . . . it is . . .

beige beige

blau blue (**himmel-/königs-/marineblau** sky/royal/navy blue; **ein blaues Auge** a black eye)

blond blonde

braun brown (**kastanienbraun** chestnut; maroon)

creme *inv*; **cremefarben** cream

fleischfarben flesh-coloured

gelb yellow

gelbbraun buff; tawny [hair]

golden gold(en)

grau grey

grün green (**grün und blau** black and blue)

hazelnußbraun hazel

indigoblau indigo (blue)

infrarot infra-red

karminrot carmine

lavendel *inv*; **lavendelblau** lavender

lila *inv* mauve (**dunkellila** purple)

mehr-/vielfarbig multicoloured

orange *inv*; **orangefarben** orange

purpurn; purpurrot crimson

rehfarben fawn

rosa *inv*; **rosafarben; rosafarbig** pink (**rosarot** deep pink)

rot red

scharlachrot scarlet

schwarz black (**schwarzweiß** black and white [film etc.]; **schwarz auf weiß** in black and white)

silbern silver

türkis *inv*; **türkisfarben** turquoise

ultraviolett ultraviolet
violett violet; purple
weiß white (**schneeweiß** white as snow)
zitronengelb lemon

dunkel- dark
hell- light; pale
leuchtend; knall- bright

blaßrosa *inv* pinkish
bläulich bluish
bräunlich brownish
gelblich yellowish; sallow
gräulich greyish
grünlich greenish
rötlich reddish (**rötlich-braun** reddish brown)
schwärzlich blackish
weißlich whitish

bräunen brown (**an|bräunen** brown [food])
grünen turn green
sich röten redden (**er'röten** blush)
schwärzen blacken
ver'gilben (turn) yellow
ver'golden gild
ver'silbern silver
weißen whiten [shoes, wall]

SEE ALSO: **Adornment; Clothing; Hair; Materials; The Senses**

10. Cooking and Eating
Kochen und Essen

Küchenausstattung Kitchen equipment

das Besteck cutlery
das Brotbrett [-er] breadboard
der Brotkasten [¨] bread-bin
die Brotmaschine [-n] bread-slicer
die Butterdose [-n] butter-dish
die Dose [-n]; die Büchse [-n] can; tin (**der Dosenöffner [-]** can-opener)
der Durchschlag [¨e] colander
der Eierbecher [-] egg-cup
die Flasche [-n] bottle (**der Flaschenöffner [-]** bottle-opener)
die Friteuse [-n] deep fryer
die Gabel [-n] fork
das Gedeck [-e] place-setting (**ein Gedeck auf|legen** lay a place)
das Geschirr dishes; crockery; kitchenware (**feuerfestes Geschirr** ovenware)
das Glas [¨er] glass; (glass) jar (**das Weinglas** wine-glass; **der Sprung [¨e]** crack)
der Herd [-e] stove; cooker (**der Elektro-/Gasherd** electric/gas cooker; **der Ofen [¨]** oven)
die Kaffeemaschine [-n] coffee-maker (**der Kaffeefilter [-]** coffee-filter; filter-paper; **die Kaffeemühle [-n]** coffee-grinder)
die Kanne [-n] pot; jug (**die Kaffee-/Teekanne** coffee-/teapot; **die Milchkanne;** [smaller] **das Milchkännchen [-]** milk jug)
die Karaffe [-n] carafe
die Kasserolle/Stielkasserolle [-n] saucepan (**der Stiel [-e]** long handle
die Kelle/Schöpfkelle [-n] ladle
der Kessel/Wasserkessel [-] kettle
die Klarsichtfolie cling-film
die Knoblauchpresse [-n] garlic press

das Kochbuch [ˌer] cookery book (**das Rezept** [-e] recipe)

der Kochtopf [ˌe]; **die Kasserolle** [-n] saucepan

der Korb [ˌe] basket

der Korken [-] cork (**der Korkenzieher** [-] corkscrew)

der Krug [ˌe] jug (**der Milchkrug** milk jug)

die Küchenmaschine [-n] food processor

der Löffel [-] spoon (**der Eß-/Servier-/Kaffee-/Teelöffel** soup- or dessert-/table/coffee-/teaspoon)

das Messer [-] knife (**das Küchen-/Brotmesser** kitchen-/bread knife; **das Schälmesser** potato peeler)

die Metallfolie foil

der Mixer [-] mixer; blender

die Pfanne/Bratpfanne [-n] frying-pan

die Pfeffermühle [-n] pepper-mill

die Platte [-n] (flat) dish

die Reibe [-n]; [coarser] **die Raspel** [-n] grater

der Salz-/Pfefferstreuer [-] salt-cellar/pepper-pot

die Sauciere [-n] sauce-boat

die Schale [-n] bowl (**die Zuckerschale** sugar-bowl)

die Schere [-n] (pair of) scissors

der Schneebesen [-] whisk

der Schnellkochtopf [ˌe] pressure-cooker

die Schnur [ˌe] (length of) string; (electric) lead

die Schüssel [-n] (large) bowl; basin

die Serviette [-n] table napkin

das/der Set [-s] place-mat

das Sieb [-e or -e] sieve; strainer

das Streichholz [ˌer] match

der Strohhalm [-e] drinking-straw

das Tablett [pl -s or -e] tray

die Tasse [-n] cup (**die Suppen-/Kaffeetasse** soup-bowl/coffee-cup)

die Teigrolle [-n]; **das Nudelholz** [ˌer] rolling-pin

der Teller [-] plate (**der Suppenteller** soup-plate)

die Terrine [-n] tureen

das Tischtuch [ˌer] tablecloth

die Thermosflasche [-n] flask; thermos ®

der Toaster [-] toaster
der Topf [ːe] pot [cooking or container]; jar; casserole; saucepan (**der Topfhandschuh** [-e] oven glove)
die Untertasse [-n] saucer
die Waage [-n] (pair of/set of) scales
die Zuckerdose [-n] sugar-bowl

Gewürze Seasonings

der Anis aniseed
das Aroma [*pl* Aromen] flavouring
das Basilikum basil
der Brüh-/Suppenwürfel [-] stock-cube
der Dill dill
der Essig vinegar
der Estragon tarragon
das Gewürz [-e] spice; herb; seasoning (**das Gewürzkraut** [ːer] herb)
die Nelke/Gewürznelke[-n] clove
der Honig honey
der Ingwer ginger
die Kaper [-n] *usually pl* capers
der Kerbel chervil
der Knoblauch garlic (**die Knoblauchzehe** [-n] clove of garlic; **die Knoblauchzwiebel** [-n] head of garlic)
das Kraut [ːer] herb
der Kümmel caraway (**der Kreuzkümmel** cumin)
das Lorbeerblatt [ːer] bay-leaf
der Majoran marjoram
der Mazis; die Muskatblüte mace
die Minze mint (**die Pfefferminze** peppermint)
die Muskatnuß [ːsse]; **der Muskat** [-e] nutmeg
der Oregano/der Origano oregano
der Paprika paprika
die Paprikaschote [-n] pepper [capsicum]
die Petersilie parsley
der Pfeffer pepper

der/das Piment; der Nelkenpfeffer pimento

der Rosmarin rosemary

der Safran saffron

der/die Salbei sage

das Salz salt

der Schnittlauch chives

der Senf [-e] mustard

der Süßstoff (artificial) sweetener

der Thymian thyme

die Vanille vanilla

der Wacholder juniper

die Würze [-n] seasoning

der Zimt cinnamon

der Zucker sugar (**das Stück [-e]** lump; **die Raffinade** granulated sugar)

Fette Fats

die Butter butter

die Margarine [-n] margarine

das Öl [-e] oil (**das Oliven-/Erdnuß-/Sonnenblumenöl** olive/ground-nut/sunflower oil)

das Schweineschmalz lard

Zubereitung Preparation

*ab|gießen drain

*an|braten brown

auf|tauen thaw

aus|beinen [meat]; **ent'gräten** [fish] bone

aus|pressen crush

*backen bake

*be'gießen baste

be'reiten prepare [food, drink]

*braten fry; roast (**am Spieß** m on a spit/skewer; **durchgebraten** well done [meat]; **halb durchgebraten** medium rare; **englisch gebraten; blutig** rare)

dämpfen; dünsten steam

ein|tauchen soak

füllen stuff

garnieren garnish

grillen grill; barbecue

hacken chop; dice

klein|hacken mince

kochen cook; boil (**es kocht** it's boiling)

marinieren marinate

panieren bread [meat]

pochieren poach

räuchern smoke

*reiben; [coarser] raspeln grate

rösten roast [coffee]; toast [bread]

rühren; um'rühren stir (**rühren in** + A mix into)

schälen peel; shell (**ent'hülsen** shell [peas])

*schlagen beat

schmoren braise

*schneiden cut (**in Scheiben schneiden** slice; **dünn** thinly)

toasten toast [bread]

*über'backen gratiné; top with cheese and brown

ver'dünnen dilute

ver'kneten knead

würzen season

*zer'lassen melt

ziehen *lassen simmer

zu|be'reiten prepare

Mahlzeiten Meals

das Abendbrot supper

das Abendessen [evening] dinner; supper

das Bankett [-e] banquet

das Festessen [-] feast

das Frühstück breakfast (**frühstücken** have breakfast)

der Imbiß [-sse]; **die Zwischenmahlzeit** [-en] snack

die Mahlzeit [-en] [the occasion]; **das Essen** [the food] meal

das Mittagessen lunch (**zu Mittag *essen** eat lunch; **zum Mittagessen** for lunch)

das Picknick [*pl* **-s** or **-e**] picnic

Essen Eating

der Appetit [**-e**] appetite (**guten Appetit!** enjoy your meal!; **den Appetit *ver'derben** spoil one's appetite)

der Geschmack [**ᵉ**] taste

die Portion [**-en**] portion; helping

*an|bieten offer

be'dienen serve (**sich be'dienen** serve oneself; **die Selbstbedienung** self-service)

*bitten um + A ask for

*essen eat (**er gern essen** like [eating] sth; **zu Mittag/zu Abend essen** have lunch/dinner)

Hunger *m* ***haben; hungrig *sein** be hungry

leben von + D live on

*mögen like

*nach|geben offer a second helping of (**die zweite Portion** [**-en**] second helping)

reichen pass (**herum|reichen** pass round)

schlucken swallow

schmecken taste (**es schmeckt gut** it tastes good; **schmeckt es?** do you like it?; **kosten; probieren** taste [= try])

*schneiden cut

*ver'schlingen devour

tranchieren; *auf|schneiden carve

es ist . . .
  altbacken stale
  angebrannt burnt
  angegangen high [meat, game]
  appetitlich appetizing
  bitter bitter
  eßbar; genießbar edible
  fade tasteless; insipid

gar cooked
geräuchert smoked
halbgar underdone; half-done
knusprig crisp
nahrhaft nourishing
pikant savoury; well-seasoned
ranzig rancid
reichhaltig ample
roh raw
salzig salty
sauer sour
scharf hot
stark strong
süß sweet
trocken dry (**getrocknet; Trocken-** dried)
ungenießbar inedible
verdaulich/unverdaulich digestible/indigestible
verkocht overcooked
würzig spicy
zäh tough
zart tender

Essen gehen Eating out

der Aschenbecher [-] ashtray
die Bedienung service (**einschließlich/inklusive Bedienung** service charge included)
die Beilage [-n] side-dish; side-salad; accompanying vegetables
die Bestellung [-en] order (**nur auf Bestellung** to order only)
die Bierhalle [-n] beer hall
das Café [-s] café (**die Café-Konditorei** [-en] pastry shop with café attached)
die Eisdiele [-n] ice-cream parlour
der Gasthof [⁼e]; **das Gasthaus** [⁼er] inn
der Gesamtbetrag [⁼e] total (**insgesamt** in total)
die Grillstube [-n] steak-house
die Imbißbude [-n] snack-stall; hot-dog stand

die Karte/Speisekarte [-n] menu (**die Weinkarte** wine list; **das Menü [-s]**; **das Gedeck [-e]** set meal; **das Tagesmenü** meal of the day)

der Kellner [-] waiter (**die Kellnerin [-nen]** waitress; **Herr Ober!/ Fräulein!** waiter!/waitress!; **der/die Weinkellner/in** wine waiter)

der Oberkellner [-] head waiter

die Pizzeria [pl -s or **Pizzerien**] pizzeria

die Raststätte [-n] motorway service restaurant

die Rechnung [-en] bill

das Restaurant [-s]; [less formal] **die Gaststätte [-n]** restaurant (**das Restaurant mit Straßenverkauf** take-away; **das Essen zum Mitnehmen** take-away food; **et zum Mitnehmen** a take-away)

der Ruhetag [-e] closing day (**dienstags Ruhetag** closed Tuesdays)

der Schnellimbiß [-sse] snack-bar (**der Imbiß** snack)

das Schnellrestaurant [-s] fast-food restaurant (**das Fast food** fast food)

die Serviette [-n] napkin

die Spezialität [-en] (**des Hauses**) speciality (of the house) (**hausgemacht** home-made)

der Stammtisch [-e] regulars' table

das Trinkgeld [-er] tip

die Weinstube [-n] wine bar

das Wirtshaus [¨er]; **die Bierstube [-n]**; **das Lokal [-e]**; colloq **die Kneipe [-n]** pub

der Zahnstocher [-] toothpick

der Zuschlag [¨e] supplement

aus|suchen choose

be'stellen order

*emp'fehlen recommend

*essen eat (**beim Chinesen/Griechen/Italiener essen** eat Chinese/ Greek/Italian)

falsch/zu viel *heraus|geben give the wrong/too much change

ins Café/Restaurant *gehen go to a café/restaurant

reservieren *lassen book

stimmen be correct (**es stimmt so** keep the change)

sich ver'rechnen make an error
zahlen pay (**getrennt zahlen** pay separately)

SEE ALSO: **Drinks; Food; The Senses; Tobacco and Drugs**

11. Crimes and Criminals
Verbrechen und Verbrecher

Verbrechen Crimes

die Alarmanlage [-n] burglar alarm

der Angriff [-e] attack

das Attentat [-e]; **der Mordanschlag** [Ꞌe] attempt on sb's life (**ver'üben** make [attempt on life])

die Bestechung bribery (**das Bestechungsgeld** [-er] bribe)

der Betrug fraud

die Beute loot

die Brandstiftung arson (**in Brand** *m* **setzen** set fire to)

der Diebstahl [Ꞌe] theft

der Drogenhandel drug-trafficking

der Einbruch [Ꞌe] burglary; break-in

die Entführung [-en] hijack; abduction

die Erpressung [-en] blackmail

die Fälschung [-en] forgery

der Faustschlag [Ꞌe] punch (**an den Kopf** to the head)

der Fußtritt [-e] kick

die Gaunerei [-en] swindle; swindling

die Geiselnahme hostage-taking (**die Geisel** [-n] [male or female] hostage; **als Geisel *nehmen/*fest|halten** take/hold sb hostage)

die Handgreiflichkeiten *f pl* scuffle (**handgreiflich *werden** come to blows; **es kam zu Handgreiflichkeiten** a scuffle broke out)

der Hausfriedensbruch; das unbefugte Betreten trespass

das Kidnapping [-s] kidnapping (**das Lösegeld** [-er] ransom)

die Kuppelei procuring

der Ladendiebstahl [Ꞌe] shop-lifting; shop theft

die Landstreicherei; [in cities] die Stadtstreicherei vagrancy

der Meineid perjury

der Mord [-e] murder

die Prostitution prostitution

der Raub [*pl* **Raubüberfälle**] robbery (**der bewaffnete Raubüberfall** robbery with violence)

das Rauschgift narcotics

die Schlägerei [**-en**]; **die Rauferei** [**-en**] fight; brawl

der Schmuggel smuggling

der Schuß [**¨sse**] shot

der Schwindel *no pl* fraud; confidence trick

die Spionage espionage

der Straßendiebstahl highway robbery

der Taschendiebstahl [**¨e**] pocket-picking

der Totschlag manslaughter; homicide

der Überfall [**¨e**] hold-up; attack

die Unterschlagung embezzlement

das Verbrechen [**-**] (**an** + D; **gegen** + A) crime (against)

die Vergewaltigung [**-en**] rape

die Vergiftung poisoning (**das Gift** [**-e**] poison)

der Verrat treason (**der Hochverrat** high treason)

die Waffe [**-n**] weapon (**bewaffnet** armed)

Verbrecher Criminals

die Bande [**-n**]; **die Gang** [**-s**] gang

der Bandit [**-en**] bandit

der/die Brandstifter/in [**-/-nen**] arsonist

der/die Dieb/in [**-e/-nen**] thief

der/die Drogenhändler/in [**-/-nen**] drug dealer

der/die Einbrecher/in [**-/-nen**] burglar

der/die Entführer/in [**-/-nen**]; **der/die Hijacker/in** [**-/-nen**] hijacker

der/die Erpresser/in [**-/-nen**] blackmailer

der/die Erst-/Rückfalltäter/in [**-/-nen**] first/persistent offender

der Gangster [**-**] gangster (**die Gangsterbraut** [**¨e**] gangster's moll)

der Gauner [**-**] crook

der/die Geiselnehmer/in [**-/-nen**] hostage-taker

der/die Hehler/in [**-/-nen**] receiver

der/die Kidnapper/in [**-/-nen**] kidnapper

der Komplize [**-n**]/**die Komplizin** [**-nen**] accomplice

der/die Kriminelle *adj n* criminal

der/die Landstreicher/in [-/-nen]; [in cities] **der/die Stadt-streicher/in** [-/-nen] vagrant

der/die Meineidige *adj n* perjurer

der/die Mörder/in [-/-nen] murderer

der/die Räuber/in [-/-nen] robber; kidnapper

der Rowdy [-s] hooligan; yob

der/die Schmuggler/in [-/-nen] smuggler

der/die Spion/in [-e/-nen] spy

der/die Taschendieb/in [-e/-nen] pickpocket

der/die Terrorist/in [-en/-nen] terrorist

der/die Übeltäter/in [-/-nen] wrong-doer

der/die Verbrecher/in [-/-nen] criminal

der Verräter [-] traitor (**die Verräterin** traitress)

der Wilderer [-]; **der Wilddieb** [-e] poacher

der Zuhälter [-] pimp

Was sie tun What they do

*an|greifen attack

*auf|brechen break into [car]

aus|rauben rob [bank, safe, etc.] (**be'rauben** rob [person])

be'drohen threaten

*be'gehen; ver'üben commit

be'lästigen importune

*be'stechen bribe

*be'stehlen um + A rob (sb) of

betroffen *sein von + D be implicated in

*be'trügen swindle

durch'suchen (nach + D) search (for)

*ein|brechen in + A break into; burgle

ent'führen hijack; abduct

*ent'kommen escape

er'morden murder

*er'schießen shoot dead (***schießen auf + A** shoot at; **das Gewehr** [-e] gun; **der Revolver** [-] revolver; **die Pistole** [-n] pistol)

*er'stechen stab to death (**das Messer** [-] knife; **der Dolch** [-e] dagger)

er'würgen strangle
gaunern swindle
kämpfen mit + D fight with
kidnappen kidnap
plündern loot
sich prostituieren prostitute oneself
sich raufen um + A fight over
rücksichtslos/unter Alkoholeinfluß *fahren drive recklessly/under
 the influence of alcohol (Alkohol m am Steuer drink-driving)
*schießen auf + A shoot at
spionieren spy
sprengen; in die Luft sprengen blow up
*stehlen steal (klauen colloq pinch)
täuschen deceive
töten; *um|bringen kill
*über'fallen attack; hold-up; mug
*unter'schlagen embezzle
ver'gewaltigen rape
ver'giften poison
*zwingen; [break open] *auf|brechen force

Ausrufe Cries

es brennt! fire!
haltet den Dieb! stop thief!
Hände hoch! hands up!
hau ab! clear off!
Hilfe! help!
hör auf! stop it!
laß mich los! let go!
Mord! murder!
Vorsicht! look out!

SEE ALSO: Describing People; Justice and Law

12. Describing People
Beschreibungen von Menschen

das Alter [-] age
das Aussehen appearance (dem Aussehen nach to judge by
  appearances)
das Benehmen; das Verhalten behaviour (D + gegenüber
  towards; das Betragen behaviour [of child])
die Beschreibung; die Schilderung description
der Charakter character
die Eigenschaft [-en] quality
die Entschuldigung [-en] excuse
der Fehler [-] fault
das Gewissen conscience (rein clear; schlecht bad)
die Gewohnheit [-en] habit
der Instinkt [-e] instinct
das Laster [-] vice
die Laune [-n]; die Stimmung [-en] mood (guter/schlechter Laune
  in a good/bad mood)
die Moral *sing* morals
die Natur; das Wesen nature (von Natur aus by nature)
die Schwäche [-n] weakness; demerit
die Tugend [-en] virtue
der Vorzug [≈e] merit

sich *be'nehmen; sich *ver'halten behave
*be'schreiben describe
*scheinen seem; appear
zeigen show

Das Äußere External appearance

die Ähnlichkeit (mit + D) resemblance (to)
der Ausdruck [≈e] expression
das Doppelkinn double chin

die Falte [-n] wrinkle
der Gang gait
die Gesichtsfarbe [-n]; **der Teint** [-s] complexion
der Gesichtszug [¨e] feature
die Geste [-n] gesture
das Gewicht weight
die Größe height
das Grübchen [-] dimple
die Haltung bearing
der Körperbau build
der Leberfleck [-e] mole
die Miene [-n] (facial) expression
die Narbe [-n] scar
der Pickel [-] spot
die Reinlichkeit; die Sauberkeit cleanliness
die Schmutzigkeit dirtiness
der Schönheitsfleck [-e] beauty spot
die Sommersprosse [-n] freckle

ähnlich sein (+ D) be like (sb)
*aus|sehen (wie) look (like)
sich *be'nehmen behave
. . . Meter groß *sein be . . . metres tall
*scheinen seem
*wiegen weigh

wie ist er/sie? what's he/she like?
  adrett smart
  aktiv active
  alt old
  auffallend striking
  bärtig bearded
  blaß pale
  blaßgelb sallow
  blind blind
  braungebrannt tanned
  bucklig hunchbacked
  dick fat

doof daft
dünn thin
eigenartig odd
einsam lonely
elegant; smart smart
ernst serious
faltig wrinkled
fett obese
fleckig blotchy
gebrechlich frail
glatt rasiert clean-shaven
groß big; tall (**der Riese** [-n]/**die Riesin** [-nen] giant/giantess)
gutaussehend good-looking
häßlich ugly
hellhäutig fair-skinned
hübsch pretty
jung young
kahl bald (**eine Glatze** a bald head)
klein small (**der/die Zwerg/in** [-e/-nen] dwarf)
komisch funny; odd
kräftig strong
kurzsichtig short-sighted
lächerlich ridiculous
lahm lame
lang long
mager thin
mittelgroß; mittlerer Größe medium-sized; of medium height
müde tired
muskulös muscular
nett nice
niedlich cute
oval oval [face]
pick(e)lig pimply; spotty
proper trim
rechtshändig right-handed (**linkshändig** left-handed)
reizend charming
rund round

sauber clean
schlank slim
schön beautiful; handsome
schmächtig weedy
schmutzig dirty
schwer heavy
seltsam; sonderbar strange
sinnlich sensual; sensuous
sonnengebräunt sun-tanned
spitz pointed [face, nose]
stumm dumb
süß sweet
taub deaf
traurig sad
weitsichtig long-sighted
winzig tiny
zart delicate
zierlich slight
zornig angry

Gute Eigenschaften Good qualities

der Adel nobility **edel** noble
die Anständigkeit decency **anständig** decent
die Aufrichtigkeit sincerity **aufrichtig** sincere
die Bescheidenheit modesty **bescheiden** modest
der Charme charm **charmant** charming
die Dankbarkeit gratitude **dankbar** grateful
die Demut humility **demütig** humble
die Ehre honour (**das Ehrenwort** word of honour) **ehrenwert**;
  ehrenhaft honourable
der Ehrgeiz ambition **ehrgeizig** ambitious
die Ehrlichkeit honesty **ehrlich** honest
der Eifer zeal **eifrig** zealous
die Einfachheit simplicity **einfach** simple
die Einsicht understanding **einsichtig** understanding
der Ernst seriousness **ernst; ernsthaft** serious

die **Exaktheit** precision   **exakt** exact; precise
der **Fleiß** industry   **fleißig** industrious
die **Freigebigkeit** generosity   **freigebig** generous
die **Freude** joy   **freudig** joyful
die **Freundlichkeit** friendliness   **freundlich** friendly
die **Fröhlichkeit** cheerfulness   **froh; fröhlich** cheerful
die **Furchtlosigkeit** fearlessness   **furchtlos** fearless
die **Geduld** patience   **geduldig** patient
der **Gehorsam** obedience   **gehorsam** obedient
der **Geist** wit   **geistreich** witty
die **Gerechtigkeit** justice   **gerecht** just
die **Geschicklichkeit; die Geschicktheit** skilfulness (**das Geschick**
   [-e] skill)   **geschickt** skilful; clever
das **Gewissen** conscience   **gewissenhaft** conscientious
die **Gnade** mercy   **gnädig** merciful
die **Großherzigkeit** magnanimity   **großherzig** magnanimous
die **Großzügigkeit** generosity   **großzügig** generous
die **Güte** goodness; kindness   **gut** good; **gütig** kindly
die **Gutmütigkeit** good nature   **gutmütig** good-natured
die **Herzlichkeit** cordiality   **herzlich** cordial
die **Höflichkeit** politeness; courtesy   **höflich** polite; courteous
der **Humor** humour (**der Sinn für Humor** sense of humour)
   humorvoll humorous [person]
die **Intelligenz** intelligence   **intelligent** intelligent
die **Klugheit** cleverness   **klug** clever
die **Kraft** [ᵉe] strength; power; energy   **kräftig** strong; powerful
die **Liebe** love   **liebevoll** loving
die **Liebenswürdigkeit** kindness   **liebenswürdig** kind
die **Mäßigkeit** moderation   **mäßig** moderate
die **Menschlichkeit; die Humanität** humanity   **menschlich**
   human; **human** humane
die **Milde** benevolence   **mild** benevolent
das **Mitgefühl** compassion   **mitfühlend** compassionate
das **Mitleid** pity   **mitleidig** pitying; sympathetic
der **Mut** bravery   **mutig** brave; courageous
die **Natürlichkeit** naturalness   **natürlich** natural
die **Nettigkeit** kindness   **nett** nice; kind

die Offenheit candour; openness   **offen** candid; open

der Optimismus optimism   **optimistisch** optimistic

die Reinheit purity   **rein** pure

der Respekt (vor + D) respect (for)   **respektvoll** respectful

die Rücksichtnahme consideration   **rücksichtsvoll** considerate

die Ruhe calmness   **ruhig** calm

die Sanftmütigkeit gentleness   **sanftmütig** gentle

der Scharfsinn astuteness   **scharfsinnig** astute

die Schlichtheit unpretentiousness   **schlicht** unpretentious

der Schneid guts   **schneidig** gutsy; daring

die Selbstsicherheit self-reliance   **selbstsicher** self-reliant

die Sensibilität sensitivity   **sensibel** sensitive

die Sorgfalt care **(die Sorgfältigkeit** carefulness)   **sorgfältig** careful

die Stärke strength   **stark** strong

der Stolz pride   **stolz (auf + A)** proud (of)

der Takt tact   **taktvoll** tactful

die Tapferkeit gallantry   **tapfer** gallant

die Toleranz tolerance   **tolerant** tolerant

die Treue loyalty; fidelity   **treu** loyal; faithful

die Umsicht circumspection   **umsichtig** circumspect

die Unschuld innocence   **unschuldig** innocent

die Vernunft reason; common sense   **vernünftig** sensible

die Verschwiegenheit discretion   **verschwiegen** discreet

das Vertrauen trust   **vertrauensvoll** trustful

die Voraussicht foresight   **vorausschauend** foresighted

die Vorsicht care; caution   **vorsichtig** careful; cautious

die Weisheit wisdom   **weise** wise

die Wohltätigkeit; die Nächstenliebe charity   **wohltätig** charitable

die Zartheit delicacy   **zart** delicate

die Zärtlichkeit tenderness   **zärtlich** tender; loving

die Zufriedenheit contentment   **zufrieden** content

die Zurückhaltung reserve   **zurückhaltend** reserved

billigen approve

be'lohnen reward

danken (+ D) thank (sb)
loben praise
miteinander *aus|kommen get along together
ruhig *bleiben; die Ruhe be'wahren keep cool
sich *zusammen|nehmen pull oneself together

Fehler Faults

die Affektiertheit affectation **affektiert** affected
die Angeberei showing-off **angeberisch** pretentious
die Ängstlichkeit timidity **ängstlich** timid; anxious
der Ärger annoyance; anger **ärgerlich (über** + A) annoyed (at)
die Arroganz arrogance **arrogant** arrogant
die Beiläufigkeit casualness; off-handedness **beiläufig** casual; offhanded
die Blödheit stupidity **blöd** stupid
die Boshaftigkeit; die Bösartigkeit maliciousness **boshaft; bösartig** malicious
die Bosheit malice **böse** wicked; malicious [also cross]
die Doofheit colloq daftness **doof** colloq daft
die Dummheit stupidity **dumm** stupid
die Eifersucht jealousy **eifersüchtig (auf** + A) jealous (of)
die Eitelkeit vanity **eitel** vain
die Falschheit deceitfulness **falsch** deceitful
die Faulheit laziness **(der/die Faulenzer/in** [-/-nen] lazybones) **faul** lazy
die Feigheit cowardice **feig(e)** cowardly
die Feindseligkeit hostility **feindlich; feindselig** hostile
die Frechheit cheek(iness) **frech** cheeky
die Gedankenlosigkeit thoughtlessness **gedankenlos** thoughtless
die Gefräßigkeit gluttony **gefräßig** gluttonous
die Gehässigkeit spite(fulness) **gehässig** spiteful
die Gerissenheit; die Schläue cunning **gerissen; schlau** cunning
die Gier greed **gierig** greedy
die Gleichgültigkeit indifference **gleichgültig** indifferent

die Grausamkeit cruelty   **grausam** cruel

die Grobheit coarseness   **grob** coarse

die Großspurigkeit boastfulness   **großspurig** boastful

die Hartnäckigkeit obstinacy   **hartnäckig** obstinate

die Hinterhältigkeit underhandedness   **hinterhältig** underhanded

der Hochmut arrogance   **hochmütig** arrogant

die Impulsivität impulsiveness   **impulsiv** impulsive

die Intoleranz intolerance   **intolerant** intolerant

die Langweiligkeit boringness (**die Langeweile** boredom)   **langweilig** boring

die Launenhaftigkeit moodiness   **launenhaft; launisch** moody

das Mißtrauen mistrust   **mißtrauisch** mistrustful

die Nachlässigkeit carelessness   **nachlässig** careless

die Naivität naïvety   **naiv** naïve

der Neid envy   **neidisch (auf + A)** envious (of)

die Neugier(de) inquisitiveness   **neugierig** inquisitive

der Pessimismus pessimism   **pessimistisch** pessimistic

die Prahlerei boasting   **prahlerisch** boastful

die Primitivität coarseness   **primitiv** coarse

die Rücksichtslosigkeit recklessness   **rücksichtslos** reckless

die Schäbigkeit meanness   **schäbig** mean

die Scheinheiligkeit hypocrisy   **scheinheilig** hypocritical

die Schlampigkeit slovenliness   **schlampig** slovenly

die Schlauheit craftiness   **schlau** crafty

die Schlechtigkeit badness   **schlecht** bad

die Schmeichelei flattery   **schmeichlerisch** flattering

die Schüchternheit shyness   **schüchtern** shy

die Schwäche [-n]; die Schwachheit [-en] weakness   **schwach** weak; **schwächlich** frail

die Selbstgefälligkeit; der Egotismus egotism   **selbstgefällig** egotistical

die Selbstzufriedenheit complacency   **selbstzufrieden** complacent

die Strenge strictness; severity   **streng** strict

die Taktlosigkeit tactlessness   **taktlos** tactless

die Treulosigkeit disloyalty   **treulos** disloyal
die Unartigkeit naughtiness   **unartig** naughty
die Undankbarkeit ingratitude   **undankbar** ungrateful
die Unehrlichkeit dishonesty   **unehrlich** dishonest
die Unfreundlichkeit unfriendliness   **unfreundlich** unfriendly
die Ungeduld impatience   **ungeduldig** impatient
der Ungehorsam disobedience   **ungehorsam** disobedient
die Ungeschicklichkeit; die Ungeschicktheit; das Ungeschick
   clumsiness   **ungeschickt** clumsy
die Ungeselligkeit unsociability   **ungesellig** unsociable
die Ungezogenheit naughtiness; insolence   **ungezogen** naughty;
   cheeky
die Unhöflichkeit rudeness   **unhöflich** rude; impolite
die Unordentlichkeit untidyness   **unordentlich** untidy
die Unsittlichkeit immorality   **unsittlich** immoral
die Unverschämtheit impudence   **unverschämt** impudent
die Unzugänglichkeit unapproachability   **unzugänglich** unap-
   proachable
die Verachtung disdain   **verachtungsvoll** disdainful
die Verdrießlichkeit sullenness   **verdrießlich; mürrisch** sullen
die Verlegenheit embarrassment   **verlegen** embarrassed
die Verlogenheit lying; mendacity   **verlogen** mendacious
die Verrücktheit madness   **verrückt** mad; crazy
die Vulgarität vulgarity   **vulgär** vulgar
die Wut rage; fury (**in Wut *ge'raten** get in a rage)   **wütend**
   furious
die Zerstreutheit absent-mindedness   **zerstreut** absent-minded
der Zorn anger   **zornig** angry

ärgern annoy (**sich ärgern** get angry)
sich auf|regen über + A get worked up about
aus|schimpfen tell off
be'dauern regret
be'leidigen insult
be'reuen + A repent of
be'strafen punish [person or deed]
sich ent'schuldigen apologize (**bei** + D to; **für** + A for)

grollen (+ D); einen Groll *haben (auf + A) hold a grudge
 (against sb)
kränken offend
kritteln an + D find fault with
*lügen lie
miß'billigen [thing]; **ab|lehnen** [person] disapprove of
sich schämen (für + A/wegen + G) be ashamed (of)
(sich) täuschen deceive (oneself)
ver'ärgern vex
*ver'geben forgive

SEE ALSO: **Clothing; Education; Hair; Health and Sickness; The
 Human Body; Identity; Jobs; Places, People, and Languages;
 Relationships**

13. Directions Auskünfte

Was man fragt What you ask

bin ich hier richtig bei Xs? is this the Xs' house?
ist es sehr weit? is it very far?
wie komme ich zu + D, bitte? how do I get to . . . ?
wo liegt die X-Straße, bitte? where is X street?

Wo es ist Where it is

am Ende *n* at the end (**am anderen Ende** at the other end)
am Verkehrskreis(el) *m* at the roundabout
an der Ecke at the corner
an der Kreuzung at the crossroads
auf der anderen/dieser (Straßen)seite on the other/this side
auf der Straße/dem Platz *m* in the street/square
bei + D at X's [= at the house/shop of X]
beinah(e); fast almost
dort; [less precise] **da** there (**dort drüben** over there; **dort unten/
oben** down/up there)
draußen outside (**drinnen** inside; indoors)
entlang + D [or preceding A] along
etwa [+ time/distance] **von hier aus** about [+ time/distance] from
here
gegen + A against
gegenüber [+ preceding D] opposite
gerade just
geradeaus straight on
hinten im Garten at the bottom of the garden
hinter + D behind; beyond
im ersten [etc.] **Stock** on the first [etc.] floor
im Nachbarhaus next door
im Norden/Süden/Osten/Westen to the north/south/east/west (**im
Nordwesten** to the north-west)

in der entgegengesetzten/dieser Richtung in the opposite/this
  direction (**in Richtung Stadt/Bahnhof** towards town/the station)
in der Mitte (+ G/**von** + D) in the middle (of)
in der Nähe von + D near (**in unmittelbarer Nähe** right next to)
irgendwo somewhere (**nirgendwo** nowhere)
links (**von** + D) on the left (of) (**nach links** to the left)
mitten in + D in the middle of
nach + D after
neben + D beside
nördlich/südlich/östlich/westlich von + D north/south/east/west
  of
oben (**auf** + D) at the top (of); on top (of)
rechts (**von** + D) on the right (of) (**nach rechts** to the right)
über + D above
überall everywhere
unter + D under; among (**unten** underneath)
unterwegs nach + D on the way to
von + D **bis** + A from . . . to
vor + D in front of; before (**kurz vor** just before)
weit von + D (**entfernt**) far from
zwanzig Meter entfernt twenty metres away
zwischen + D **und** + D between . . . and

Was man tut What you do

*ab|biegen turn off (**rechts/links abbiegen** turn left/right)
*biegen turn (**um die Ecke biegen** turn/take the corner)
deuten/hin|deuten auf + A; *hin|weisen auf + A point to
*fahren [in vehicle]; *gehen [on foot] go (**entlang|gehen**;
  entlang|fahren go along; **hinunter|gehen**; **hinunter|fahren** go
  down; **hinauf|gehen**; **hinauf|fahren** go up; **vorbei|gehen**; **vor-
  bei|fahren an** + D go past; **vorwärts|gehen**; **vorwärts|fahren** go
  forwards; **rückwärts|gehen**; **rückwärts|fahren** go backwards;
  weiter|gehen; **weiter|fahren** (**bis**) keep going (until); **zur-
  ück|gehen**; **zurück|fahren** go back)
folgen + D follow
fragen ask

*nehmen take
*sehen see
suchen look for (***finden** find)
zeigen show
zurück|setzen reverse; back (**wenden** turn around)

SEE ALSO: **Holidays**; **Places, People, and Languages**; **Shops and Shopping**; **Towns**; **Transport**

14. Disasters Katastrophen

Was sie sind What they are

der Blitzschlag [ː̈e] thunderbolt
die Dürre [-n] drought
die Epidemie [-n] epidemic
das Erdbeben [-] earthquake (**der Erdrutsch [-e]** landslide)
das Feuer [-]; der Brand [ː̈e] fire
die Flutwelle [-n] tidal wave
die Hungersnot no pl; **die Knappheit [-en]** famine
die Lawine [-n] avalanche
der Notfall [ː̈e] emergency (**der Ausnahmezustand [ː̈e]** state of
  emergency)
der Orkan [-e]; [tropical storm] der Hurrikan [-s] hurricane
die Pest no pl plague
der Sturm [ː̈e] gale; tempest (**der Wirbelsturm [ː̈e]** cyclone)
der Taifun [-e] typhoon
der Tornado [-s] tornado
die Überschwemmung [-en] flood
das Unwetter [-] storm (**das Gewitter [-]** thunderstorm)
der Vulkanausbruch [ː̈e] volcanic eruption (**der Vulkan [-e]**
  volcano; **die Lava** lava)

Was sie veranlassen What they cause

*ab|schneiden cut off (**durch den Schnee/durch die Flut** by snow/
  flood; **von der Außenwelt** from the outside world)
*aus|brechen erupt
beben tremble; shake
be'schädigen damage
*ein|brechen; ein|stürzen cave in; collapse
ent'wurzeln uproot
er'sticken (an + D) suffocate (on)
explodieren explode

*fallen fall
herunter|strömen flow down [lava]
in Schutt und Asche *liegen lie in ashes (**der Schutt** rubble)
*nieder|brennen burn down
platzen burst
rutschen slide
*schlagen/ein|schlagen in + A strike [lightning]
*sinken sink
töten kill
*über|laufen overflow (**über die Ufer** n pl ***treten** overflow its
   banks; **über'fluten** flood)
ver'nichten; kaputt|machen destroy
*zer'brechen smash
zer'stören demolish

Ihre Folgen Their results

der/die Ertrunkene adj n drowned person
die Explosion [-en] explosion
das Koma [pl -s or **Komata**] coma (**im Koma *liegen** be in a
   coma)
die Lebensgefahr danger of death
der Mangel an + D lack of
das Opfer [-] victim (**der/die Tote** adj n dead person; **der/die
   Überlebende** adj n survivor; **der/die Verwundete** adj n casualty;
   injured person)
die Panik panic
der Schaden [¨] often pl damage
der Schock [-s] shock
der Sturz [¨e] fall
die Unterernährung malnutrition
die Verbrennung [-en] burn
die Verletzung [-en] injury
die Vernichtung destruction
die Wunde [-n]; wound
die Zerstörung demolition

sich [D] **das Bein** [etc.] ***brechen** break one's leg [etc.]

das Bewußtsein *ver'lieren lose consciousness **(wieder zu Bewußtsein *kommen** regain consciousness)

bluten bleed **(Blut** n ***ver'lieren** lose blood)

eingeklemmt *sein be trapped

sich *er'brechen vomit; be sick

*er'trinken drown

*leiden an + D suffer from

schwer verletzt *sein be seriously injured

*sterben die **(an Hunger/Durst/seinen Verletzungen** of hunger/ thirst/one's injuries)

*ver'schwinden disappear

Hilfe! Help!

der Arzt [ˑe]/**die Ärztin** [-nen] doctor

die Bergwacht; der Bergrettungsdienst mountain rescue service

die Erste Hilfe first aid **(die Sanitätswache** [-n] first-aid post)

die Feuerwehr fire brigade **(der Feuerwehrmann** [pl ˑe or -leute] fireman; **das Löschfahrzeug** [-e] fire-engine; **der Schlauch** [ˑe] hose; **der Feuermelder** [-] fire-alarm)

der/die Freiwillige adj n volunteer

die Hilfe help **(die Hilfsorganisation** [-en] relief organization)

der Hubschrauber [-] helicopter

der Krankenwagen [-] ambulance **(der/die Sanitäter/in** [-/-nen] ambulance man/woman; **die Trage** [-n] stretcher)

die künstliche Beatmung artificial respiration **(die Mund-zu-Mund-Beatmung** kiss of life; **der Mund** [ˑer] mouth)

die Leiter [-n] ladder

der Notfall [ˑe] emergency **(der Notausgang** [ˑe] emergency exit; **die Nothilfe** emergency assistance)

die Rettung rescue; rescuing **(die Rettungsaktion** [-en] rescue (operation); **der Rettungs-/Seerettungsdienst** ambulance/life-boat service; **der Seenotrettungseinsatz** air-sea rescue)

der/die Rettungs-/Katastrophenhelfer/in [-/-nen] relief worker

das Rote Kreuz Red Cross **(der Rote Halbmond** Red Crescent)

das SOS SOS **(SOS funken** send an SOS)

Alarm *schlagen raise the alarm
jm zu Hilfe *kommen come to sb's aid
löschen put out [fire]
retten rescue

SEE ALSO: **Accidents; Crimes and Criminals; Health and Sickness; War, Peace, and the Armed Services; The Weather**

15. Drinks Getränke

das Getränk [¨e]; **der Drink** [-s] drink
zwei Glas Wein two glasses of wine (**zwei Flaschen Bier** two
   bottles of beer [only f containers pluralize])
zwei Kaffee; zweimal Kaffee two coffees

Alkoholfreie Getränke Non-alcoholic drinks

das Coke [-s]; **das/die Cola** [-s] coke®
der Espresso [pl -s or **Espressi**] espresso coffee
das Fruchtsaftgetränk [¨e] squash
der Kaffee coffee (**Kaffee kochen** make coffee; **die Kaffeesahne**
   coffee cream; **mit/ohne Sahne** white/black; **koffeinfrei** decaf-
   feinated; **der Instant-/Pulverkaffee** instant coffee; **der Filter-
   kaffee** filter coffee; **der Mokka** strong black coffee)
der Kakao cocoa
die Limonade [-n] fizzy drink (**die Zitronenlimonade** lemonade)
die Milch milk (**entrahmt** skimmed; **das Milchmixgetränk** [¨e]
   milk shake)
die Orangeade orangeade
der Saft [¨e] (fruit) juice (**der Frucht-/Apfel-/Orangen-/Zitronen-/
   Tomaten-/Grapefruit-/Traubensaft** fruit/apple/orange/lemon/
   tomato/grapefruit/grape juice; **frisch ausgepreßt** freshly
   squeezed)
die Schokolade chocolate
das Soda(wasser) soda
der Tee tea (**mit Zitrone/Milch** with lemon/milk; **der Kräuter-/
   Eistee** herb/iced tea)
das Tonic tonic (water)
das Wasser water (**das Mineralwasser** mineral water; **mit/ohne
   Kohlensäure** sparkling/still)

Alkoholische Getränke Alcoholic drinks

der Aperitif [-s] aperitif

der Apfelwein [-e] cider (der Cidre [-s] Normandy/Brittany cider;
der Apfelschnaps apple brandy)

das Bier [-e] beer (das Pils [-] Pils(ner); das Malzbier malt beer;
das Faßbier/Bier vom Faß draught beer; das Faß [¨sser] barrel;
das Flaschenbier bottled beer; dunkel dark; hell light)

der Branntwein [-e] spirit(s)

der Burgunder burgundy

der Champagner champagne® (der Sekt [-e] [quality] sparkling
wine)

der Gin gin (Gin (und) Tonic n gin and tonic)

der Glühwein mulled wine

der Kirsch; das Kirschwasser kirsch; white cherry brandy

der Korn corn schnapps

der Kümmel caraway brandy

der Likör [-e] liqueur (der Eierlikör egg-flip)

der Portwein port

die Radlermaß; der Radler; das Alsterwasser shandy

der Rum rum

der Schaumwein [-e] sparkling wine

der Schnaps [-e] spirits; schnapps

der Schoppenwein [-e] wine by the glass; draught wine (der
Schoppen [-] large glass of wine/beer)

die Schorle spritzer

der Sherry sherry

der Wein [-e] wine (der Weiß-/Rotwein white/red wine; der Rosé
[-s] rosé wine; die Spät-/Auslese late vintage)

der Weinbrand [¨e]; der Kognak [-s] brandy (der Cognac [-s]
cognac®)

der Wermut vermouth

der Whisky [-s] (Scotch) whisky (der Whiskey [-s] (American/
Irish) whiskey)

der Wodka vodka

Ihre Behälter Their containers

eine Dose Bier a can of beer
eine Flasche Wein a bottle of wine
ein Glas *n* Limonade a glass of lemonade
eine Kanne/[smaller] ein Kännchen Kaffee a pot of coffee
ein Krug *m*/eine Kanne Wasser a jug of water
eine Tasse Tee a cup of tea
eine Tüte Milch a carton of milk

Wie man sie lieber trinkt How you prefer them

der/die/das Halbe half (litre of beer)
die halbe Flasche [-n] half bottle
der Viertelliter quarter-litre

auf Zimmertemperatur *f* at room temperature
berauschend heady [wine]
frisch crisp
fruchtig fruity
halbtrocken medium-dry
herb very dry [wine]
mild light [wine]; smooth [brandy]
mit Blume *f* with a head [beer]
mit Wasser *n*/Eis *n* with water/ice (der Eiswürfel [-] ice-cube)
pur neat
schäumend; sprudelnd bubbly
schaumig frothy
süß; lieblich sweet
trocken [wine] dry
vollmundig full-bodied [wine]
würzig full-flavoured [beer, wine]

Was man tut What you do

betrunken *sein/*werden (von + D) be/get drunk (on) **(sich
*be'trinken** get [intentionally] drunk; **der/die Trinker/in** [-/-nen]/
[more derogatory] **der/die Säufer/in** [-/-nen] drunk; drunkard)

Durst *m* ***haben; durstig *sein** be thirsty

seinen Durst löschen/stillen quench one's thirst

ein|schenken pour (out)

herunter|kippen swig down

nippen (an + D) sip (from)

nüchtern *sein/*werden be/get sober

eine Runde kaufen buy a round [of drinks]

schlucken swallow

einen Schuß *geben in + A lace [drink]

*trinken (auf + A) drink (to) **(einen Schluck Wasser trinken**
have a drink of water; **einen trinken** have a drink; **jn unter den
Tisch trinken** drink sb under the table)

die Weinkarte ver'langen ask for the wine-list

Was man sagt What you say

auf dein/Ihr Wohl! good health!

das ist aber gut für dich! but it's good for you!

das schmeckt gut! that tastes good!

das tut gut! that does you good!

köstlich delicious

trinkbar/nicht trinkbar drinkable/not drinkable

ungenießbar undrinkable

was trinken Sie? what will you have?

zum Wohl!; [less formal] **pros(i)t!** cheers!

SEE ALSO: **Cooking and Eating; Food; The Senses; Tobacco and
Drugs**

16. Education Erziehung

Anstalten Institutions

die Berufsschule [-n] vocational school

die Fachhochschule [-n] specialist tertiary college

die Fachschule [-n] technical college (**die kaufmännische Fachschule** business school)

die Gesamtschule [-n] comprehensive school

die Grundschule [-n] primary school

das Gymnasium [*pl* **Gymnasien**] academic secondary school (= grammar school)

die Handelsschule [-n] commercial college

die Hauptschule [-n] non-academic secondary school

das Internat [-e] boarding-school

der Kindergarten [ä] kindergarten; nursery school

die Mittel-/Realschule [-n] practical secondary school

die pädagogische Hochschule [-n] teacher-training college

die Privatschule [-n] private school

die Schule [-n] school (**zur/in die Schule *gehen** go to school; **die höhere Schule** secondary school; **die Schule *ver'lassen** leave school)

die Universität [-en]; die Hochschule [-n]; *colloq* **die Uni [-s]** university (**die technische Hochschule** technical college/university)

Wer man ist Who people are

der/die Direktor/in [G -s/- *pl* -en/-nen] head/principal

der/die Grundschullehrer/in [-/-nen] primary-school teacher

der/die Gymnasiast/in [-en/-nen] grammar-school boy/girl

der/die Hauptschüler/in [-/-nen] secondary (modern)-school boy/girl

der/die Hochschüler/in [-/-nen] college/university student

der/die Internatschüler/in [-/-nen] boarder (**der/die externe Schüler/in [-/-nen]** day-boy/-girl)

der/die Klassenkamerad/in [-en/-nen] class-mate

der/die Klassensprecher/in [-/-nen] class representative

der/die Lehrbeauftragte *adj n* university teacher; lecturer (**der/die Dozent/in** [-en/-nen] senior lecturer)

der/die Lehrer/in [-/-nen] teacher (**der Lehrkörper** staff; **der/die Deutschlehrer/in** German teacher)

der/die Mitschüler/in [-/-nen] fellow pupil

die Null [-en] dunce

der/die Professor/in [G -s/- *pl* -en/-nen] (**für** + A) professor (of)

der/die Prüfer/in [-/-nen] examiner

der/die Rektor/in [G -s/- *pl* -en/-nen] [school] head; [university] = vice-chancellor

der/die Schulabgänger/in [-/-nen] school-leaver

der/die Schulanfänger/in [-/-nen] child starting school

der/die Schüler/in [-/-nen] pupil

der/die Schulfreund/in [-e/-nen] schoolfriend

der Schuljunge [-n] schoolboy (**das Schulmädchen** [-] schoolgirl; **das Schulkind** schoolchild)

der/die Schulkamerad/in [-en/-nen] schoolfriend

der/die Schulleiter/in [-/-nen] head

der Schulrat [¨e]/**die Schulrätin** [-nen] schools inspector

der/die Schulschwänzer/in [-/-nen] truant

der/die Schulsprecher/in [-/-nen] pupils' representative

der/die Student/in [-en/-nen] student

der/die Studienassessor/in [G -s/- *pl* -en/-nen]; **der/die Studienreferendar/in** [-e/-nen] probationary teacher

der Studienrat [¨e]/**die Studienrätin** [-nen] post-probationary secondary teacher

Was man tut What they do

*ab|schreiben (bei + D) copy (from sb)

antworten answer

anwesend/abwesend *sein be present/absent

arbeiten work

*auf|haben have as homework

auf|passen pay attention

be'antworten; antworten auf + A answer
be'fragen über + A question on
begabt/unbegabt *sein be talented/untalented
sich *be'nehmen; brav *sein behave (well) (sich schlecht benehmen behave badly)
be'strafen punish
buchstabieren spell (aloud) (wie schreibst du das? how do you
spell that?)
*durch|sehen read through
ein|sammeln collect in
faul/fleißig/gewissenhaft *sein be lazy/hard-working/conscien-
tious
faulenzen idle (about)
fragen ask (Fragen f pl stellen ask questions)
*geben teach [a subject]
gut *können be good at
klingeln ring (es hat schon geklingelt the bell's gone)
lehren; unter'richten teach [a person or a subject]
lernen learn (auswendig lernen learn by heart)
*lesen read
loben praise
sich melden put one's hand up
*nach|sitzen be in detention (nachsitzen *lassen put in detention)
prüfen test; examine
*schreiben write (eine Arbeit schreiben do a test)
die Schule *ver'lassen leave school
schwänzen truant (eine Stunde schwänzen cut a lesson)
*sitzen|bleiben repeat a year
studieren be at university; study
ver'bessern; korrigieren correct
*ver'weisen expel
wieder'holen revise
*wissen know [facts]
zur Schule *gehen attend/be at school

Was man lehrt und lernt
What they teach and learn

die Algebra algebra
die Arithmetik; das Rechnen arithmetic (**das Kopfrechnen** mental arithmetic)
die Biologie biology
die Chemie chemistry
die Computerwissenschaft computer science
das Deutsch German
die Dichtung poetry
die Elektronik electronics
das Englisch English
die Erdkunde; die Geographie geography
das Fach [¨er] subject (**das Pflichtfach** compulsory subject; **das Wahlfach** option)
das Französisch French
die Fremdsprache [-n] foreign language
die Geometrie geometry
der Gesang(s)unterricht singing
die Geschichte history
die Grammatik grammar
das Handarbeiten needlework
die Hauswirtschaftslehre domestic science
die Kunst art
das Latein Latin
das Lesen reading
die Literatur literature
die Mathematik; *colloq* die **Mathe** *both sing* maths
die Medizin medicine
die Musik music
die Pharmazie pharmacy
die Philosophie philosophy
die Physik physics
die Psychologie psychology
die Rechtschreibung spelling

die Rechtswissenschaft law
die Religion; der Religionsunterricht religious education
das Schreiben writing
der Schulunterricht *no pl* lessons (**der Unterricht** teaching)
das Spanisch Spanish
die Sprache [-n] language (**neuere Sprachen** modern languages)
die Technik technology
das Turnen; der Sportunterricht physical education
das Werken craft
der Werkunterricht woodwork and metalwork
die Wirtschaftslehre business studies
die Wissenschaft [-en]/die Naturwissenschaft *usually pl* science
(**rein** pure; **angewandt** applied; **die Sozialwissenschaften** *pl*
social science; **die exakten Naturwissenschaften** *pl* physical
science)
der Zeichenunterricht drawing

Die Umgebung Things around them

die Aufgabe [-n] exercise
der Aufsatz [ẍe] essay
die Aula [*pl* -s or Aulen] (assembly) hall
die Bibliothek [-en] library
der Bleistift [-e] pencil (**der Spitzer [-]** pencil-sharpener)
das Buch [ẍer] book (**das Schulbuch** school-book)
der Computer [-] computer
die Disziplin discipline
der Entwurf [ẍe]; das Konzept [-e] rough copy
die Erziehung education
das Feder-/Schreibmäppchen [-] pencil-case
der Filzstift [-e] felt pen
die Frage [-n] question (**die Antwort [-en]** answer; **stellen** ask;
be'antworten answer)
der Füllhalter [-]; der Füller [-]; der Federhalter [-] fountain-pen
(**die Feder [-n]** nib; quill-pen)
der Gang [ẍe] corridor
die Garderobe [-n] cloakroom

der **Gummi/Radiergummi** [-s] rubber; eraser
die **Hausaufgabe** [-n] (piece of) homework (**machen** do)
das **Heft** [-e] exercise book
der **Hof/Schulhof** [ːe] playground
die **Kantine** [-n]; das **Kasino** [-s] canteen
das/der **Katheder** [-]; das **Pult** [-e] (lecturer's) lectern
die **Klasse** [-n]; der **Kurs** [-e] class
das **Klassenbuch** [ːer] class register (and work record)
das **Klassenzimmer** [-] class-room
die **Klingel** [-n] bell
die **Kreide** [-n] chalk
der **Kugelschreiber** [-]; der **Kuli** [-s] ball-point
das **Laboratorium** [pl **Laboratorien**]; das **Labor** [pl -s or -e]
lab(oratory) (**das Sprachlabor** language laboratory)
das **Lehrerzimmer** [-] staff room
das **Lexikon** [pl **Lexika** or **Lexiken**] encyclopaedia
das **Lineal** [-e] ruler
die **Mappe** [-n] briefcase (**die Schulmappe**; **die (Schul)tasche** [-n];
der **(Schul)ranzen** [-] schoolbag; satchel)
die **Nachhilfe** coaching (**die Nachhilfstunde** [-n] private lesson)
das **Nachsitzen** detention (**eine Stunde /nachsitzen *müssen** have
an hour's detention)
das **Notizbuch** [ːer] notebook
das **Papier** paper (**das Blatt** [ːer] sheet)
die **Pause** break (**klein** short; **groß** long)
die **Preisverleihung** prize-giving
die **Prügelstrafe** corporal punishment
der **Rechner** [-] calculator (**der Taschenrechner** pocket calculator)
die **Reinschrift** [-en] fair copy (**ins reine *schreiben** make a fair
copy of)
das **Schließfach** [ːer] locker
der **Schrank** [ːe] cupboard
der **Schreibblock** [pl -s or ːe] pad
die **Schulaufgabe** [-n]; die **Schularbeit** [-en] (item of) homework
der **Schüleraustausch** [-e] school exchange
der **Schulfunk** schools broadcasting

das Schulgelände school grounds

der/die Schulleiter/in [-/-nen] head

die Schulordnung *sing* school rules

die Schultüte [-n] cone of sweets [given to child on first day at school]

der Schwamm [ˉe] sponge; duster

der Speisesaal [*pl* -säle] dining-hall

das Staubtuch [ˉer] duster

die Strafe [-n] punishment (**zur Strafe** as a punishment; **die Strafarbeit** [-en] imposition)

das Studentenheim [-e] hall of residence

das Studium [*pl* Studien] study

die Stunde [-en] lesson (**die Lektion** [-en] lesson [in book]; **der Stundenplan** [ˉe] timetable)

die Tafel [-n] blackboard (**an die Tafel *schreiben** write on the board)

die Tinte [-n] ink (**der Klecks** [-e] blot)

der Tisch [-e] [school] desk (**der Lehrertisch** teacher's desk)

das Tonbandgerät [-e] tape recorder

die Turnhalle [-n] gymnasium (**das Seil** [-e] rope; **das Reck** [*pl* -e or -s] horizontal bar; **der Barren** [-] (set of) parallel bars; **das (Sprung)pferd** [-e] vaulting-horse)

die Übersetzung [-en] translation

der Vortrag [ˉe]; [university] **die Vorlesung** [-en] lecture (***halten** give)

das Wörterbuch [ˉer] dictionary

das Zeugnis [-se] (school) report; certificate

der Zirkel [-] (pair of) compasses

Prüfungen Examinations

das Abitur [-e] *sing* = A-levels (**das Abitur machen** = take A-levels)

die Arbeit/Klassenarbeit [-en]; **der Test** [*pl* -s or -e] test (***schreiben** take; **schreiben *lassen** give)

das Attest [-e] doctor's certificate

das Diplom [-e] diploma; first science degree

der Doktorgrad [-e] doctorate; PhD (**die Doktorarbeit [-en]** PhD thesis)

der Erfolg [-e] success

das Ergebnis [-se] result

der Fehler [-]; der Irrtum [¨er] mistake

der Fortschritt [-e] *often pl* progress

der Grad [-e] degree

der Hochschulabschluß [¨sse] first degree [at university]

die Leistung [-en] performance; achievement

der Magister master's degree (**Magister Artium/rerum naturalium** MA/MSc; **den Magister machen** get one's master's degree)

die Mindestpunktzahl [-en] pass-mark

die mittlere Reife leaving certificate from *Realschule*

die Note [-n] mark (**ungenügend** unsatisfactory; **mangelhaft** poor; **befriedigend** fair; **(sehr) gut** (very) good)

der Preis [-e] prize (**die Preisverleihung [-en]** prize-giving; award ceremony)

das Problem [-e] problem

der/die Prüfer/in [-/-nen] examiner

die Prüfung [-en]; das Examen [*pl* - or Examina]; die Klausur [-en] examination (**machen/*schreiben** take; ***be'stehen** pass; ***durch|fallen in** + D fail; **schriftlich** written; **mündlich** oral)

der Schulabschluß [¨sse] school-leaving qualification

das Staatsexamen finals [at university]

die Urkunde [-n] certificate

Das Schul- und Universitätsjahr
The academic year

der Feiertag [-e] (day's) holiday (**der freie Tag** day off; **heute haben wir schulfrei** there's no school today)

die Ferien *pl* holidays (**die Schulferien** school holidays; **die großen Ferien/die Sommerferien** summer holidays; **die Weihnachts-/Oster-/Herbstferien** Christmas/Easter/autumn holidays)

das Halbjahr [-e] [school] term

die Klassenfahrt [-en] school trip

der Schulanfang first day at school; school starting time

das Schuljahr [-e] school year (**das Universitätsjahr** university year)

der Schulschluß end of school (**nach Schulschluß** after school)

der Schultag [-e] school day

das Semester [-] [university] term (**das Trimester** [-] term [three per year]; **das Quartal** term [-e] [four per year])

der Stundenplan [ẅe] timetable

SEE ALSO: **Identity; Reading and Writing; Science**

17. Feelings Gefühle

die Empfindlichkeit [-en] sensitivity
das Gefühl [-e] feeling; emotion (**die Ergriffenheit** [deep] emotion)
der Geisteszustand [ᴂe] state of mind
die Leidenschaft [-en] passion
die Sentimentalität sentimentality
die Stimmung [-en]; die Laune [-n] mood (**die Verstimmung [-en]**; **die schlechte Laune** bad mood; **Launen *haben** be moody)
das Temperament disposition

Glück Happiness

die Befriedigung; die Genugtuung satisfaction
die Begeisterung enthusiasm
die Ekstase [-n] ecstasy
die Freude [-n] joy
die Fröhlichkeit cheerfulness
die gehobene Stimmung *sing* high spirits
das Gelächter; das Lachen laughter (**ein lautes Lachen** a loud laugh; **die Lachsalve [-n]** roar of laughter; **in Gelächter *aus|brechen** burst out laughing)
die Gelassenheit serenity
das Glück happiness; luck (**Glück *haben** be lucky/in luck; **Glück *bringen** bring good luck)
die Heiterkeit cheerfulness
die Hoffnung [-en] hope
der Humor humour
das Lächeln *no pl* smile
die Leidenschaft [-en] passion
die Lust [ᴂe] desire
der Optimismus optimism
die Ruhe calm
die Seligkeit/Glückseligkeit bliss

die Sorglosigkeit carefreeness
der Spaß [≈e] joke; (piece of) fun; prank (**Spaß machen** be fun;
  Spaß *haben an + D take pleasure in)
das Vergnügen [-]; **die Vergnügung** [-en] pleasure; delight (**ein**
  Vergnügen a treat)
die Verzückung rapture
der Witz [-e] joke
die Zufriedenheit contentment

sich amüsieren enjoy oneself
auf|heitern cheer (sb) up
sich be'geistern für + A be enthusiastic about
ent'zücken enchant
er'freuen delight; gladden
freuen please (**es freut mich, zu . . .** I'm pleased/glad to . . .)
*ge'nießen enjoy
guter Laune ƒ ***sein** be in a good mood
hoch erfreut *sein be delighted
kichern giggle (**der Kicheranfall** [≈e] fit of the giggles)
lächeln smile
lachen (über + A) laugh (about)
scherzen joke

begeistert enthusiastic
erfreut (über + A) delighted (at)
freudig; freudvoll joyful
froh; fröhlich; heiter cheerful
gelassen serene
glücklich happy; lucky
lustig merry
munter lively
optimistisch optimistic
selig blissful (**selig *sein über** + A be over the moon about)
sorglos happy-go-lucky
strahlend radiant
überglücklich overjoyed
zufrieden; vergnügt pleased; content

Unglück Unhappiness

die Angst [⁼e] anxiety
das Bedauern regret
die Bedrängnis affliction
die Depression [-en] (fit of) depression
die Desillusionierung disillusionment
das Elend misery
die Enttäuschung [-en] disappointment
die Erregung agitation
das Heimweh homesickness
der Kummer; das Leid grief; sorrow (**es tut mir sehr leid** I'm very sorry)
das Leiden [-] suffering
die Melancholie melancholy
die Niedergeschlagenheit dejection
die Not need; hardship; poverty
das Pech bad luck
die Qual [-en] torment (**die Qualen** pl anguish; torture)
die Rastlosigkeit restlessness
die Reue remorse
der Schluchzer [-] sob
der Seufzer [-] sigh
die Sorge [-n] worry; sorrow; trouble; preoccupation
die Träne [-n] tear (**in Tränen *aus|brechen** burst into tears)
die Trauer sadness
das Unglück [-e] misfortune
die Unruhe disquiet
die Unzufriedenheit dissatisfaction
das Versagen no pl failure
die Verzweiflung despair

be'kümmern trouble
be'stürzen dismay
betroffen *sein von + D be affected by
be'unruhigen worry; disturb
deprimieren depress

ent'täuschen disappoint
*er'tragen suffer; put up with
fehlen be missing (**du fehlst mir** I miss you)
klagen (über + A) complain (of/about)
kränken hurt (sb's) feelings
den Mut *ver'lieren lose heart (**der Mut** courage)
*nahe|gehen + D; *mit|nehmen distress
schlechter Laune *f* *sein be in a bad mood
schluchzen sob
schmerzen pain
schockieren shock
seufzen sigh
sich sorgen; sich [D] Sorgen machen worry
stöhnen; auf|stöhnen groan
stören disturb
trösten comfort
ver'stören disconcert
ver'zweifeln despair (**die Hoffnung *auf'geben auf** + A despair of
sth; give up hope of sth)
weinen weep

ängstlich anxious
bedrückt despondent
bekümmert worried; distressed
berührt touched
besorgt preoccupied
bestürzt upset
betrübt gloomy; dismayed
deprimiert depressed
elend miserable; wretched
entsetzt appalled
enttäuscht disappointed
ernüchtert disenchanted
frustriert frustrated
gequält pained
im Stich gelassen let down (**der Stich** the lurch)
leidvoll distressed

melancholisch melancholy; gloomy
mißmutig sullen; morose
mitgenommen worn out; grieved (**schwer mitgenommen** shattered)
niedergeschlagen dejected
rastlos restless
traurig sad
trübsinnig gloomy
überwältigt overwhelmed
unglücklich unhappy; miserable
unleidlich; grantig grumpy
untröstlich disconsolate
unzufrieden dissatisfied
verletzt hurt
verzweifelt despairing

Überraschung Surprise

das Erstaunen astonishment
die Überraschung [-en] surprise
die Verblüffung amazement; stupefaction
die Verwirrung bewilderment
die Verwunderung amazement

Aufsehen *n* **er'regen; Sensation** *f* **machen** make a sensation
be'eindrucken; Eindruck machen auf + A impress (**der Eindruck [ˈɛ]** impression)
***durcheinander|bringen** throw into confusion
er'schrecken startle (***er'schrecken** be startled)
er'staunen astonish
mit offenem Mund *m* **staunen** stand open-mouthed (in amazement)
die Sprache *ver'schlagen + D stupefy; stagger (sb)
über'raschen surprise
ver'blüffen amaze; take aback
ver'wirren bewilder; baffle
ver'wundern amaze; astonish
sich wundern wenn . . . /über + A be surprised if . . . /at

benommen dazed
erstaunt astonished (**erstaunlich** surprising)
mit großen Augen *n pl* wide-eyed
sprachlos dumbfounded
überrascht surprised
umgehauen *colloq* flabbergasted
verblüfft amazed; taken aback
verstört disconcerted
verwirrt bewildered
verwundert amazed
wie vom Donner gerührt thunderstruck
wie vor den Kopf geschlagen stupefied

Angst Fear

die Angst [ˀe] fear; anxiety (**die panische Angst** terror)
die Besorgnis alarm; apprehension
die Bestürzung consternation
das Entsetzen; der Horror horror
die Furcht fear
die Hysterie hysteria
die Panik panic
der Schau(d)er [-] shiver; shudder
der Schreck [-e]; **der Schrecken** [-] fright
die Sorge [-n] worry
die Todesqualen *f pl* agony
das Unbehagen uneasiness
die Unruhe disquiet
das Zittern trembling

Angst haben vor + D be afraid of
ängstigen frighten
be'drohen threaten
be'unruhigen worry (sb); alarm
ein|schüchtern intimidate
er'schrecken frighten (**zu Tode erschrecken** scare to death)

fürchten fear (**ich fürchte, daß . . .** I'm afraid that . . . ; **sich fürchten vor** + D be afraid of)

schaudern shudder (**mich schaudert bei diesem Gedanken** I shudder at the thought)

schrecken fill with dread (**mich schreckt der Gedanke** I dread the thought)

vor Schreck *m* ***sterben** die of fright

zittern tremble; shiver

zum Fürchten ***sein be (quite) frightening

ängstlich anxious

bange afraid

bedroht threatened (**bedrohend** menacing)

bekümmert troubled

besorgt worried

beunruhigt alarmed

eingeschüchtert intimidated

entsetzt horrified

erschrocken frightened (**zu Tode erschrocken** terror-stricken)

furchtbar; fürchterlich dreadful

furchterregend frightening

furchtlos fearless

furchtsam timid

nervös nervous

starr (**vor** + D) petrified (with)

verängstigt scared

versteinert petrified

von Panik erfaßt panic-stricken

Zorn Anger

der Ärger annoyance

die Boshaftigkeit spite

die Entrüstung indignation

die Fassung self-control (**die Fassung ***ver'lieren** lose one's composure)

die Feindschaft enmity
die Feindseligkeit hostility; antagonism
der Groll *no pl* (**auf** + A) grudge (against)
die Reizbarkeit irritability
der Schrei [-e] cry
der Streß stress
die Verärgerung vexation
die Verzweiflung exasperation
die Wut fury; rage (**der Wutausbruch** [¨e] fit of rage)
der Zorn anger

ärgern irritate (**sich ärgern** get cross)
auf die Nerven *m pl* ***gehen** (+ D) get on (sb's) nerves
sich auf|regen get worked up
brüllen roar
sich ent'rüsten become indignant
er'zürnen; er'bosen incense
Luft *f* **machen** + D give vent to
meckern; mosern *colloq* grouse
*schreien shout
*übel|nehmen be resentful of
ver'ärgern vex
ver'zweifeln exasperate
vor Wut schäumen fume
wüten rage

böse angry; cross
boshaft malicious
entrüstet; indigniert indignant
erbost; erzürnt incensed
feindlich; feindselig hostile
fuchsteufelswild *colloq* hopping mad
haßerfüllt filled with hatred
jähzornig hot-tempered
mieser Laune *f* in a foul temper
mürrisch sullen
übelnehmerisch; nachtragend resentful
verärgert annoyed (**ärgerlich** cross; annoying)

wütend furious
zornig (very) angry

SEE ALSO: **Describing People; Liking, Dislike, Comparing**

18. Food Nahrungsmittel

die Beilage [-n] side-dish
der Fisch [-e] fish (**der Fischgang** [ˑe] fish course)
das Fleisch meat
das Gemüse [-] vegetable(s)
das Gericht [-e] dish (**das Haupt-/Tagesgericht** main course/dish of the day)
der Imbiß [-sse] snack
der Käse [-] cheese
die Konserven *f pl* preserved/canned food
der Nachtisch [-e]; **die Nach-/Süßspeise** [-n]; **das Dessert** [-s] dessert
die Nahrung food [= nourishment] (**die Lebensmittel** *pl* food [as commodity]; **das Essen** food [as eaten]; **das Futter** food [for animals])
der Salat [-e] salad (**grün** green; **gemischt** mixed)
die Suppe [-n] soup (**die Tagessuppe** soup of the day)
der/die Vegetarier/in [-/-nen] vegetarian (**vegetarisch** vegetarian *adj*)
die Vorspeise [-n] hors-d'œuvre; starter

Gerichte Dishes

der Aufschnitt [-e]; **die kalte Platte** assorted cold meats (and cheeses)
das Bauernfrühstück; **das Hoppelpoppel** fried potatoes and bacon in scrambled egg
der Bauernschmaus ['peasant's feast'] sauerkraut with pork, sausage, and dumplings
der Bismarckhering pickled herring with onions
die Bouillon; **die Fleischbrühe** broth
die Brühe-/Kraftbrühe mit Einlage *f* clear soup with meatballs/ dumplings
das Curry(gericht) curry

der Eintopf [≃e]; **das Ragout** [-s] stew

das Eisbein knuckle of pork

das/die Fondue fondue [melted cheese in white wine]

die Galantine galantine [cold meat in aspic]

das Geschnetzelte *adj n* small slices of veal in wine sauce

das/der Gulasch [*pl* -e or -s] goulash

der Hackbraten meat loaf

das Hacksteak [-s]; **die Frikadelle** [-n]; **die B(o)ulette** [-n] rissole; hamburger (**der Hamburger** [-] hamburger [in roll])

(der) Handkäse mit Musik marinaded curd-cheese

das Häppchen [-] canapé

(der) Himmel und Erde apple and potato purée with liver sausage and black pudding

das Holsteiner Schnitzel [-] veal ecalope with fried egg on top

das Jägerschnitzel escalope chasseur [veal escalope in mushroom and wine sauce] (**der Jäger** [-] huntsman)

der/das Kasseler Rippenspeer cured pork ribs

die Königsberger Klopse *m pl* meatballs in caper sauce

das Labskaus = lobscouse [beef and vegetable stew with gherkins, with fried egg]

der Leberkäse meat loaf [made with minced liver and eggs]

die Leberpastete [-n] liver pâté

das Matjesfilet fillet(s) of salted herring

die Pastete [-n] vol-au-vent; pâté; pie (**die Königinpastete** chicken vol-au-vent)

die Pizza [*pl* -s or Pizzen] pizza

das Pökelfleisch salt meat

das Roastbeef [-s] roast sirloin of beef

die Rouladen *f pl* beef/pork/veal olives

die russischen Eier *n pl* egg mayonnaise

der Sauerbraten braised beef marinaded in vinegar

der/das Schaschlik [-s]; **der Kebab** *no pl* kebab

der Schmorbraten pot-roast

der Spieß [-e] kebab; spit (**am Spieß** spit-roasted)

der stramme Max fried egg on spiced minced pork and onions, on bread

die Sülze brawn (**das Sülzkotelett** [-s] boned pork chop in aspic)

das Wiener Schnitzel [-] veal escalope fried in breadcrumbs
das Wiener Würstchen [-] frankfurter

Soßen Sauces

die Mayonnaise mayonnaise
nach Hausfrauenart in sour-cream sauce with wine and onions
[sometimes simply = home-made]
nach Jägerart in red-wine sauce with mushrooms and root
vegetables (for game)
die Minz-/Pfefferminzsoße mint sauce
die Remoulade tartare sauce [mustardy mayonnaise with
shallots or capers]
die Soße [-n]; **die Sauce** [-n] sauce (**die Braten-/Salatsoße** gravy/
vinaigrette dressing)
der/das Tomatenketchup tomato sauce

Fleisch Meat

der Braten [-] joint; roast (**der Schweine-/Rinderbraten** roast
pork/beef; **die Scheibe** [-n] slice)
das Bries [-e] sweetbread
die Brust breast [of chicken etc.]
das Eisbein [-e] pork knuckle
der Fleischkloß [=e]; [smaller] **das Fleischklößchen** [-] meatball
die Hachse/Haxe [-n] shank; knuckle
das Hackfleisch mince
das Herz heart
die Innereien pl offal
die Kaldaune [-n] (piece of) tripe (**die Kutteln** pl tripe)
der Kamm; [as dish] **das (Schäl)rippchen** spare ribs
die Keule [-n] leg; haunch (**die Lamm-/Kalbskeule** leg of lamb/
veal)
das Kotelett [-s] chop; cutlet
die Leber [-n] liver (**die Geflügelleber** chicken liver)
das Lendenstück [-e] tenderloin (steak)
die Niere [-n] kidney (**das Nierenstück** [=e] loin)

das Rippchen [-] pork rib
das Rippenstück [-e] rack [of lamb]
der Rostbraten grilled steak
das Rückenstück [-e] saddle (**der Lammrücken** saddle of lamb)
das Schnitzel [-] escalope [veal, pork]
die Schulter [-n] shoulder (**die Lamm-/Kalbsschulter** shoulder of lamb/veal)
das Steak [-s]; **das Beefsteak** [-s] steak (**das Filetsteak** fillet steak; **das deutsche Beefsteak** = beefburger; **das Tatarsteak** steak tartare [raw mince]; **englisch gebraten** rare; **halb durchgebraten** medium rare; **durchgebraten** well done; **verbraten** overdone)
die Zunge [-n] tongue

FLEISCHARTEN NAMES OF MEATS

die Ente [-n] duck (**die Mastente** specially fattened duck)
der Frühstücks-/Schinkenspeck bacon (**der Speck** bacon fat)
die Gans [-e] goose
das Geflügel poultry
das Hammelfleisch mutton
das Huhn [-er] chicken (**das (Brat)hähnchen** [-] roast chicken; **das junge Hähnchen** spring chicken; **das Masthuhn** fattened chicken)
das Kalbfleisch veal
der Kapaun [-e] capon
das Lammfleisch lamb
der Puter [-]; **der Truthahn** [-e] turkey
das Rindfleisch beef
der Schinken [-] ham
das Schweinefleisch pork
die Wurst [-e] sausage

WURSTSORTEN NAMES OF SAUSAGES

die Bierwurst smoked beef and pork sausage
die Blutwurst [cold] black pudding
die Bockwurst [hot] large frankfurter heated in water
die Bratwurst [hot] large fried or grilled sausage

die Currywurst sliced fried sausage served with curry and ketchup

der Fleischkäse bologna sausage

die Frankfurter [-] frankfurter

die Jagdwurst smoked sausage with garlic and mustard

die Knackwurst [hot] smoked minced-meat sausage in tight skin that snaps [**knacken**] when bitten

die Leberwurst liver sausage

die Nürnberger [hot] veal and pork sausage

die Regensburger spicy smoked sausage

die Salami [*pl* - or -s] salami

die Schinkenwurst ham sausage

die Weißwurst [hot] veal, bacon, and parsley sausage

das (Wiener) Würstchen [-] [hot] wiener; small frankfurter

die Zervelatwurst smoked pork, beef and bacon sausage

die Zungenwurst tongue sausage

Wild Game

der Fasan [G -(e)s *pl* -e(n)] pheasant

der Hase [-n] hare (**der Hasenpfeffer** jugged hare; **der falsche Hase** meat loaf)

das Kaninchen [-] rabbit

das Perlhuhn [¨er] guinea-fowl

das Rebhuhn [¨er] partridge

das Rehfleisch; **der Hirsch** venison

die Schnepfe [-n] snipe

die Taube [-n] pigeon

die Wachtel [-n] quail

das Waldhuhn [¨er] grouse

die Waldschnepfe [-n] woodcock

das Wild game

der Wildbraten roast venison

das Wildschwein [-e] wild boar

Fisch Fish

die Fischfrikadelle [-n] fishcake
der Fischkloß [ꞏe] fish dumpling; fish ball
das Fischstäbchen [-] fish finger
die Meeresfrüchte *f pl* seafood; shellfish
die Scheibe [-n] (fish) steak

FISCHARTEN NAMES OF FISH

der Aal [-e] eel (**der Räucheraal** smoked eel)
die Auster [-n] oyster
der Barsch [-e] perch (**der Rotbarsch** rose-fish; red sea-bass)
der Brachsen [-] bream
die Flunder [-n] flounder
die Forelle [-n] trout
die Garnele [-n] shrimp; prawn
der Hecht [-e] pike
der Heilbutt [-e] halibut
der Hering [-e] herring (**mariniert** pickled)
der Hummer [-] lobster
die Hummerkrabbe [-n] king prawn
die Jakobsmuschel [-n] scallop
der Kabeljau [*pl* -e or -s]; **der Dorsch** [-e] cod
der Kalmar [-e] squid
der Karpfen [-] carp
die Klaffmuschel [-n] clam
die Krabbe [-n] crab; *colloq* prawn/shrimp
der Krebs [-e] crayfish; crab
der Lachs [-e]; **der Salm** [-e] salmon (**der Räucherlachs** smoked salmon)
die Languste [-n] langouste
die Makrele [-n] mackerel
die Sprotte [-n] sprat (**Kieler Sprotten** smoked sprats)
der Steinbutt [-e] turbot
der Thunfisch [-e] tuna
der Wittling [-e] whiting
der Zander [-] pike-perch

Eier Eggs

das Ei [-er] egg **(hart-/weichgekocht** hard-/soft-boiled; **verlorene Eier** poached eggs; **Eier mit Speck** *m*/**mit Schinken** *m* bacon/ham and eggs)

das Eigelb [-] yoke

das Eiweiß [-] white of egg

das Omelett [*pl*** -e** or **-s]** omelette

das Rührei [-er] scrambled egg

das Spiegelei [-er] fried egg

Gemüse, Nüsse und Salate
Vegetables, nuts, and salads

das Gemüse [-] vegetable(s) **(eingemacht/tiefgekühlt** canned/frozen)

die Nuß [¤sse] nut **(der Kern [-e]** kernel)

der Salat [-e] salad **(gemischter/russischer Salat** mixed/Russian salad; **an|machen** dress [salad])

GEMÜSESORTEN NAMES OF VEGETABLES

die Artischocke [-n] artichoke **(der/die Topinambur [***pl*** -s, -e** or **-en]** Jerusalem artichoke)

die Aubergine [-n] aubergine

die Avocado [-s] avocado

der Blumenkohl cauliflower

die Bohne [-n] bean **(die grüne Bohne** French bean; **die Stangen-/Feuerbohne** runner bean; **die Saubohne; die dicke Bohne** broad bean; **die Garten-/Kidneybohne** kidney/red kidney bean)

die Brokkoli *pl* broccoli

der/die Chicorée [-] chicory

die Endivie [-n] endive

die Erbse [-n] pea **(junge Erbsen** petits pois; **die Zuckererbse** sugar-pea; mange-tout; **die Schote [-n]; die Hülse [-n]** pod)

der Fenchel *no pl* fennel

der Grün-/Krauskohl kale

die Gurke [-n] cucumber (**die Essig-/Gewürzgurke** pickled gherkin)

die Kartoffel [-n] potato (**die Salz-/Brat-/Petersilienkartoffeln** boiled/fried/parsley potatoes; **die Pellkartoffeln** pototoes boiled in their jackets; **der Kartoffelbrei/das Kartoffelpüree** mashed potatoes; **der Kartoffelpuffer** [-] potato pancake; **der Kartoffelsalat** potato salad; **die Pommes frites** *pl* chips; **das** (**Kartoffel)stäbchen** [-] [single] chip; **der Chip** [-s] crisp)

der Kohl cabbage (**der Rotkohl/das Blaukraut** red cabbage; **der Weißkohl** white cabbage)

der Kohlrabi [*pl* - or -s] kohlrabi

die Kohl-/Steckrübe [-n] turnip

der Kopfsalat [-e] lettuce

die Kresse cress (**die Brunnenkresse** watercress)

das Leipziger Allerlei mixed vegetables [peas, carrots, celery, beans, kohlrabi, and asparagus]

die Linse [-n] lentil

der Mais/Zuckermais sweetcorn (**der Maiskolben** [-] corncob; corn-on-the-cob)

der Mangold *no pl* spinach beet/Swiss chard

der Meerrettich horse-radish

die Möhre [-n]; **die Mohrrübe** [-n]; **die Karotte** [-n] carrot

die Olive [-n] olive

die Paprikaschote [-n] (sweet) pepper

der Pfifferling [-e] chanterelle (mushroom)

der Pilz [-e]; [cultivated] **der Champignon** [-s] mushroom

der Porree [-s]; **der Lauch** [-e] leek(s) (**magst du Porree?** do you like leeks? [*German sing = English pl*])

das Radieschen [-]; [larger] **der Rettich** [-e] raddish (**das Bund** [-e] bunch)

der Reis rice

der Rosenkohl *no pl* Brussels sprouts

die rote Rübe [-n]/**Be(e)te** [-n] beetroot

das Sauerkraut pickled white cabbage (**das Kraut** [ˮer] herb; [in S. Germany] cabbage)

die Schalotte [-n] shallot
die Schwarzwurzel [-n] salsify
der/die Sellerie celeriac (**der/die Stangensellerie** celery; **die Stange** [-n] stick; **der Kopf** [≈e] head)
der Spargel [-] asparagus; stick of asparagus (**die Spitze** [-n] tip)
der Speisekürbis [-se] marrow (**der Kürbis** [-se] pumpkin)
der Spinat spinach
der Steinpilz [-e] cepe (mushroom)
die Tomate [-n] tomato
die/der Trüffel [-n] truffle
der Zucchino [*pl* Zucchini] courgette
die Zwiebel [-n] onion

NUSSARTEN NAMES OF NUTS

die Cashewnuß [≈sse] cashew nut
die Erdnuß [≈sse] peanut
die Haselnuß [≈sse] hazelnut
die Kastanie [-n] chestnut
die Mandel [-n] almond
die Muskatnuß [≈sse] nutmeg
die Paranuß [≈sse] Brazil nut
die Pistazie [-n] pistachio
die Walnuß [≈sse] walnut

Brot und Teigwaren Bread and pasta

das Brot [-e] bread; loaf (**das Butterbrot** slice of bread and butter; **der/das Sandwich** [-(e)s] sandwich; **das belegte Brot** open sandwich; **das Schinkenbrot** ham sandwich)
die Corn-flakes *pl* cornflakes
das Getreide [-] cereal (**die Getreideflocken** *f pl* breakfast cereal)
der Kloß [≈e]; **der Knödel** [-]; [smaller] **das Klößchen** [-] dumpling
die Krume [-n] crumb
die Kruste [-n] crust
der Laib [-e] loaf (**ein Laib Brot** a loaf of bread)
das Mehl flour

das Nockerl [G -s pl -n] semolina dumpling (**Salzburger Nockerl**
  sweet vanilla soufflé)
die Nudeln f pl; **die Teigwaren** f pl pasta
der Pfann-/Eierkuchen [-] pancake
der Teig [-e] dough; pastry (**der Blätterteig** puff pastry)
die Waffel [-n] wafer

BROTARTEN NAMES OF BREADS

das Brötchen [-]; **die Semmel** [-n] roll
das Graubrot brown bread [made with rye and wheat flour]
das Hörnchen [-] croissant
das Knäckebrot [-e] crispbread
der Pfefferkuchen [-] gingerbread
der Pumpernickel pumpernickel [rich black rye bread]
das Roggenbrot rye bread
das Schwarzbrot black bread; rye bread
der Toast [pl -e or -s] toast
das Vollkornbrot wholemeal bread
das Weißbrot white bread
der Zwieback [pl -e or ⸚e] (breakfast) rusk

TEIGWARENARTEN NAMES OF PASTA

die Makkaroni pl macaroni
die Nudeln f pl pasta; [in soup] noodles
die Ravioli pl ravioli
die Spaghetti pl spaghetti
die Spätzle pl spaetzle; homemade gnocchi

Käse Cheeses

der Altenburger Altenburger cheese [mild; made from goat's
  milk]
der Emmentaler Emmenthal cheese [boiled, with holes]
der Frischkäse fromage frais
der Kümmelkäse cheese with caraway seeds
der Münsterkäse Münster cheese [hard, yellow]

der Quark curd cheese
der Räucherkäse smoked cheese
der Tilsiter Tilsit cheese [mild]
der Ziegenkäse goat's cheese

Obst Fruit

die Beere [-n] berry
das Dörr-/Backobst dried fruit
die Frucht [≈e] fruit [of a plant]
der Kern [-e] pip; stone
das Obst *no pl* fruit (**ein Stück** *n* **Obst** a piece of fruit)
die Schale [-n] peel; skin

OBSTSORTEN NAMES OF FRUITS

die Ananas [*pl* - or -se] pineapple
der Apfel [≈] apple
die Aprikose [-n] apricot
die Back-/Dörrpflaume [-n] prune
die Banane [-n] banana
die Birne [-n] pear
die Brombeere [-n] blackberry
die Dattel [-n] date
die Erdbeere [-n] strawberry (**die Walderdbeere** wild strawberry)
die Feige [-n] fig
der Granatapfel [≈] pomegranate
die Grapefruit [-s]; **die Pampelmuse** [-n] grapefruit
die Heidel-/Blaubeere [-n] bilberry; blueberry
die Himbeere [-n] raspberry
die Kirsche [-n] cherry
die Kiwifrucht [≈e] kiwi
die Korinthe [-n] currant
die Limone [-n] lime
die Mandarine [-n] tangerine; mandarin
die Mango [-s] mango

die Melone [-n] melon
die Mirabelle [-n] mirabelle plum
die Nektarine [-n] nectarine
die Orange [-n]; **die Apfelsine** [-n] orange
der Pfirsich [-e] peach
die Pflaume [-n]; **die Zwetsch(g)e** [-n] plum
die Preiselbeere [-n] cranberry
die Quitte [-n] quince
die Reineclaude [-n] greengage
der Rhabarber rhubarb
die Rosine [-n] raisin
die schwarze/rote/weiße Johannisbeere [-n] black/red/white
  currant
die Stachelbeere [-n] gooseberry
die Sultanine [-n] sultana
die Wassermelone [-n] watermelon
die Weintraube [-n] grape (**eine Traube** a bunch of grapes)
die Zitrone [-n] lemon

Nachtische und Süßwaren
Puddings and sweets

der Apfelkuchen [-] apple flan/cake
der Apfelstrudel [-] apfelstrudel
die Apfeltasche [-n] apple turnover
das Baiser [-s] meringue
der Berliner [-] jam doughnut
der Bienenstich [-e] honey and almond cake
der/das Bonbon [-s] sweet (**der Pfefferminzbonbon** mint)
der Cracker [-s] cracker (biscuit)
die Cremeschnitte [-n] cream slice
das Eclair [-s] éclair
das Eis [-] ice-cream (**der Eisbecher** [-] ice-cream sundae; **das Eis
am Stiel** ice-lolly; **das Eishörnchen** [-] cornet; **das Mokkaeis**
coffee-ice; **die Eisbombe** [-n] bombe glacée)

der Honig honey (**der Honigkuchen** [-] honey cake)

das Gebäck [-e] cakes; pastries; biscuits

die Götterspeise [-n] jelly

der Gugelhupf [-e] large ring-shaped raisin cake

der/das Joghurt [*pl* - or -s] yogurt

die Kaltschale [-n] chilled fruit-and-wine soup

der Käsekuchen [-] cheesecake

der Kaugummi chewing-gum

der Keks [G - or -es; *pl* - or -e]; **das Plätzchen** [-] biscuit

das Kompott stewed fruit

der Kuchen [-] cake

die Makrone [-n] macaroon

die Marmelade [-n]; [better quality] **die Konfitüre** [-n] jam (**die Orangenmarmelade** marmalade)

das Marzipan marzipan

der Mohrenkopf [⸚e] chocolate whipped-cream meringue

das Mus [-e] purée (**das Apfelmus** puréed apple)

der Obstsalat fruit salad

der Pfannkuchen [-] pancake

die Printe [-n] sweet spiced honey-cake

der Pudding [*pl* -e or -s] = blancmange

die Quarkspeise curd cheese and fruit dessert

die rote Grütze red-fruit blancmange

das Rumbaba [-s] rum baba

die Sahne; der Rahm cream (**die Schlagsahne** whipped cream)

die Schokolade chocolate (**die Tafel** [-n] bar; **eine Praline** [-n] a chocolate; **halbbitter** plain; **Milch-** milk)

der/das Sorbet [-s] sorbet; water-ice

das Soufflé [-s]; **der Auflauf** [⸚e] soufflé

der Spekulatius [-] spiced figure-shaped Christmas biscuit

der Stollen [-] nut and fruit Christmas cake

der Streuselkuchen [-] cake topped with crumble

die Torte [-n] flan; gateau (**die Obsttorte** fruit flan; **die Schwarzwälder Kirschtorte** Black Forest gateau; **die Sachertorte** rich chocolate gateau)

das Trifle trifle

die Vanillesoße = custard
der Windbeutel [-] cream puff

SEE ALSO: **Cooking and Eating; Drinks; The Home; The Senses; Tobacco and Drugs**

19. Furniture Möbel

die Einrichtung [-en] furnishings; *pl* fittings
das Möbelstück [-e]; das Möbel [-] piece of furniture (**die Möbel** *pl* furniture)
die Tapete [-n] wallpaper
der Teppichboden [∺] fitted carpet
der Umzug [∺e] removal

aus|räumen clear out
*aus|ziehen move out
*ein|ziehen move in
möblieren furnish
um|räumen rearrange
*um|ziehen move house

bequem/unbequem comfortable/uncomfortable
eng cramped
geräumig roomy

Die Diele The hall

der Briefkasten [∺] letter-box
die Fußmatte [-n]; der Abtreter [-] doormat
die Kleiderablage [-n]; die Garderobe [-n] coat-rack (**der Kleiderhaken [-]** coat-hook)
der Läufer [-] [long, narrow] rug
der Schirmständer [-] umbrella-stand
das Telefon [-e] telephone
die Truhe [-n] chest
die Türklingel [-n] doorbell

Das Wohnzimmer The living-room

das Bild [-er] picture (**das Gemälde [-]** painting; **der Rahmen [-]** frame)

das Brett [-er]; **das Bord** [-e] shelf

das Büchergestell [-e] (set of) bookshelves

der Bücherschrank [ː-e] bookcase

die Chaiselongue [*pl* -n or -s] chaise longue

der Couchtisch [-e] coffee-table

der Fernsehapparat [-e]; **der Fernseher** [-] television

das Foto [-s] photograph

der Heizkörper [-]; *colloq* **die Heizung** [-en] radiator (**der Speicherofen** [ː] storage heater)

der Kaffeetisch [-e] = tea table (**den Kaffeetisch decken** lay the table for coffee and cakes)

der Kamin [-e] fireplace (**das Feuer** fire; **an|zünden** light; **der Kohleneimer** [-] coal-scuttle; **die Schürstange** [-n]; **das Schüreisen** [-] poker)

das Kissen [-] cushion

das Klavier [-e] piano (**der Flügel** [-] grand piano; **der Klavierschemel** [-] piano-stool)

die Lampe [-n] lamp (**die Stehlampe** standard lamp; **die Wandlampe** wall-light; **der (Lampen)schirm** [-e] lampshade; **die Birne** [-n] bulb)

der Lehnstuhl [ː-e]; **der Sessel** [-] armchair

die Liege [-n] sofa-bed

der Plattenspieler [-] record-player (**die (Schall)platte** [-n] record; **die CD-Platte** CD; **der CD-Spieler** [-] CD player)

die Polstergarnitur [-en] three-piece suite

das Radio [-s] radio (**das Transistorrradio** transistor)

das Regal [-e] (set of) shelves; shelving

der Schaukelstuhl [ː-e] rocking-chair

der Schmuckgegenstand [ː-e] ornament

der Schreibschrank [ː-e]; **der Sekretär** [-e] writing-bureau

das Sofa [-s]; **die Couch** [-es] sofa; settee

die Stereoanlage [-n] stereo (**der Verstärker** [-] amplifier; **der Lautsprecher** [-] loudspeaker)

der Teppich [-e] rug; carpet (**der Teppichboden** wall-to-wall carpeting)

das Tonbandgerät [-e] tape recorder (**die Kassette** [-n] cassette)

die Uhr [-en] clock (**die Kuckucks-/Standuhr** cuckoo/grandfather clock)

die Vase [-n] vase

der Videorecorder [-] video (recorder) (**die Videokassette [-n]** video cassette)

die Vitrine [-n] display cabinet

der Vorhang [ᵉe] curtain (**die Gardine [-n]** net curtain; ***auf|ziehen** open; draw back; ***zu|ziehen** draw)

der Wandschirm [-e] (folding) screen

der Zeitschriftenständer [-] magazine rack; canterbury

die Zimmerpflanze [-n] house-plant

an|zünden light (**das Feuer** fire)

ein|schalten switch on (**aus|schalten** switch off)

sich ent'spannen relax

*fern|sehen watch television

hören/an|hören listen to

*lesen read

*schreiben write

Das Eßzimmer The dining-room

die Anrichte [-n]; das Sideboard [-s]; das Büfett [pl -s or -e] sideboard; dresser

der Eßtisch [-e] dining-table

der Hochstuhl [ᵉe] (baby's) high chair

der Kerzenhalter [-] candlestick (**die Kerze [-n]** candle)

der Servierwagen [-] trolley

die Serviette [-n] (table) napkin

der Stuhl [ᵉe] chair

der Tisch [-e] table (**die Platte [-n];** [for inserting] **das Einlegebrett [-er]** leaf; **bei Tisch** at table)

das Tischtuch [ᵉer] table-cloth

ab|räumen clear [table]

decken lay [table]

*heran|ziehen draw up [chair]

sich zu Tisch setzen sit down at table

Die Terrasse The patio

die Bank [≃e] bench
der Blumentopf [≃e] flowerpot
der Grill [-s]; **das Barbecue** [-s] barbecue (**die Holzkohle** charcoal)
der Klappstuhl [≃e] folding chair
der Liegestuhl [≃e] deck-chair
die Markise [-n] awning
der Sonnen-/Gartenschirm [-e] sunshade; garden umbrella
die Terrasse [-n] patio; terrace (**die Terrassengarnitur** patio furniture)
die Veranda [*pl* **Veranden**] veranda; porch; patio

Die Küche The kitchen

das Abflußrohr [-e] drain
das Brett [-er]; **das Bord** [-e] shelf
das Element [-e] unit (**das Hängeelement** wall-unit)
das Gestell [-e] clothes-horse; wine-rack
die Heizungsanlage central heating
der Herd [-e] stove; cooker (**der Elektro-/Gasherd** gas/electric cooker; **der (Back)ofen** [≃] oven; **der Grill** [-s] grill; **die Kochplatte** [-n] hotplate; **die Abzugshaube** [-n] cooker hood)
der Hochstuhl [≃e] [baby's] high chair
der Hocker [-] stool
die Kaffeemühle [-n] coffee-grinder
der Kühlschrank [≃e] refrigerator
der Mikrowellenherd [-e] microwave
der Schrank [≃e] cupboard
das Spülbecken [-]; **die Spüle** [-n] sink
die Spül-/Geschirrspülmaschine [-n]; **der Geschirrspüler** [-] dishwasher
die Spül-/Abwaschschüssel [-n] washing-up bowl
das Tablett [*pl* -s or -e] tray (**das Teebrett** [-er] tea-tray)
die Tiefkühltruhe [-n]; [upright] **der Tiefkühlschrank** [≃e] deep-freeze; freezer

der Toaster [-] toaster

der Ventilator [G -s *pl* -en] ventilator; fan

die Waschmaschine [-n] washing-machine

der Wäschetrockner [-] tumble-drier (**die Wäscheschleuder** [-n] spin-drier)

der Wasserhahn [ᵉe] tap

Das Schlafzimmer The bedroom

das Bett [-en] bed

die Bettwäsche bed-linen

das Bettzeug bedclothes

die Brücke [-n] rug

das Bücherregal [-e] (set of) bookshelves

das Daunenbett [-en] eiderdown

die Decke [-n] blanket

das Federbett [-en] duvet

die Frisierkommode [-n]; **die Frisiertoilette** [-n] dressing-table

die Heizdecke [-n] electric blanket

der Kassettenrecorder [-] cassette recorder (**die Kassette** [-n] cassette)

das Kinderbett [-en] cot; child's bed

das Kissen/Kopfkissen [-] pillow (**der Kissenbezug** [ᵉe] pillowcase)

der Kleiderschrank [ᵉe] wardrobe (**der Kleiderbügel** [-] coat-hanger; **die Kleiderbürste** [-n] clothes-brush)

die Kommode [-n] chest of drawers (**die Schublade** [-n]; **das Schubfach** [ᵉer] drawer)

das Laken [-]; **das Bettuch** [ᵉer] sheet

die Matratze [-n] mattress

das Nachtlicht [-er] night-light

der Nachttisch [-e] bedside table (**die Nachttischlampe** [-n] bedside lamp)

die Nackenrolle [-n]; [wedge-shaped] **das Keilkissen** [-] bolster

die Nähmaschine [-n] sewing-machine (**die Strickmaschine** knitting-machine)

der Papierkorb [ᵉe] waste-paper basket

das/der Poster [*pl* - or -s] poster

der Schrank [=e] cupboard
der Schreibtisch [-e] writing-desk
der Spiegel [-] mirror
die Steppdecke [-n] continental quilt
die Tagesdecke [-n] quilt; coverlet; bedspread
die Truhe [-n] chest
die Wärmflasche [-n] hot-water bottle
der Wecker [-] alarm clock (**der Radiowecker** radio alarm; **stellen auf** + A set for)
die Wiege [-n] cradle

auf|räumen tidy up
das Bett machen make the bed
im Bett *sein/*liegen be in bed
ins Bett/zu Bett *gehen go to bed
weg|räumen put away (**seine Sachen** *f pl* one's things)

Das Badezimmer The bathroom

die Badematte [-n] bath-mat
die Badewanne [-n] bath (**ein Bad** [=er] ***nehmen** take a bath)
der Badezimmerschrank [=e] bathroom cabinet
das Bidet [-s] bidet
die Dusche [-n] shower
die Haarbürste [-n] hairbrush
der Haartrockner [-]; **der Fön**® [-e] hair-drier
das Handtuch [=er] towel (**das Badetuch** bath towel; **der Handtuchhalter** [-] towel-rail)
der Heißwasserbereiter [-] immersion heater (**das Kontrollämpchen** [-] pilot-light)
die Jalousette [-n]; **die Jalousie** [-n] Venetian blind
der Kamm [=e] comb
der Rasierapparat [-e] razor; shaver (**die Klinge** [-n] blade; **der Rasierpinsel** [-] shaving-brush; **der Rasierspiegel** [-] shaving-mirror)
das Rouleau [-s] blind
das Schaumbad [=er] bubble bath

der Schwamm [¨e] sponge

die Seife [-n] soap

das Shampoo(n) shampoo

der Stöpsel [-] plug

die Toilette [-n] lavatory (**auf die Toilette *gehen** go to the lavatory; **das Klo** [-s] *colloq* loo; **das Klo-/Toilettenpapier** toilet-roll; **spülen** flush the lavatory)

die Waage [-n] scales

das Waschbecken [-] wash-basin

der Waschlappen [-] flannel

die Zahnbürste [-n] toothbrush

die Zahnpasta [*pl* **-pasten**] toothpaste

baden; ein Bad *nehmen have a bath

sich [D] **die Haare bürsten/kämmen** brush/comb one's hair

sich duschen have a shower (**sich kalt duschen** have a cold shower)

putzen clean (**sich** [D] **die Zähne putzen** clean one's teeth)

sich rasieren shave

trocknen dry [hair] (**sich ab|trocknen** dry oneself; **sich** [D] **die Hände ab|trocknen** dry one's hands)

sich *waschen wash (**sich** [D] **die Hände waschen** wash one's hands)

SEE ALSO: **The Home; Materials**

20. Greetings and Replies
Grüße und Antworten

Ankunft Arrival

bitte, nehmen Sie Platz! please take a seat

darf ich mal vorbei, bitte? may I get past?

Entschuldigung! excuse me!

grüß (dich) Gott! hello! [in S. Germany]

guten Abend good evening

guten Morgen good morning

guten Tag good day/morning/afternoon; hello

hallo! hi!; hello!

herein! come in!

verzeihen Sie bitte, können Sie mir sagen . . . ? excuse me, can you tell me . . . ?

Vorsicht!; Achtung!; paß auf! watch out!

was darf es sein? can I help you? [in shop]

wie geht es Ihnen?; wie geht's how are you? **((es geht mir) gut, danke, und Ihnen/dir?** very well, thank you, and you?; **so lala** so-so)

willkommen (bei + D) welcome (to)

Abfahrt Departure

alles Gute! all the best!

bis gleich/bis bald see you soon

bis heute abend/morgen [etc.] see you tonight, tomorrow [etc.]

bis später see you later

grüße(n Sie) X von mir all the best to X

gute Nacht good night

gute Reise!; gute Fahrt! safe journey!

hau ab! clear off!

ich muß mich verabschieden I have to go now

raus! get out!

schlaf gut! sleep well! (**gut geschlafen?** did you sleep well? **ausgeschlafen?** did you have a long enough sleep?)

tschüs! bye!

viel Spaß! have a good time!

(auf) Wiedersehen goodbye (**auf Wiederhören** goodbye [on phone])

(auf) Wiedersehen in Köln/nächsten Montag goodbye, see you in Cologne/next Monday

Vorstellung Introduction

darf ich vorstellen: X? can I introduce X? (**darf ich mich vorstellen? Ich heiße . . .** may I introduce myself? My name is . . .)

kennen Sie X? do you know X? (**kennen Sie sich?** do you know each other?; **nur vom Sehen** only by sight)

möchten Sie . . . ? would you like to . . . ?

(sehr) angenehm; (es) freut mich pleased to meet you

Entschuldigungen Apologies

bedaure! sorry!

entschuldigen Sie, bitte! please excuse me (**die Störung** for disturbing you; **die späte Störung** for disturbing you at this hour)

Entschuldigung!; Verzeihung! excuse me (**oh, Verzeihung!** sorry!; **Verzeihung?** (I beg your) pardon?)

es tut mir (sehr) leid I'm (very) sorry

es war nicht böse gemeint I didn't mean it nastily

ich bedaure sehr, daß . . . I'm very sorry that . . .

lassen Sie sich nicht stören don't let me disturb you

Pardon! I beg your pardon

seien Sie mir bitte nicht böse, aber . . . please don't be angry with me, but . . .

störe ich? am I intruding/disturbing you?

stört es, wenn ich rauche? do you mind if I smoke?

verzeihen Sie, daß ich es sage, aber . . . forgive me for saying so, but . . .

wie bitte? what?; pardon?

Einladungen Invitations

bedienen Sie sich! serve yourself

darf ich dich/Sie hereinbitten/herüberbitten/zu mir einladen? may I invite you in/over/round? (zu + D for)

darf ich dich/Sie nach Hause begleiten? may I see you home?

erlauben Sie? may I?; would you mind?

gehen wir! let's go

ich möchte Ihnen keine Umstände machen I don't want to put you to any trouble

machen Sie sich nicht allzuviel Umstände don't go to a lot of trouble (**das macht keine Umstände** it's no trouble)

nur zu! go ahead!

was möchten Sie trinken? what will you have?

werden wir uns wiedersehen? shall we see each other again?

Festliche Anlässe Special occasions

alles Gute (zum Geburtstag etc.) all the best (for your birthday, etc.)

bravo! well done

frohe Ostern! happy Easter

fröhliche/frohe Weihnachten! merry Christmas

Gesundheit! bless you! [after sneeze]

gute Besserung! get well soon

gute Reise! safe journey (**gute Heimfahrt!** safe journey home)

guten Appetit!; Mahlzeit! enjoy your meal!

herzlichen Glückwunsch (zum Jahrestag etc.)! happy anniversary etc.

herzliches/aufrichtiges Beileid! heartfelt/sincere condolences (**darf ich Ihnen mein Beileid aussprechen?** may I offer you my sympathy?; zu + D on)

ich gratuliere! congratulations!

mit den besten Wünschen (zu + D) with best wishes (for; on)
pros(i)t! cheers!
**pros(i)t Neujahr!; ein glückliches neues Jahr!; frohes neues Jahr!;
guten Rutsch (ins neue Jahr)!** happy New Year (**der Rutsch [-e]**
slide)
viel Glück! best of luck!
viel Spaß!; viel Vergnügen! have a good time!
zum Wohl! good health!

Antworten Replies

aber doch [contradicting negative statement] you're wrong, it is
aber nein [contradicting positive statement] no, you're wrong, it
isn't
(ach) du lieber Himmel! good heavens!
ach je!; ach du liebe (Zeit)! oh dear!
also so was! well, really!
beruhige dich! calm down!
besser nicht better not
bitte (sehr/schön) please; here you are [offering sth]; don't
mention it (**bitte nicht!** please don't!)
danke (schön/sehr/vielmals) thank you (very much) (**danke;
danke, ja** yes thank you; **danke; danke, nein** no thank you)
danke, gleichfalls thank you, and the same to you [not rude]
das/es ist mir egal/einerlei/gleich it's all the same to me
das ist sehr nett von Ihnen that's very kind of you
das kann ich mir vorstellen I can quite believe it
das macht mir nichts aus I don't mind
das soll wohl ein Witz sein you must be joking
(das) stimmt nicht that's not so
das tut mir sehr leid I'm sorry to hear it
das versteht sich (von selbst) that goes without saying
desto besser so much the better
einverstanden! agreed!
es geht it's all right
es ist nicht der Mühe wert it's not worth it
es kommt darauf an it depends

(es) macht nichts it doesn't matter
ganz im Gegenteil quite the reverse
ganz recht quite right
gar nicht; durchaus nicht not at all
gern geschehen my pleasure
genau! exactly!
Gott sei Dank! thank God!
großartig terrific
hocherfreut delighted
ich habe es satt I'm fed up with it
ich habe nichts dagegen I don't mind
ich komme gleich I'm just coming
ich weiß nicht so recht I'm not really sure
im Gegenteil quite the reverse
in Ordnung OK
ja bitte; bitte ja yes please
(ja) doch oh yes (it is)
ja sicher of course
ja, stimmt! that's right!
jawohl certainly
keine Ahnung no idea
keineswegs by no means; not at all
keine Ursache not at all **(die Ursache [-n])** cause)
kein Problem! no problem!
kommt nicht in Frage out of the question
laß mich in Ruhe! leave me alone
leider nicht unfortunately not
lieber nicht better not
mach dir keine Sorgen don't worry
macht keine (großen) Umstände please don't go to any trouble
  (das macht gar keine Umstände it's no trouble at all)
mein Gott! good Lord!
mit Vergnügen with pleasure
na gut; also gut OK then
na bitte! there you are!
(na/nein/also) so was! well I never!
nanu well, there's a surprise

natürlich of course

na, und? well, so what?

na und ob! and how!

nein danke no thank you

nichts zu danken don't mention it

nichts zu machen! nothing doing!

nicht wahr? absolutely!; how true!

nie im Leben! not on your life!

noch besser so much the better

noch schlimmer even worse

okay OK

Pech gehabt! hard luck!

prima!; Klasse! great!

recht/gut so right, that's fine

schön fine

sei doch nicht so! don't be like that!

so? really?

so eine Frechheit! what cheek!

so ein Pech! too bad!

so ist es that's right (**so ist es nun einmal** that's the way it is)

so, so! oh, I see

so, und nun? right, and now what?

tatsächlich? really?

um Gottes/Himmels willen! for God's/heaven's sake!

um so besser so much the better

verflucht (noch mal)! blast it! (**verdammt!** bloody hell!; **verflixt!** [weaker] damn it all!)

vielen Dank (für + A) thank you very much (for)

was du nicht sagst! you don't say!

was ist zu tun? what shall we do?

was kümmert mich das? I should worry!

weiß Gott!; weiß der Himmel! heaven knows!

wie ärgerlich! what a nuisance!

(wie) bitte? what?

(wie) schade! what a pity!

wie schrecklich! how dreadful!
wirklich? really?

SEE ALSO: **Directions; Identity; Post and Telephone; Reading and Writing; Shops and Shopping**

21. Hair Haar

der Backenbart side-whiskers
der Bart [≈e] beard (**bärtig** bearded; **glatt rasiert** clean-shaven)
die Glatze [-n] bald head (**eine Glatze *haben** be bald; **der Skinhead** [-s] skinhead)
das Haar [-e] *often pl* hair
die Koteletten *pl* sideboards
der Schnurrbart [≈e] moustache

Wie man es beschreibt How to describe it

blond blond; fair
braun brown
dunkel dark
dunkelblond light brown
dunkelbraun dark brown
grau grey
graumeliert [**grau meliert** after verb] greying
kastanienbraun chestnut
rot red
rotblond sandy
rötlichbraun auburn
silbern silver
schwarz black
weiß white

bis in den Nacken down the back of one's neck
blondiert bleached
dicht thick
dünn thin
fein fine
fettig greasy
gefärbt dyed
geflochten plaited

gestutzt cropped
gewellt; wellig wavy
glänzend glossy
glatt straight
-haarig -haired
kahl bald
kraus frizzy
kurz short
lang long
lockig curly
matt dull
mittellang medium-length
trocken dry

Wie man es trägt How it's worn

die Bürste [-n] crew cut
die Frisur [-en] hairstyle; hair-do
das Haarteil [-e] hair-piece
der Knoten [-] bun
die Locke [-n] curl
die Perücke [-n] wig
der Pferdeschwanz [ᴇe] pony-tail
der Pony [-s] fringe
der Scheitel [-] parting
der Schnitt/Haarschnitt [-e] cut/haircut
das Strähnchen [-] highlight (**die Strähne** [-n] streak; strand)
der Zopf [ᴇe] plait; pigtail

blondieren bleach
bürsten brush (**sich** [D] **die Haare bürsten** brush one's hair)
sich [D] **die Haare auf|drehen** put one's hair in rollers
färben dye
sich frisieren; sich [D] **das Haar machen** do one's hair
kämmen comb (**sich** [D] **die Haare kämmen** comb one's hair)
sich rasieren shave

Was man darauf verwendet What's used on it

das After-shave; das Rasierwasser aftershave
das Frisiermittel [-] conditioner
das Gel [-e] gel
das Haarband [⸚er] hairband
die Haarbürste [-n] hairbrush
der Haarfestiger [-] setting-lotion
die Haarnadel [-n] hairpin
die Haarspange [-n] hair-slide
das/der Haarspray [-s] hair-spray
der Haartrockner [-]; der Fön® [-e] hair-drier (**mit dem Fön
trocknen; fönen** blow-dry)
der Kamm [⸚e] comb
der Lockenstab [⸚e] (electric) curling-tongs
der Lockenwickler [-] hair-curler/roller
der Rasierapparat [-e] shaver
die Rasierklinge [-n] razor-blade
das Rasiermesser [-] razor
der Rasierpinsel [-] shaving-brush
der Rasierschaum shaving-foam
das Shampoo(n) [-s] shampoo (**shampoonieren** shampoo; **die
Schuppen** *f pl* dandruff)
die Schere [-n] (pair of) scissors

Beim Friseur At the hairdresser's

die Dauerwelle [-n] perm (**sich** [D] **eine Dauerwelle machen
*lassen** have one's hair permed)
das Einlegen set
das Farbmittel [-] dye (**die Aufhellung** bleach; **die Farbspülung**
colour-rinse; **die Farbtabelle** [-n] colour chart)
der Friseur/Frisör [-e]/die Friseuse/Frisöse [-n] hairdresser (**zum
Friseur *gehen** go to the hairdresser's)
der Friseursalon [-s] hairdressing salon
die Frisur [-en] hair-do
der Haarschnitt [-e] haircut

das Strähnchen [-] highlight
der Termin [-e] appointment (**sich** [D] **einen Termin geben
*lassen** make an appointment)
die Tönung [-en] rinse (**der Töner** [-] rinse [the substance])
die Trockenhaube [-n] [hairdresser's] drier

sich an|melden make an appointment
sich [D] **das Haar färben *lassen** have one's hair dyed
sich [D] **das Haar in Locken** *f pl* **legen *lassen** have one's hair
curled
ein|legen set
frisieren do sb's hair (**mit dem Fön frisieren *lassen** have a blow-
dry)
legen shape
***nach|schneiden; stutzen** trim
***schneiden** cut (**sich** [D] **die Haare schneiden *lassen** have one's
hair cut)
tönen tint

an der Seite [-n] at the side
hinten at the back
im Nacken at the neck
oben on top

SEE ALSO: **Adornment; Colours; Describing People; The Human
Body**

22. Health and Sickness
Gesundheit und Krankheit

Symptome Symptoms

was hast du?; was fehlt dir? what's wrong?

der Abszeß [-sse] abscess
die Allergie [-n] allergy
der Anfall [¨e] attack; fit
die Ansteckung contagion
der Ausschlag [¨e] rash (**Ausschlag *be'kommen** break out in spots)
die Beule [-n]; [cancerous] **der Knoten [-]** lump
das Bewußtsein consciousness (**das Bewußtsein *ver'lieren** lose consciousness; **wieder zum Bewußtsein *kommen** regain consciousness)
die Bißwunde [-n] bite
die Blase [-n] blister
das blaue Auge [-n] black eye
der blaue Fleck [-e]; die Quetschung [-en] bruise
die Blindheit blindness
der Blutdruck blood pressure (**hoch** high; **niedrig** low)
die Blutung haemorrhage; bleeding
die Brandwunde [-n] burn
der Bruch [¨e] fracture
das Eitern suppuration
die Entzündung [-en] inflammation
das Erbrechen vomiting
die Erfrierung frost-bite
die Erschöpfung exhaustion
das Fieber fever; high temperature (**Fieber *haben** have a temperature)
die Frostbeule [-n] chilblain
der/das Furunkel [-] boil

die **Gebrechlichkeit** infirmity

die **Gehirnerschütterung** [-en] (case of) concussion

das **Geschwür** [-e] ulcer

die **Halsschmerzen** *m pl*; das **Halsweh** sore throat

das **Herzklopfen** *no pl* palpitations

das **Hühnerauge** [-n] corn

der **Husten** [-] cough (**Husten *haben** have a cough)

die **Infektion** [-en] infection

das **Jucken** itch(ing) (**es juckt mich** I itch)

der **Katarrh** catarrh

das **Koma** coma (**im Koma *liegen** be in a coma)

die **Kopfschmerzen** *m pl*; das **Kopfweh** headache

der **Krampf** [ːe] cramp; spasm

die **Krampfader** [-n] varicose vein

der **Kratzer** [-]; die **Schramme** [-n] scratch

die **Lahmheit** lameness (die **Lähmung** paralysis)

die **Lebensmittelvergiftung** food poisoning

die **Magenschmerzen** *m pl*; die **Bauchschmerzen** *m pl* stomach-ache (die **Magenverstimmung** [-en] stomach upset)

die **Mikrobe** [-n] microbe

die **Muskelzerrung** [-en] muscle strain; pulled muscle

die **Narbe** [-n] scar

das **Nasenbluten** nosebleed

die **Ohnmacht** [-en] faint (in **Ohnmacht *fallen** faint; **ohnmächtig *werden** pass out)

der **Pickel** [-] spot

die **Rückenschmerzen** *m pl* backache

der **Rückfall** [ːe] relapse (**einen Rückfall *be'kommen** have a relapse)

der **Rülpser** [-] belch

der **Schmerz** [-en] pain; ache (**Schmerzen *haben** be in pain; **dumpf** dull; **scharf** sharp; **anhaltend** constant; **unregelmäßig** irregular)

die **Schnittwunde** [-n] cut

der **Schock** [-s] shock (**unter Schock *stehen** be in shock)

die **Schürfwunde** [-n]; die **Abschürfung** [-en] graze

die **Schwäche** [-n] weakness

der Schweiß sweat

die Schwellung [-en] swelling

der Schwindel giddiness; dizziness (**das Schwindelgefühl** feeling of dizziness)

das Seitenstechen *no pl* stitch (**Seitenstechen *haben** have a stitch)

der Splitter [-] splinter

der Stich [-e] sting; insect bite

das Symptom [-e] symptom

die Todesqualen *f pl* agony; death throes

der Tumor [G -s *pl* -en] tumour

die Übelkeit nausea

die Unpäßlichkeit indisposition; upset

die Unterernährung malnutrition

die Verbrennung [-en] burn

die Verdauungsstörung [-en] (attack of) indigestion

die Vergiftung [-en] (case of) poisoning (**das Gift** poison)

die Verletzung [-en] injury

die Verstauchung [-en] sprain

das Virus [*pl* Viren] virus (**die Virusinfektion [-en]** virus infection)

die Warze [-n] wart; verruca

die Wehwehchen *n pl* aches and pains

die Wunde [-n] wound

die Zahnschmerzen *m pl*; **das Zahnweh** toothache

das Zittern trembling; shivering

Krankheiten Diseases

(das) AIDS; (das) Aids Aids (**die HIV-Infektion [-en]** HIV infection; **HIV-negativ** HIV-negative; **HIV-positiv** HIV-positive)

die Akne acne

die Angina pectoris angina

die Arthritis arthritis

das Asthma asthma

die Bindehautentzündung conjunctivitis

die Blähungen *f pl* flatulence

die Blasenentzündung cystitis

die Blinddarmentzündung appendicitis

die Blutarmut; die Anämie anaemia

die Bronchitis bronchitis

der Bruch [⁼e] hernia

die Brustfellentzündung pleurisy

die Cholera cholera

die Diphtherie diphtheria

der Durchfall diarrhoea

die Epidemie [-n] epidemic

die Epilepsie epilepsy

die Erkältung [-en] cold; chill (**erkältet *sein** have a cold)

der Gallen-/Nierenstein [-e] gall/kidney stone

die Gastritis gastritis

die Geisteskrankheit insanity

die Gelbsucht jaundice

die Geschlechtskrankheit venereal disease

die Gicht gout

die Grippe flu

die Hämorrhoiden *pl* haemorrhoids

der Herzanfall [⁼e]; **der Herzinfarkt** [-e]; [fatal] **der Herzschlag** [⁼e] heart attack

der Heuschnupfen; das Heufieber hay fever

der Hexenschuß lumbago

der Hitzschlag [⁼e] heat-stroke

der Keuchhusten whooping cough

die Kinderlähmung polio

die Kolik colic

die Krankheit [-en] illness

der Krebs cancer

die Lebensmittelvergiftung [-en] (case of) food poisoning

das Leiden [-] illness; complaint (**ein Herzleiden** a heart complaint)

der Leistenbruch [⁼e] hernia

die Lepra leprosy (**der/die Leprakranke** *adj n* leper)

die Leukämie leukaemia

die Lungenentzündung pneumonia

die Mandelentzündung tonsillitis

die Masern *pl* measles

die Migräne [-n] migraine

der Mumps mumps

der Nervenschmerz neuralgia

der Nervenzusammenbruch [¨e] nervous breakdown

die Pocken *f pl* smallpox

die Reisekrankheit travel sickness (**die See-/Luftkrankheit** sea/air sickness)

der Rheumatismus; das Rheuma rheumatism

die Röteln *pl* German measles

die Ruhr dysentery

die Salmonellenvergiftung (case of) salmonella poisoning

der Scharlach scarlet fever

die Schlaflosigkeit insomnia

der Schlaganfall [¨e] stroke

der Schluckauf hiccups (**den/einen Schluckauf *be|kommen** get hiccups)

der Schnupfen (head) cold ((**den**) **Schnupfen *haben; sich [D] einen Schnupfen holen** have/catch a cold)

die Sepsis septicaemia

die Seuche [-n] plague (**die Pest** bubonic plague)

das Sodbrennen heartburn

der Sonnenbrand sunburn (**der Sonnenstich** sunstroke; **einen Sonnenstich *be'kommen** get sunstroke)

der Starrkrampf/Wundstarrkrampf tetanus

die Tollwut rabies

die Tuberkulose tuberculosis

der Typhus typhoid

die Verdauungsstörungen *f pl* (chronic) indigestion

die Verstopfung constipation

der Wahnsinn madness

die Windpocken *f pl* chicken-pox

die Zuckerkrankheit diabetes

Wie man ist How you are

allergisch gegen + A allergic to
anämisch anaemic
ansteckend contagious; infectious
asthmatisch asthmatic
atemlos breathless
behindert disabled; handicapped (**körperbehindert** physically
  handicapped; **geistig behindert** mentally handicapped; **der/die
  Behinderte** *adj n* handicapped person)
bewußtlos unconscious
blind blind (**der/die Blinde** *adj n* blind person; **der Blindenstock**
  [ⁿe] white stick; **der Blindenhund** [-e] guide-dog)
bucklig humpbacked
deprimiert depressed
diabetisch diabetic
einäugig one-eyed
epileptisch epileptic
ernst serious
erschöpft exhausted
farbenblind colour-blind
fiebrig feverish
fit fit
gebrechlich frail
gebrochen broken
geheilt cured
geisteskrank mentally ill
gelähmt lamed; crippled; paralysed
gerissen torn
geschwollen swollen
gestochen stung
gesund/ungesund healthy/unhealthy
heiser hoarse
infiziert infected
krank ill (**kränklich** sickly)
lahm lame
müde tired

reisekrank travel-sick (**see-/luftkrank** sea-/airsick)

schläfrig sleepy

schlecht; schlimm bad (**mir ist schlecht** I feel sick; **ich fühle mich schlecht** I feel unwell)

schmerzhaft painful

schwach weak

schwanger pregnant

schwerhörig hard of hearing (**das Hörgerät [-e]** hearing-aid)

schwindlig dizzy (**mir ist schwindlig** I feel dizzy)

stark strong

taub deaf (**taubstumm** deaf and dumb)

träge lethargic

übel sick (**mir ist/wird übel** I feel sick)

unversehrt unscathed

verkrüppelt crippled

verletzt hurt

verrenkt dislocated

verstaucht sprained

verstopft constipated

wach alert

wahnsinnig insane; mad

wohl/unwohl well/unwell (**mir ist nicht wohl** I'm not feeling well)

zuckerkrank diabetic

Was man tut What you do

sich an|melden bei + D make an appointment to see

sich an|stecken (bei + D) catch sth (from)

***an|schwellen** swell

aus|renken; aus|kugeln dislocate

sich aus|ruhen take a rest

***be'kommen** catch

***besser|gehen** + D improve (**mir geht es besser** I'm better; **auf dem Wege der Besserung *sein** be getting better)

bluten bleed

***brechen** break (**sich [D] das Bein** etc. **brechen** break one's leg etc.)

*ein|reiben rub in

sich ent'zünden become infected

*er'brechen bring up (**sich erbrechen; sich *über'geben** vomit; be sick)

sich er'holen von + D; ***ge'nesen von** + D recover from

sich er'kälten catch a cold (**erkältet *sein** have a cold)

*er'tragen; *aus|halten bear; put up with

fiebern be feverish

sich fühlen feel (**krank** ill; **besser** better)

*ge'nesen recover

holen *lassen send for

husten cough

eine Kur machen take a cure/take the waters

leichtes/hohes Fieber *haben run a slight/high temperature

*leiden an + D suffer from

mir ist kalt/warm/schwind(e)lig I feel cold/hot/dizzy

*nehmen; *ein|nehmen take [medicines]

niesen sneeze

ohnmächtig *werden faint

operiert *werden (**an** + D) have an operation (on)

schwitzen sweat

stöhnen; ächzen groan

ver'heilen heal up

sich ver'letzen injure oneself (**sich am Bein verletzen** hurt one's leg)

ver'renken twist (**sich** [D] **den Knöchel** etc. **verrenken** twist one's ankle etc.)

sich ver'schlimmern; sich ver'schlechtern get worse (**mir geht es schlechter** I'm getting worse)

ver'stauchen sprain (**sich** [D] **den Knöchel** etc. **verstauchen** sprain one's ankle etc.)

sich ver'wöhnen coddle oneself

warm *bleiben; sich warm *halten keep warm

sich [D] **weh *tun** hurt oneself (**es tut weh** it hurts)

zittern shiver

*zu|nehmen put on weight (***ab|nehmen** lose weight)

Ärzte Doctors

der Arzt [≃e]/**die Ärztin** [-nen] doctor (**der/die praktische Arzt/
Ärztin** general practioner; **der Hausarzt/die Hausärztin** family
doctor; **den Arzt *rufen**; **den Arzt kommen *lassen** call the
doctor)

der Augenarzt [≃e]/**die Augenärztin** [-nen] oculist; eye-specialist

der Chefarzt [≃e]/**die Chefärztin** [-nen] consultant

der/die Chirurg/in [-en/-nen] surgeon

der Frauenarzt [≃e]/**die Frauenärztin** [-nen] gynaecologist

der/die Fußpfleger/in [-/-nen] chiropodist

der Hals-Nasen-Ohren-Arzt [≃e]/**-Ärztin** [-nen] ear, nose, and
throat specialist

der Hautarzt [≃e]/**die Hautärztin** [-nen] dermatologist

der Kinderarzt [≃e]/**die Kinderärztin** [-nen] paediatrician

der Nervenarzt [≃e]/**die Nervenärztin** [-nen] neurologist

der Orthopäde [-n]/**die Orthopädin** [-nen] orthopaedist

der/die Psychiater/in [-/-nen] psychiatrist

der Psychologe [-n]/**die Psychologin** [-nen] psychologist

der Quacksalber [-] quack

der/die Spezialist/in [-en/-nen] specialist

der Zahnarzt [≃e]/**die Zahnärztin** [-nen] dentist

Was sie tun What they do

ab|horchen sound the chest

ärztlich ver'sorgen give medical care to

be'handeln treat

diagnostizieren diagnose

eine Diät *ver'schreiben + D put on a diet

heilen cure [disease or person]

impfen vaccinate

ins Krankenhaus schicken send to hospital

*messen measure (**den Blutdruck/den Puls/die Temperatur
messen** take sb's blood pressure/pulse/temperature)

operieren + A operate on

*raten + D advise

sorgen für + A; **pflegen** look after
jm einen Termin *geben give sb an appointment
unter'suchen examine
*ver'binden bandage
ver'ordnen; *ver'schreiben prescribe

Beim Arzt At the doctor's

die Behandlung [-en] (course of) treatment
die Beratung [-en] consultation
der Blutdruck blood pressure
die Blutgruppe [-n] blood group
die Blutprobe [-n] blood test/sample (**die Harnprobe** urine test/ sample; **das Blut** blood; **der Harn** urine)
die Diagnose [-n] diagnosis
die Empfängnisverhütung contraception
die Erste Hilfe first aid (**Erste Hilfe leisten** give first aid)
die Gesundheit health
die Impfung [-en] vaccination (**der Impfstoff [-e]** vaccine)
der/die Kranke *adj n* sick person
die Krankenkasse [-n] health insurance scheme/company (**der Krankenschein [-e]** health insurance certificate)
das Medikament [-e] medicine (**die Medizin** medecine [the science])
die Menstruation menstruation (**menstruieren** menstruate)
das Mittel/Heilmittel [-] [thing that cures]; **die Heilung** [restoration to health] cure
der/die Patient/in [-en/-nen] patient
die Pille [-n] the [contraceptive] pill
die Praxis/Arztpraxis [*pl* **-praxen**] practice; surgery
der Puls pulse (**fühlen** feel; ***messen** take)
das Rezept [-e]; die Verschreibung [-en] prescription
das Sprechzimmer [-] consulting room (**die Sprechstunden** *pl* surgery; surgery hours)
die Spritze [-n]; die Injektion [-en] injection
das Stethoskop [-e] stethoscope

die Temperatur temperature (***messen** take; **(erhöhte) Temperatur *haben** be running a temperature)
der Termin [-e] appointment
das Thermometer [-] thermometer
die Untersuchung [-en] examination
das Wartezimmer [-] waiting-room
der Zustand [≈e] condition

Im Krankenhaus At the hospital

die Abmagerungskur [-en] slimming diet (**eine Abmagerungskur machen** go on a diet; **die Diät** [-en] special diet; **auf Diät setzen** put on a diet)
die Abtreibung [-en] abortion (**die Fehlgeburt** [-en] miscarriage)
die Armbinde [-n] sling
der Arzt [≈e]/**die Ärztin** [-nen] doctor (**der diensthabende Arzt/die diensthabende Ärztin** duty doctor)
die Bahre/Tragbahre [-n]; **die Trage** [-n] stretcher
die Besserung improvement; recovery (**gute Besserung!** get well soon!)
die Besuchszeit [-en] visiting hours/period
die Bettpfanne [-n] bedpan
die Bluttransfusion [-en] blood transfusion (**das Blutbild** blood count)
die Entlassung discharge [from hospital]
die Erholung recovery
die Genesung convalescence
der Gipsverband [≈e] plaster cast
die Hygiene hygiene
die Intensivpflege intensive care (**die Intensivstation** [-en] intensive-care unit; **auf der Intensivstation *sein** be in intensive care)
die Klinik [-en] hospital; clinic
das Krankenhaus [≈er] hospital
der Krankenwagen [-] ambulance
die Krücke [-n] crutch
die Kur [-en] health cure (**der Kurort** [-e] health spa)

der Masseur [-e] masseur (**die Masseurin [-nen]** masseuse)

die Narkose general anaesthetic **die örtliche Betäubung** local anaesthetic)

der Notfall [ˑe] emergency

die Oberin [-nen]; die Oberschwester [-n] matron

die Operation [-en] operation

der Operationssaal [pl -säle] operating-theatre

der/die Patient/in [-en/-nen] patient

die Poliklinik out-patients' department

der Rollstuhl [ˑe] wheelchair

die Röntgenaufnahme [-n] X-ray

der Rückfall [ˑe] relapse

die Ruhe rest

das Sanatorium [pl Sanatorien] sanatorium

die Schiene [-n] splint

das Schlammbad [ˑer] mud-bath (**das Dampfbad** steam bath)

die Schlinge [-n] sling

die Schwangerenfürsorge antenatal care

die Schwester/Krankenschwester [-n] nurse (**der (Kranken)pfleger [-]** male-nurse; **die diensthabende Schwester** duty nurse)

die Station [-en]; der Krankensaal [pl -säle] ward (**die Unfallstation** casualty (ward))

die Therapie [-n] therapy

der Ultraschall ultrasound; ultrasonics (**mit Ultraschall unter'suchen** give an ultrasound scan)

be'handeln treat

massieren massage

operieren operate (on sb) (**jn am Bein** etc. **operieren** operate on sb's leg etc.; **operiert *werden; sich operieren *lassen** have an operation)

röntgen X-ray

sorgen für + A look after

*ver'binden; ver'sorgen dress [wound]

In der Apotheke At the chemist's

das Abführmittel [-] laxative
das Antibiotikum [*pl*** Antibiotika]** antibiotic
das Antidepressivum [*pl*** Antidepressiva]** antidepressant
das Antiseptikum [*pl*** Antiseptika]** antiseptic (**antiseptisch** antiseptic)
die Apotheke [-n] (dispensing) chemist's; pharmacy
der/die Apotheker/in [-/-nen] (dispensing) chemist; pharmacist
die Augentropfen *m pl* eye-drops (**die Ohrentropfen** ear-drops)
das Beruhigungsmittel [-] tranquilizer
die Damenbinde [-n] sanitary towel
die Droge [-n] drug
die Drogerie [-n] (non-dispensing) chemist's
das Einreib(e)mittel [-] liniment
das Gurgelmittel [-] gargle (**gurgeln** gargle)
das homöopathische Mittel [-] homoeopathic remedy
das Hühneraugenpflaster [-] corn-plaster
die Husten-/Halspastillen *f pl* cough-drops
der Hustensaft cough mixture
das/der Kondom [-e] condom
die Kopfschmerztablette [-n] headache tablet; aspirin
das Kortison cortisone
das Medikament [-e] medicine
das Mittel [-] remedy
der Mull lint; gauze
das Mundwasser mouthwash
die Pastille [-n] lozenge
das Pflaster/Heftpflaster [-] sticking plaster
die Salbe [-n] ointment
die Schlaftablette [-n] sleeping-pill
das Schmerzmittel [-] pain-killer
die Tablette [-n] pill; tablet
der Tampon [-s] tampon
das Tonikum [*pl*** Tonika]** tonic
die Vaseline vaseline®

der Verband [¨e] bandage; dressing
der Verbandskasten [¨] first-aid kit
die Vitamintablette [-n] vitamin pill
die Watte cotton wool
die Wundsalbe [-n] antiseptic cream
das Zäpfchen [-] suppository

auf|lösen dissolve
kauen chew
schlucken swallow

**dreimal täglich/nach dem Essen/auf nüchternen Magen einzu-
nehmen** to be taken three times a day/after meals/on an empty
stomach
ich möchte etwas gegen + A I'd like something for . . .
nicht zur innerlichen Anwendung not be taken internally

Beim Zahnarzt At the dentist's

der Abszeß [-sse] abscess
der Backenzahn [¨e] molar
der Eck-/Augenzahn [¨e] canine/eye-tooth
die Füllung [-en] filling
das (künstliche) Gebiß [-e]; **die Zahnprothese** [-n] (set of)
dentures/false teeth
die Infektion [-en] infection
die Karies caries
die Krone [-n] crown
der Milchzahn [¨e] milk-tooth
die Spritze [-n] injection
der Weisheitszahn [¨e] wisdom tooth
die Wurzel [-n] root
der Zahn [¨e] tooth (**Vorder-** front; **Hinter-** back; **locker** loose)
der Zahnarzt [¨e]/**die Zahnärztin** [-nen] dentist
die Zahnarztpraxis [*pl* **-praxen**] dental surgery
der Zahnbelag; die Plaque plaque
das Zahnfleisch gum(s) (**wund** sore)
die Zahnspange [-n]; **die Zahnklammer** [-n] brace

der Zahnstein tartar
das Zahnweh; die Zahnschmerzen *m pl* toothache

an|passen fit [dentures]
*an|schlagen chip
füllen fill
spülen; aus|spülen rinse (**bitte mal (aus)spülen!** please rinse)
*ziehen draw; take out (**ziehen *lassen** have out)

Beim Optiker At the optician's

das Auge [-n] eye (**sich [D] die Augen *ver'derben** ruin one's
  eyesight)
die Brille [-n] (pair of) spectacles (***tragen** wear)
das Brillenetui [-s] spectacle case
das Fernglas [ːer] (pair of) binoculars
das Gestell/Brillengestell [-e] frame
das Glas [ːer] lens [in spectacles] (**getönt** tinted)
das Glaukom; der grüne Star glaucoma (**der graue Star** cataract)
der Kneifer [-] pince-nez
die Kontaktlinse [-n] contact lens (**hart** hard; **weich** soft)
die Lupe [-n] magnifying glass
das Monokel [-] monocle
der/die Optiker/in [-/-nen] optician (**der/die Augenoptiker/in**
  ophthalmic optician)
der Sehtest [*pl* -s or -e] eye-test (**unter'suchen; testen** test)
das Sehvermögen sight (**gut** good; **schwach** weak; **der Verlust des
  Sehvermögens** loss of sight)
die Sonnenbrille [-n] (pair of) sun-glasses

bebrillt wearing glasses
farbenblind colour-blind
kurzsichtig short-sighted (**weitsichtig** long-sighted)

SEE ALSO: **Accidents; Disasters; The Human Body; Science; The
Senses; Tobacco and Drugs**

die Antike; das Altertum antiquity (**im Altertum; in der Antike** in antiquity)

die Ära [*pl* **Ären**] era

der Archäologe [-n]/**die Archäologin** [-nen] archaeologist

die Archäologie; die Altertumskunde archaeology (**die Unterwasser-/Industriearchäologie** marine/industrial archaeology)

die Ausgrabung excavation [action] (**die Ausgrabungsstätte** [-n] excavation [place])

die Chronologie chronology

das Denkmal [¨er] monument

das Dokument [-e]; **die Urkunde** [-n] document

die Eiszeit Ice Age (**die Stein-/Bronze-/Eisenzeit** Stone/Bronze/Iron Age)

die Entwicklung [-en] development

die Epoche [-n] epoch

das Ereignis [-se] event

der Feudalismus feudalism (**feudalistisch; Feudal-** feudal)

die Gegenwart present (**gegenwärtig** present)

die Geschichte [-n] history; story (**geschichtlich; historisch** historical)

der/die Historiker/in [-/-nen]; [writer] **der/die Geschichtsschreiber/in** [-/-nen] historian

der Höhepunkt [-e] high point

der Imperialismus imperialism

das Jahrhundert [-e] century (**im neunzehnten Jahrhundert** in the nineteenth century)

das Jahrzehnt [-e] decade

der Kreuzzug [¨e] crusade

das Mittelalter Middle Ages (**im Mittelalter** in the Middle Ages; **mittelalterlich** medieval)

das Museum [*pl* **Museen**] museum

die Periode [-n] period

die Quelle [-n] source

die Reformation Reformation
die Renaissance Renaissance
die Revolution [-en] revolution
die Ruine [-n] ruin
die Tatsache [-n] fact
der Untergang [≈e] fall
der Ursprung [≈e] origin
der Verfall *no pl* decline
die Vergangenheit past (**in der Vergangenheit** in the past;
 vergangen past)
die Verschwörung [-en] conspiracy (**die Pulververschwörung**
 Gunpowder Plot)
die Vorgeschichte prehistory (**vorgeschichtlich** prehistoric)
die Zeit [-en] time (**zu der Zeit** at that time; **in früheren Zeiten** in
 former times; **das waren noch Zeiten** those were the days; **das
 Zeitalter [-]** age; **das goldene Zeitalter** golden age)
die Zivilisation [-en] civilization (**zivilisiert** civilized)
die Zukunft future (**(zu)künftig** future)

dauern last
***ent'stehen aus** + D originate from
***ge'schehen; passieren** happen
stammen aus + D date from
***ver'gehen** pass [of time]
***vor|kommen** occur

aktuell current
chronologisch chronological
damals at that time
ehemalig former
einmal once (**es war einmal . . .** once upon a time there was . . .)
früher former(ly); in the past
heutzutage nowadays
in diesem/dem Moment at the/that moment
legendär; sagenhaft legendary
modern modern
seit + D since (**seit X Jahren** for X years)
traditionell; [handed down] **überkommen** traditional

vor/nach Christus; v./n. Chr. BC/AD
vor X Jahren X years ago

SEE ALSO: **Art and Architecture; Politics; Time; War, Peace, and the Armed Services**

24. Holidays Ferien

Vorbereitungen Preparations

die **Anzahlung** [-en]; die **Kaution** [-en] deposit
der **Aufenthalt** [-e] stay
die **Bestätigung** confirmation
die **Broschüre** [-n]; der/das **Prospekt** [-e] brochure
die **Fahrkarte** [-n] ticket (die **Flugkarte** plane ticket)
das **Gepäck** luggage
das **Hotelverzeichnis** [-se] hotel guide
die **Karte** [-n] map; ticket
der **Koffer/Reisekoffer** [-] suitcase
der **Kulturbeutel** [-] sponge-bag
die **Liste** [-n] list
der **Paß/Reisepaß** [¨sse] passport (ver'**längern** renew; das **Visum** [pl **Visen**] visa)
der **Rabatt** [-e] discount
die **Reise** [-n] journey; trip
das **Reisebüro** [-s] travel agent's
der **Reisescheck** [-s] traveller's cheque
die **Reiseroute** [-n] itinerary
die **Reiseversicherung** travel insurance (eine **Versicherung** *ab|schließen take out insurance; die **grüne Karte** green card)
die **Reservierung** [-en] reservation
der **Rucksack** [¨e] rucksack
die **Saison** [-s] (holiday) season (während/außerhalb der **Saison** during the season/off-season)
die **Unterkunft** [¨e] accommodation
der **Urlaub**; die **Ferien** pl holiday(s) (in **Urlaub** *fahren go on holiday; auf/im/in **Urlaub** *sein; **Urlaub machen** be on holiday; **urlaubsreif** *sein need a holiday; der **freie Tag** [-e]; [public holiday] der **Feiertag** day's holiday)

ab'**sagen** cancel
be'**stätigen** confirm (**schriftlich** in writing)

buchen; [rooms] **vor|be'stellen** book (**voll belegt; ausgebucht** fully booked)

sich er'kundigen (**nach** + D) enquire (about)

*****fahren; reisen** travel

sich impfen *****lassen be vaccinated

mieten rent

*****mit|nehmen** take (with you)

packen pack (**die Koffer** *m pl* **packen** pack one's bags)

Reiseziele Destinations

der Austausch/Schüleraustausch [-e] exchange/school exchange

der Campingplatz [ᵍe] campsite

die Ferien *pl* **auf dem Lande** country holiday

die Ferienreise [-n] holiday trip/journey

die Ferienwohnung [-en] holiday flat

die Frühstückspension [-en] bed-and-breakfast place (**ein Zimmer** *n* **mit Frühstück** bed and breakfast; *****unter|bringen** put up)

der Gasthof [ᵍe] inn

das Hotel [-s] hotel (**das Hotel garni** [G - -; *pl* -s -s] bed-and-breakfast hotel)

die Jugendherberge [-n] youth hostel

die Kreuzfahrt [-en] cruise (**eine Kreuzfahrt machen** go on a cruise)

der Kurort [-e] health resort; spa

das Motel [-s] motel

die Pauschalreise [-n] package tour (**die Gruppe** [-n] group)

die Pension [-en]; **das Fremdenheim** [-e] guest-house

die Selbstversorgung self-catering

der Urlaubs-/Aufenthalts-/Ferienort [-e] resort (**der Skiurlaubsort** ski resort; **das Seebad** [ᵍer] seaside resort)

Was man dort findet What you find there

der Aufenthalt [-e] stay (**ein fünftägiger Aufenthalt** a five-day stay)

der Ausflug [≃e] outing; excursion (**das Ausflugsziel** [-e] destination; **das Ausflugsziel am Ort** local beauty-spot)

der Besuch [-e] visit (**der/die Besucher/in** [-/-nen] visitor)

die Busreise [-n] coach trip

der/die Fremde *adj n* foreigner; stranger; visitor

das Fremdenverkehrsbüro [-s] tourist office (**die Broschüre** [-n]; **der/das Reiseprospekt** [-e] brochure)

die Führung [-en] guided tour

die Gastfreundlichkeit hospitality

die Gastronomie gastronomy

die Grenze [-n] frontier; border

der Karneval [*pl* -e or -s]; [pre-Lent] **der Fasching** [*pl* -e or -s] carnival

das Konsulat [-e] consulate

die Küche cuisine; cooking

das Kunsthandwerk crafts

das Picknick [*pl* -e or -s] picnic (**Picknick machen/*halten** have a picnic)

der Reiseführer [-] guide(book)

der/die Reiseleiter/in [-/-nen] guide [the person]

die Rundfahrt [-en] tour

die Sehenswürdigkeit [-en] sight (**die Sehenswürdigkeiten be'sichtigen** see the sights)

das Souvenir [-s]; **das Reiseandenken** [-] souvenir

der Spaziergang [≃e] walk

die Spezialität [-en] (**des Hauses**) speciality (of the house)

der Sprachführer [-] phrase-book

der Tourismus tourism

der/die Tourist/in [-en/-nen] tourist (**ermäßigte Preise für Touristen** tourist rates)

der Zoll customs (**der Zollbeamte** *adj n*/**die Zollbeamtin** [-nen] customs officer; **die Zollkontrolle** customs check; **zollfrei** duty-free; **ver'zollen** pay duty on)

sich amüsieren; sich ver'gnügen enjoy oneself (**sich vergnügen damit, et zu tun** enjoy oneself doing sth)

be'suchen visit

neppen rip off

beeindruckend impressive
berühmt famous
häßlich ugly
malerisch picturesque
romantisch romantic
Touristen- tourist
vergnügt having a good time

Im Hotel At the hotel

das Anmeldeformular [-e] registration form (**aus|füllen** fill in)
das Badezimmer [-] bathroom
der Balkon [*pl* -s or -e] balcony (**die Aussicht** [-en] view)
die Bar [-s] bar
die Bedienung service (**der Zimmerservice; die Zimmerbedienung**
  room service; **mit/ohne Bedienung** including/excluding service)
die Beschwerde [-n]; **die Reklamation** [-en] complaint
das Bett [-en] bed (**das Kinderbett** cot)
das Büro [-s] office
der Direktor [G -s *pl* -en]/**die Direktorin** [-nen] manager (**die
  Direktion** the management)
das Einzelzimmer [-] single room (**das Doppel-/Zweibettzimmer**
  double/twin-bedded room)
der Empfang reception
der Empfangschef [-s]/**die Empfangsdame** [-n] receptionist
die Empfangshalle [-n]; **das Foyer** [-s] foyer
das Essen [-]; **die Mahlzeit** [-en] meal
der Fahrstuhl [ː e]; **der Aufzug** [ː e]; **der Lift** [*pl* -e or -s] lift
das Fremden-/Gästebuch [ː er] hotel register (**sich ins Fremden-
  buch *ein|tragen** register)
das Fremdenzimmer [-] room (to let) (**Übernachtung** *f* **mit
  Frühstück** *n* bed and breakfast)
der Gast [ː e] guest; patron; resident
das Gasthaus [ː er]/**Gasthof** [ː e] inn
die Gaststätte [-n] public house; restaurant

die Heizung [-en] *colloq* heating; radiator

das Hotel [-s] hotel

die Hotelgarage [-n] hotel garage

der Hotelier [-s] hotelier

die Hotelpreise *m pl* tariff

der/die Inhaber/in [-/-nen] proprietor

die Klimaanlage air-conditioning

die Kneipe [-n]; **die Schenke** [-n] pub (**die Theke** [-n] bar [counter])

der Küchenchef [-s] chef

die Kurtaxe [-n] (spa) visitor's tax

die Lounge [-s]; **die Hotelhalle** [-n] lounge

der Notausgang [≈e] emergency exit

der Parkplatz [≈e] car-park

die Pension [-en] full board (**halbe/volle Pension** half/full board)

der Portier [-s]; **der Hausdiener** [-] porter (**der Nachtportier** night-porter)

die Quittung [-en] receipt

die Rechnung [-en] bill (**das Trinkgeld** [-er] tip; **die Mehrwertsteuer** VAT)

das Restaurant [-s] restaurant (**der Speisesaal** [*pl* -säle] dining-room)

die Rezeption reception (desk/counter)

der/das Safe [-s] safe

das Schwimmbecken [-] swimming-pool (**das Freibad** [≈er] open-air swimming-pool)

der Stock [-] floor (**im ersten/obersten Stock** on the first/top floor; **im Erd-/Kellergeschoß** *n* on the ground/basement floor)

der/die Telefonist/in [-en/-nen] switchboard operator

die Terrasse [-n] terrace

die Toilette [-n] toilet (**eine eigene Toilette** a private toilet)

die Treppe [-n] (flight of) stairs

das Waschbecken wash-basin (**der Stöpsel** [-] plug)

der Wäscheservice laundry service

der Wirt/Gastwirt [-e] host; landlord (**die Wirtin/Gastwirtin** [-nen] hostess; landlady)

das Zimmer [-] **(mit Dusche** *f*/**mit Bad** *n*/**mit Frühstück** *n*) room
  (with shower/bath/breakfast) **(vorne/zur Straße** at the front;
  hinten/zum Hof at the back; **der Hof** [¬e] yard; **mit Blick**
  auf + A facing . . . ; **Zimmer frei** vacancies)
das Zimmermädchen [-] chambermaid **(das Zimmer machen** do
  the room)
die Zimmernummer [-n] room number
der Zimmerpreis [-e] price of room **(pro Tag** per day)
der Zimmerschlüssel [-] (room) key **(das Schloß** [¬sser] lock)
der Zuschlag [¬e] supplement

auf das Zimmer *bringen take up to one's room
sich be'schweren/sich be'klagen über + A complain
*bleiben bis** + A stay until
*emp'fehlen** recommend
fertig|machen make up; prepare [bill]
hinauf|-/-/hinunter|tragen** take up/down **(hinauf|-/-hinunter-**
  schicken send up/down)
klingeln ring
*liegen zu** + D **hin** look out on
nach|prüfen check [bill] **(richtig|stellen** put right)
reservieren *lassen; vor|be'stellen book
stören disturb
über'nachten put up; spend the night
wecken wake
zahlen pay **(im voraus zahlen** pay in advance)

auf open **(zu** closed)
ausgebucht full up
belegt hotel full; no vacancies
bequem comfortable
inbegriffen in + D included in
laut noisy
zur Verfügung available

Auf dem Campingplatz On the campsite

der Abfall [ˉe] *often pl* rubbish (**die Abfalltonne [-n]** rubbish bin)

das Abwaschbecken washing-up sink

der Anhänger [-] trailer

die Bodenplane [-n]; **der Zeltboden** [ˉ] groundsheet (**die Plane** flysheet)

der/die Camper/in [-/-nen] camper

das Camping; **das Zelten** camping (**zum Camping *fahren** go camping; **Zelten verboten** no camping)

der Campingbus [-se] motor-caravan; camper

der Campingführer [-] camping-guide (book)

das Campinggas camping-gas (**das Butangas** butane; **die Nachfüllflasche [-n]** refill)

der Campinghocker [-] camp-stool

die Campingliege [-n] camp-bed

der Campingplatz [ˉe] campsite (**der Campingplatz für Wohnwagen** caravan site; **die Gebühren** *f pl* charges)

das Feldbett [-en] camp-bed

die Feldflasche [-n] water-bottle

das Freie *adj n* the open air (**im Freien über'nachten** spend the night in the open)

der Herd [-e] stove

der Klapptisch [-e] folding table (**der Klappstuhl** [ˉe] folding chair)

die Kühltasche [-n] cool box/bag

das Lagerfeuer [-] camp-fire

die Luftmatratze [-n] air-bed

das Mückennetz [-e] mosquito-net

der Preis [-e] charge (**der Tages-/Wochenpreis** daily/weekly charge)

die sanitären Anlagen showers and toilets

das Seil [-e] rope

der Spielplatz [ˉe] playground

der Stromanschluß electricity connection

die Taschenlampe [-n] torch

das Taschenmesser [-] pocket-knife

das Trinkwasser drinking-water
der Waschsalon [-s] launderette
der Wasserkanister [-] water container
das Wohnmobil [-e] mobile home
der Wohnwagen [-] caravan (**Urlaub im Wohnwagen machen** go caravanning)
das Zelt tent
der Zeltpflock [ːe]; **der Hering** [-e] tent-peg
der Zeltplatz [ːe] (tent) site
die Zeltstange [-n] tent-pole

auf|bauen; *****auf|schlagen** put up; pitch (**ab|bauen**; *****ab|schlagen** take down; strike)
trampen hitch-hike
zelten; **campen** camp (**wild zelten** camp off-site)

In der Jugendherberge At the youth hostel

die Bettwäsche bed-linen (**die Decke** [-n] blanket; **das Laken** [-] sheet)
der Herbergsvater [ː]/**die Herbergsmutter** [ː] warden
die Jugendherberge [-n] youth hostel
die Kochgelegenheit *sing* cooking facilities (**die Waschgelegenheit** *sing* washing facilities)
der Mitgliedsausweis [-e] membership card
der Schlafraum [ːe] dormitory
der Schlafsack [ːe] sleeping-bag
der Spielraum [ːe] games room
der Tagesraum [ːe] day-room
die Vorschriften *f pl* rules
der Waschraum [ːe] wash-room

SEE ALSO: **Cinema and Photography; Furniture; The Home; Leisure and Hobbies; Nature; Places, People, and Languages; Sports and Games; Transport; The Weather**

25. The Home Das Heim

der/die Eigentümer/in [-/-nen] owner
der/die Hausbesitzer/in [-/-nen] (home-)owner
der/die Hausverwalter/in [-/-nen] caretaker
die Hypothek [-en] mortgage (*auf|nehmen take out)
die Miete [-n] rent (der/die Mieter/in [-/-nen] tenant; der
  Mietvertrag [⁼e] lease; der/die Untermieter/in [-/-nen] subtenant)
der/die Nachbar/in [-n/-nen] neighbour (die unmittelbaren
  Nachbarn; die Nachbarn von nebenan next-door neighbours)
der Umzug [⁼e] move; removal (der Möbelpacker [-] removal
  man)

ab|stellen cut off [electricity, gas]
*an|schließen (an die Strom-/Gasversorgung) connect (the
  electricity/gas)
auf|drehen turn on [water, gas] (zu|drehen turn off)
bauen *lassen have built
sich ein|leben settle in
*ein|ziehen move in (*aus|ziehen move out)
heizen heat
kündigen give notice; foreclose [mortgage] (jm die Wohnung
  kündigen give sb notice to quit the flat)
*liegen be situated
mieten rent
möblieren furnish
nach Hause *gehen go home (zu Hause *sein be at home)
räumen vacate
*um|ziehen move house
ver|mieten let; rent out
wohnen (in + D) live (in)
*zu|schließen lock (up)

außen outside
gemütlich cosy
innen inside

möbliert furnished (**möbliert wohnen** live in a furnished flat)

nebenan next door

oben upstairs (**die Treppe *hinauf|gehen** go upstairs)

schön gelegen nicely situated

unten downstairs (**die Treppe *hinunter|gehen** go downstairs)

Wohnungen Dwellings

der Altbau [*pl* **-bauten**] old house/building (**der Neubau** new house/building)

das Altersheim [**-e**]/**das Altenheim** [**-e**] old people's home

der Bauernhof [ˀe] farm

der Bungalow [**-s**] bungalow

das Chalet [**-s**] chalet

das Cottage [**-s**] cottage (**strohgedeckt** thatched)

die Doppelhaushälfte [**-n**] semi-detached house (**das Doppelhaus** [ˀer] pair of semis)

das Einfamilienhaus [ˀer] private house [as opposed to **das Mehrfamilienhaus**, house split into flats]

das Einzelhaus [ˀer] detached house

die Einzimmerwohnung [**-en**]; **das Apartment** [**-s**] studio flat

das Gebäude [**-**] building

das Haus [ˀer] house; building

die Kellerwohnung [**-en**] basement flat

das Landhaus [ˀer] country house

das Reihenhaus [ˀer] terraced house

das Stadthaus [ˀer] town house

die Villa [*pl* **Villen**] villa

der Wohnblock [**-s**] block of flats

die Wohnung [**-en**] flat (**die Sozialwohnung** = council flat)

der Wolkenkratzer [**-**] skyscraper

Teile eines Hauses Parts of a house

der Abstellraum [ˀe] box-room

das Arbeitszimmer [**-**] study

das Bad [ˀer]; **das Badezimmer** [**-**] bathroom

der **Balken** [-] beam (**freigelegt** exposed)

der **Balkon** [*pl* -s or -e] balcony

der **Boden/Fußboden** [ⁿ] floor (**das Parkett** [-e]; **der Parkettboden**
parquet floor)

die **Bibliothek** [-en] library

das **Dach** [ⁿer] roof (**der Dachziegel** [-] roof tile; **die Schieferplatte**
[-n] slate; **der Dachboden** [ⁿ] attic; loft; **die Dachkammer** [-n]; **die**
Mansarde [-n] attic room; **der Dachausbau** [-bauten] loft
conversion; **das Dachfenster** [-] rooflight; skylight)

die **Decke** [-n] ceiling

die **Diele** [-n] hall(way); floor-board

das **Erdgeschoß** [-sse] ground floor (**im Erdgeschoß** on the
ground floor)

das **Eßzimmer** [-] dining-room (**die Eßecke** [-n] dining-area)

der **Fahrstuhl** [ⁿe]; **der Aufzug** [ⁿe] lift (**außer Betrieb** *m* out of order)

die **Fassade** [-n]; **die Front** [-en] façade; house front

das **Fenster** [-] window (**das Erker-/Mansarden-/Schiebe-/**
Flügelfenster bay/dormer/sash/casement window; **das franzö-**
sische Fenster French window)

die **Fensterbank** [ⁿe] [internal]; **der/das Fenstersims** [-e] [external]
window-ledge

die **Fensterscheibe** [-n] window pane

die **Fliese** [-n] tile

der **Flur** [-e] entrance hall; corridor

der **Gang** [ⁿe]; **der Korridor** [-e] corridor

die **Garage** [-n] garage

das **Gast-/Gästezimmer** [-] guest-room

der **Giebel** [-] gable (**die Giebelseite** [-n] gable-end)

das **Haus** [ⁿer] house

der **Kamin** [-e] fireplace (**der/das Kaminsims** [-e] mantelpiece; **das**
Feuer [-] fire; **der Rauch** smoke; **die Kohle** [-n] coal; **das**
Holzscheit [*pl* -e or -er] log; **der Schornstein** [-e] chimney; **der**
Schornsteinkopf [ⁿe] chimney-pot; **der Schornsteinfeger** [-]
chimney-sweep)

der **Keller** [-] cellar (**das Kellergeschoß** [-sse]; **das Souterrain** [-s]
basement)

das **Kinderzimmer** [-] children's room; nursery

die **Küche** [-n] kitchen
die **Mauer** [-n] [outside]; die **Wand** [¨e] [inside] wall
das **Obergeschoß** [-sse] upper storey
das **Oberlicht** [-er] fanlight
die **Rumpelkammer** [-n] junk room
das **Schlafzimmer** [-] bedroom
die **Schwelle** [-n] threshold
der **Sparren** [-] rafter
die **Speisekammer** [-n] larder (der **Speiseschrank** [¨e] larder cupboard)
der **Stock** [-]; das **Stockwerk** [-e]; die **Etage** [-n] floor; storey (im ersten Stock on the first floor)
die **Toilette** [-n]; das **WC** [pl - or -s] lavatory (das **Klo** [-s] colloq loo)
die **Trennwand** [¨e] partition (wall)
die **Treppe** [-n] staircase; flight of stairs (die **Stufe** [-n] step; das **Treppenhaus** [¨er] stairwell; das **Geländer** [-] (set of) bannisters; die **Treppe** *hinauf-/hinunter|gehen go up-/downstairs; der **Treppenabsatz** [¨e] half-landing; der **Treppenflur** [-e] landing; die **Wendeltreppe** spiral staircase)
die **Tür** [-en] door (die **Türstufe** [-n] doorstep; die **Eingangs-/Haus-/Hintertür** entrance/front/back door; die **Dreh-/Schiebe-/Pendel-/Doppeltür** revolving/sliding/swing/double door)
die **Veranda** [pl **Veranden**] veranda; patio
die **Vorderfront** [-en]; die **Frontseite** [-n] front; façade
der **Waschraum** [¨e] laundry room (die **Wäscherei** [-en] laundry)
das **Wohnzimmer** [-] living-room; sitting-room
das **Zimmer** [-] room (der **Raum** [¨e] room [especially unfurnished]; der **Saal** [pl **Säle**] (public) room)

Der Garten The garden

das **Beet** [-e] bed; plot (das **Blumenbeet** flower-bed)
der **Boden** soil
die **Erde** earth
der **Faulraum** [¨e] septic tank
die **Gartenbank** [¨e] garden seat
die **Gartenmöbel** n pl garden furniture

der Gemüsegarten [¨] kitchen garden

der Geräteschuppen [-] garden shed

das Gewächshaus [¨er] greenhouse

die Gießkanne [-n] watering-can

das Gitter [-] trellis

die Hecke [-n] hedge

der Hof [¨e] courtyard (**der Hinterhof** backyard)

die Laube/Gartenlaube [-n]; **das Gartenhaus** [¨er] summer-house;
  garden house

der Obstgarten [¨] orchard

der Pfad [-e]; **der Weg** [-e] path

die Pflanze [-n] plant

die Pforte [-n] gate (**die Gartenpforte** [-n] garden gate)

die Rabatte [-n] border

der Rasen [-] lawn (**das Gras** [¨er] grass; **der Rasenmäher** [-] lawn-
  mower)

der Schlauch [¨e] hose

die Schubkarre [-n]/**der Schubkarren** [-] wheelbarrow

die Sonnenuhr [-en] sundial

der Steingarten [¨] rockery

der Teich [-e] pond

die Terrasse [-n] terrace; patio

das Unkraut weeds

der Vorgarten [¨] front garden (**der Hintergarten** back garden)

die Walze [-n] (garden) roller

der Wintergarten [¨] conservatory

der Zaun [¨e] fence (**der Gitterzaun** railings; lattice fence)

blühen blossom

jäten weed

mähen mow

pflanzen plant

pflücken pick

*um|graben dig over

*wachsen grow

SEE ALSO: **Plants; Tools**

Ausstattung und Installationen
Fixtures and fittings

der Abfluß [ⁱsse] waste-pipe

die Abwasserleitung [-en] drain-pipe; soil-pipe

die Antenne [-n] aerial

der Aschenbecher [-] ashtray

die Batterie [-n] battery

der Boiler [-] boiler; water-heater

der Briefkasten [ⁱ] letter-box

die Dachrinne [-n] gutter

der Fensterladen [*pl* ⁱ or -] shutter (**der Rolladen** roller shutter)

die Fensterscheibe [-n] window pane

der Fensterverschluß [ⁱsse] window catch

die Fliese [-n] tile [floor/wall]

die Garderobe [-n] coat-rack

das Geländer [-] handrail; banisters

der Griff [-e] [bucket, jug, cup]; **der Henkel** [-] [broom, pan, axe]; **der Stiel** [-e] handle

der Hahn/Wasserhahn [ⁱe] tap (**der Abstellhahn** mains stopcock; **auf**-/**zu|drehen** turn on/off)

der Haken [-] hook

der Hausrat household goods

der Heißwasserbereiter [-] water-heater (**der Heißwasserspeicher** [-] hot-water tank with immersion heater)

die Jalousette [-n]; **die Jalousie** [-n] Venetian blind

der Kachelofen [ⁱ] tiled stove (**die Kachel** [-n] tile)

der Kamin [-e] fireplace

die Kanalisation sewage system

das Kissen [-] cushion

der Kleiderbügel [-] coat-hanger

die Lampe [-n] light; lamp (**die Birne** [-n] bulb; **die Fassung** [-en] (lamp) socket)

die Leitungen *f pl* wiring (**die Gas-/Wasserleitung** gas-/water-pipe; gas-/water-main)

die Lüftung ventilation

der Ofen [ː] stove; heater

der Putz/Verputz plaster; [external] rendering

der Riegel [-] bolt (**die Tür ver'riegeln** bolt the door)

das Rohr [-e] pipe (**das Regen(abfall)rohr** rain-water pipe)

das Rouleau [-s]; **das Rollo** [-s] (roller) blind

der Schalter [-] switch (**an-/aus|schalten** switch on/off)

das Scharnier [-e] hinge

das Schloß [ːsser] lock (**der Schlüssel** [-] key; **das Schlüsselbund** [-e] bunch of keys; **das Schlüsselloch** [ːer] keyhole)

der Schnapper [-] door latch

die Schnur [ːe] lead (**die Verlängerungsschnur** extension lead)

der Schrank [ːe] cupboard

der Sicherungskasten [ː] fuse-box (**die Sicherung** [-en] fuse)

das Spülbecken [-]; **die Spüle** [-n] sink

die Steckdose [-n] socket (**die Zweifachsteckdose** double socket; adaptor; **der Stecker** [-] plug; ***an|schließen** plug in; **den Stecker *heraus|ziehen** unplug)

das Stromnetz [electric] mains (**der Hauptschalter** [-] mains switch; **die (Hoch-/Nieder)spannung** (high/low) voltage)

der Stromzähler [-] electricity meter (**der Gaszähler** gas meter; **die Wasseruhr** [-en] water meter)

die Tapete [-n] wallpaper

der Türgriff [-e]; **die Klinke/Türklinke** [-n] door-handle

die Türklingel [-n] doorbell

der Türklopfer [-] door-knocker

das Vorhängeschloß [ːsser] padlock

der Wetterhahn [ːe] weathercock

die Zentralheizung central heating (**die Gas-/Öl-/Elektroheizung** gas/oil/electric heating; **der Heizkörper** [-]; **der Radiator** [G -s *pl* -en]; *colloq* **die Heizung** [-en] radiator)

Hausarbeit Housework

WER SIE MACHT THOSE WHO DO IT

das Au-pair-Mädchen [-] au pair
der/die Babysitter/in [-/-nen] baby-sitter (**die Tagesmutter** [≃])
baby-minder)
das Dienstmädchen [-] maid
der/die Gärtner/in [-/-nen] gardener
die Hausfrau [-en] housewife
die Haushaltshilfe [-n] home help
der Hausmann [≃er] house-husband
der/die Hausmeister/in [-/-nen] caretaker
die Putzfrau [-en]; **die Reinemachefrau** [-en] cleaning woman;
daily

WAS SIE TUN WHAT THEY DO

ab|decken clear the table
ab|stauben dust [a piece of furniture] (**im Wohnzimmer Staub** *m*
wischen dust the living room)
*****ab|waschen; spülen** wash up (**das Geschirr** the dishes)
auf|räumen tidy up
babysitten *only inf* baby-sit
die Betten machen make the beds
bügeln; plätten iron; do the ironing
fegen; kehren sweep (**zusammen|fegen; zusammen|kehren** sweep
up)
flicken patch
die Hausarbeit machen do the housework
*****helfen** + D; **Hilfe** *f* **leisten** + D help
kochen cook
polieren; [floor] **bohnern** polish
reinigen [carpets, clothes]; **sauber|machen/putzen** [house, shoes]
clean (**der Frühjahrsputz** spring-clean)
reparieren mend
scheuern scour
spülen rinse

staub|saugen vacuum
stopfen darn
den Tisch decken lay the table
trocknen dry (**im Automaten trocknen** tumble-dry; **ab|trocknen**
dry [dishes])
***waschen** wash; do the washing
***weg|werfen** throw away

WAS SIE GEBRAUCHEN WHAT THEY USE

der Abfalleimer [-] bin
das Abtropfbrett [-er] draining-board
die Abwaschschüssel [-n] washing-up bowl
der Besen/Kehrbesen [-] long-handled brush; broom
das Bleichmittel [-] bleach
der Bodenwischer [-] [for floors]; **der Fensterwischer** [for
windows] squeegee
das Bügel-/Plätteisen [-] iron (**das Bügel-/Plättbrett** [-er] ironing-
board)
die Bürste [-n] brush
das Desinfektionsmittel [-] disinfectant
der Eimer [-] bucket
der Geschirrspüler [-] dishwasher
das Geschirrtuch [ːer] tea-towel
der Handfeger [-]; **der Handbesen** [-] (short-handled) brush
die Kehrschaufel [-] dustpan
der Lappen [-] cloth (**der Putzlappen** floor-cloth)
der Mop [-s] mop
der Mülleimer [-] waste-bin (**der Müll; der Abfall** refuse; **die
Müllabfuhr** refuse collection)
die Mülltonne [-n] dustbin
die Nähmaschine [-n] sewing-machine
die Scheuerbürste [-n] scrubbing-brush
das Seifenpulver soap powder
die Spülbürste [-n] washing-up brush
das Spülmittel [-] washing-up liquid
der Staubsauger [-] vacuum cleaner

das Staubtuch [≅er] duster
der Teppichkehrer [-] carpet-sweeper
der Topfreiniger [-]; **der Topfkratzer** [-] scourer
die Wäscheleine [-n] washing-line (**die Wäscheklammer** [-n] peg)
der Wäscheständer [-] clothes-horse
die Waschmaschine [-n] washing-machine
das Waschpulver [-] washing-powder

SEE ALSO: **Accidents; Cooking and Eating; Furniture; Plants; Relationships**

26. The Human Body
Der menschliche Körper

Der Kopf The head

der Augapfel [≃] eyeball
das Auge [-n] eye
die Augenbraue [-n] eyebrow
das Augenlid [-er] eyelid
die Falte [-n] wrinkle
der Gaumen [-] palate (**hart** hard; **weich** soft)
das Gehirn *no pl* brain
das Gesicht [-er] face (**der Gesichtszug [≃e]** feature)
die Gesichtsfarbe [-n]; der Teint [-s] complexion
die Grimasse [-n] grimace (**eine Grimasse *schneiden** make a
  face)
das Grübchen [-] dimple
das Haar [-e] hair
der Hals [≃e] neck; throat
die Kehle [-n] throat
der Kiefer [-] jaw (**der Ober-/Unterkiefer** upper/lower jaw)
das Kinn [-e] chin (**das Doppelkinn** double chin)
der Kopf [≃e] head (**von Kopf bis Fuß** from head to foot)
die Lippe [-n] lip
die Miene [-n] look; facial expression
der Mund [≃er] mouth
der Nacken [-]; das Genick [-e] nape (of neck)
die Nase [-n] nose (**sich [D] die Nase putzen** blow one's nose; **das
  Nasenloch [≃er]** nostril)
das Ohr [-en] ear (**das Ohrläppchen [-]** ear-lobe)
die Pupille [-n] pupil
der Schädel [-] skull
die Schläfe [-n] temple
der Speichel [-] saliva
die Stimme [-n] voice

die Stirn [-en] forehead (**die Stirn runzeln** frown)

die Wange [-n]; **die Backe** [-n] cheek (**der Backenknochen** [-] cheekbone)

die Wimper/Augenwimper [-n] eyelash

der Zahn [≈e] tooth (**der Milch-/Weißheitszahn** milk-/wisdom tooth)

das Zahnfleisch *sing* gum(s)

die Zunge [-n] tongue

Der Körper The body

die Achselhöhle [-n] armpit

die Ader [-n]; **die Vene** [-n] vein (**die Arterie** [-n]; **die Schlagader** artery)

der Arm [-e] arm (**der Unterarm** forearm)

der Atem breath (**ein Atemzug** [*m; pl* ≈e] a breath)

das Atmen breathing

das Band [≈er] ligament

die Bandscheibe [-n] (inter-vertebral) disc

die Bauchspeicheldrüse [-n] pancreas

das Becken [-] pelvis

das Bein [-e] leg

die Blase [-n] bladder

der Blinddarm [≈e] appendix

das Blut blood (**der Kreislauf** circulation)

die Brust [≈e] breast; chest (**die Büste** [-n]; **der Busen** [-] bust)

der Darm bowels

der Daumen [-] thumb

die Drüse [-n] gland

der Ell(en)bogen [-] elbow

die Faust [≈e] fist (**der Faustschlag** [≈e] punch)

die Ferse [-n] heel

die Figur [-en] figure

der Finger [-] finger (**der Zeige-/Mittel-/Ringfinger** index/middle/ring-finger; **der kleine Finger** little finger)

das Fleisch flesh

der Fuß [≈e] foot (**zu Fuß** on foot; **barfuß** barefoot)

die Galle [-n] gall-bladder; bile

das Gelenk [-e] joint

das Gerippe [-]; **das Skelett** [-e] skeleton

die Geschlechtsorgane n pl genitals

das Glied [-er] limb

die Hand [≈e] hand (**sich** [D] **die Hand** *geben shake hands)

die Handfläche [-n]; **der Handteller** [-] palm

das Handgelenk [-e] wrist

der Harn; der Urin urine

die Haut [≈e] skin

das Herz [-en] heart (**klopfen** beat)

die Hinterbacke [-n] buttock

der Hintern [-]; **das Gesäß** [-e] backside; bottom

der Hoden [-] testicle

die Hüfte [-n] hip

der Kehlkopf [≈e] larynx

das Knie [-] knee (**die Kniescheibe** [-n] kneecap)

der Knöchel [-] ankle; knuckle (**der Fußknöchel; die Fessel** [-n] ankle; **sich** [D] **den Knöchel ver'stauchen** sprain one's ankle)

der Knochen [-] bone

der Knorpel [-] cartilage

der Körper [-] body

die Leber [-n] liver

die Luftröhre [-n] windpipe

die Lunge [-n] lung

der Magen [pl ≈ or -]; **der Bauch** [≈e] stomach

die Mandel [-n] tonsil

die Menstruation menstruation (**die Periode** [-n]; **die Regel** [-n] period)

der Muskel [G -s pl -n] muscle

der Nagel [≈] nail

der Nerv [-en] nerve (**das Nervensystem** nervous system)

die Niere [-n] kidney

das Organ [-e] organ

der Penis [-se] penis

die Rippe [-n] rib

der Rücken [-] back

das Rückgrat [-e] spine (**die Wirbelsäule [-n]** spinal column)

der Rumpf [⁼e] trunk

die Scheide [-n] vagina

der Schenkel [-] thigh

das Schienbein [-e] shin

das Schlüsselbein [-e] collar-bone

die Schulter [-n]; die Achsel [-n] shoulder (**die/mit den Achseln zucken** shrug)

der Schweiß sweat

die Sehne [-n] sinew; tendon (**die Achillessehne** Achilles tendon)

die Seite [-n] side

die Sohle/Fußsohle [-n] sole

der Spann [-e]; der Fußrücken [-] instep

der Stoffwechsel; der Metabolismus metabolism

die Taille [-n] waist

das Trommelfell [-e] ear-drum

die Verdauung digestion

die Wade [-n] calf

der Zeh [-e]; die Zehe [-n] toe (**auf Zehenspitzen** on tiptoe)

Körperbewegungen Actions of the body

*an|sehen look at

atmen breathe

*auf|schrecken; *auf|fahren start

*auf|stehen stand/get up

aus|strecken stretch out (**sich ausstrecken** stretch (oneself))

ballen clench [fist]

sich be'eilen hurry (up)

*beißen bite

be'rühren touch

beugen bend

be'wegen move (**die Bewegung [-en]** movement)

blicken; schauen glance (**der Blick [-e]** glance)

blinzeln blink

boxen punch

*brechen break (**sich [D] das Bein** etc. **brechen** break one's leg etc.)

sich bücken bend down; stoop

eilen rush

er'sticken choke

*fallen fall

*fallen|lassen drop

*fangen catch

gähnen yawn (**das Gähnen** *no pl* yawn; yawning)

*gehen walk

gestikulieren gesture (**die Geste [-n]** gesture)

grinsen grin (**das Grinsen** *no pl* grin)

*halten hold

*heben raise

*herab|lassen; [gaze] **senken** lower

hinken limp

sich hin|legen lie down

sich hocken squat down

hören hear

hüpfen hop

kauen chew

keuchen pant

kosten; schmecken taste

kratzen scratch

lächeln smile (**das Lächeln** *no pl* smile)

lachen laugh (**das Lachen** *no pl* laugh; laughter)

laufen run; walk

sich lehnen lean (**gegen** + A against; **sich vor|-/zurück|lehnen** lean forwards/backwards)

*nehmen take

nicken nod (**das Nicken** *no pl* nod)

nieder|knien; sich knien; sich hin|knien kneel down

*riechen smell

ruhen; sich aus|ruhen rest

runzeln wrinkle (**die Stirn runzeln** frown)

*schlagen hit; slap; [heart] beat (**der Schlag [ːe]** blow)

schlucken swallow

schütteln shake (**den Kopf schütteln** shake one's head; **das Kopfschütteln** shake of the head)

schwanken stagger

*sehen see

sich setzen; sich hin|setzen sit down

*sprechen speak

*springen jump; leap

starren stare (**finster starren** glare; **finster** darkly)

stolpern (über + A) trip (over)

sich strecken stretch (**das Bein strecken** stretch one's leg)

*treten kick (**der Tritt [-e]** kick)

sich um|drehen turn round

ver'dauen digest

ver'stauchen sprain

weinen (vor + D) weep (with) (**die Träne [-n]** tear)

*werfen throw

winken wave

zeigen (auf + A) point (at) (**das Zeichen [-]** sign)

zu|hören listen

*zurück|treten step back

zwinkern wink; blink (**das Zwinkern** no pl wink)

Stellungen Positions

Arm m **in Arm** arm in arm

ausgestreckt stretched out

hängend hanging

gebückt bent

gekrümmt bent double

gelehnt gegen + A; angelehnt an + A or D leaning against/on

Hand f **in Hand** hand in hand

hängend hanging

hockend squatting

kauernd crouching

kniend; auf den Knien kneeling (**auf allen vieren** on all fours)

krumm bent [finger]

liegend lying (**auf dem Bauch** face down)

nebeneinander side by side
Schulter *f* **an Schulter** shoulder to shoulder
sitzend sitting
stehend standing
verschränkt [arms]; **gefaltet** [hands] folded

SEE ALSO: **Accidents; Adornment; Clothing; Describing People; Hair; Health and Sickness; Identity; The Senses; Tobacco and Drugs**

27. Identity Identität

Name Name

ich heiße ... my name is ...

wie heißen Sie?; wie nennen Sie sich?; wie ist Ihr Name? what is your name?

wie heißen Sie mit Vor-/Nachnamen? what is your first name/surname?

wie schreiben Sie sich? how do you spell your name?

die Identität [-en] identity
die Initiale [-n] initial
der Name [G -ns _pl_ -n] name (**der Vor-/Mädchen-/Ehename** first/maiden/married name; **der Familien-/Nach-/Zuname** surname; **der Schriftsteller-/Künstlername** pen-/stage-name; **der Spitzname** nickname)
die Unterschrift [-en] signature

Frau X Mrs/Ms X
Fräulein/Frl. X Miss X
Herr [A, G, D -n] X Mr X
Herr/Frau Doktor X Dr X [**Frau Doktor** also found meaning 'wife of Dr X']

(die) Damen _f pl_ ladies (**meine Damen und Herren** ladies and gentlemen)
(die) Herren _m pl_ gentlemen

buchstabieren spell
*heißen be called
*nennen name (**sich nennen** be called)
paraphieren initial
taufen christen
*unter'schreiben sign

Adresse Address

wo wohnen Sie? where do you live?
**ich wohne in der Bismarckstraße Nummer 17; ich wohne
  Bismarckstraße 17** I live at 17 Bismarckstraße

die Adresse [-n]; die Anschrift [-en] address
die Allee [-n]; die Avenue [-n]; der Boulevard [-s] avenue
das Branchenverzeichnis [-se] trade directory
die Etage [-n]; der Stock [-]; das Stockwerk [-e] storey
der Geburtsort [-e] place of birth
die Hausnummer [-n] number
der/die Mieter/in [-/-nen] tenant (**der/die Untermieter/in** subtenant)
der Ort [-e] place [town]
der Platz [ːe] square
die Postleitzahl [-en] postcode
die Staatsangehörigkeit [-en] nationality
die Straße [-n] street
das Telefonbuch [ːer] telephone directory (**die Telefonnummer [-n]**
  phone number)
der Vermieter [-]; der Hauswirt [-e] landlord (**die Vermieterin
  [-nen]; die Hauswirtin [-nen]** landlady)
der Wohnort [-e] place of residence

*be'sitzen own
leben live
mieten rent
teilen mit + D share with
ver'mieten let
wohnen live [in a specific place]

am Meer _n_; **an der See** by the sea (**die Seestadt [ːe]** seaside town;
  der Badeort [-e] seaside resort; spa)
am Stadtrand on the edge of town; in the suburbs
auf dem Lande in the country
bei X [D] at X's
in der Stadt in town

Alter Age

wie alt sind Sie? how old are you?
ich bin 17 Jahre alt I'm 17
ich bin Mitte (der) Dreißig I'm in my mid-thirties

die Adoleszenz adolescence (**der/die Heranwachsende** *adj n*
adolescent)
der/die Alte *adj n* old man/woman (**die Alten** *pl* the old; **alte
Leute** *pl* old people)
das Alter [-] age; old age (**im Alter von** + D at the age of; **ein
älterer Herr/eine ältere Dame** an elderly man/woman; **in
fortgeschrittenem Alter** at an advanced age)
die Altersgrenze [-n] age limit
das Baby [-s] baby
der/die Erwachsene *adj n* adult
die Geburt [-en] birth (**das Geburtsdatum** [*pl* **-daten**] date of birth;
der Geburtstag [-e] birthday; **gebürtige(r) Deutsche(r)** *adj n*
German by birth)
der/die hundertjährige Greis/in [-e/-nen] centenarian; hundred-
year-old
das Jahr [-e] year
die Jugend youth [the state] (**der/die Jugendliche** *adj n* youth;
young person; **junge Leute** *pl* young people)
die junge Dame [-n] young woman/lady
der junge Mann [¨er] young man
das Kid [-s] kid
das Kind [-er] child
die Langlebigkeit longevity
das Mädchen [-] girl
der Monat [-e] month
der Teenager [-]; der Teen [-s] teenager
der Zeitgenosse [-n]/die Zeitgenossin [-nen] contemporary

altern age; grow old
*auf|wachsen; [reach maturity] **erwachsen *werden** grow up
geboren *sein be born
mündig/volljährig *werden come of age

*sterben die

alt old (**älter** elderly; **älter als** older than)
altersschwach; senil senile
erwachsen adult
jugendlich; [derogatory] **infantil** juvenile
jung young (**jünger als** younger than)
kindlich; [derogatory] **kindisch** childish
-jährig -year-old (**siebenjährig** seven-year-old)
mit X Jahren at the age of X
mittleren Alters middle-aged
reif mature (**im reiferen Alter** of mature years)
unmündig; minderjährig under-age
zeitgenössisch; gleichaltrig contemporary

Geschlecht Sex

die Dame [-n] lady; woman
der Feminismus feminism
die Frau [-en] woman
der Herr [A, G, D *sing* -n; *pl* -en] (gentle)man
der Junge [-n] boy
das Mädchen [-] girl
der Mann [╌er] man
die Männlichkeit masculinity
die Weiblichkeit femininity

damenhaft ladylike
gentlemanlike gentlemanly
heterosexuell heterosexual
homosexuell homosexual (**der/die Homosexuelle** *adj n* homosexual; **schwul** *colloq* gay)
lesbisch Lesbian (**die Lesbierin** [-nen] Lesbian)
männlich male; masculine
weiblich female; feminine

SEE ALSO: **Birth, Marriage, and Death; Describing People; The Human Body; Jobs; Places and Languages; Relationships**

JOBS

der/die Büchsenmacher/in [-/-nen] gunsmith
der/die Büroangestellte *adj n* office worker
der/die Busfahrer/in [-/-nen] bus driver
der/die Cartoonist/in [-en/-nen]; **der/die Karikaturist/in** [-en/-nen] cartoonist
der/die Caterer/in [-/-nen] caterer
der/die Chirurg/in [-en/-nen] surgeon
der/die Dichter/in [-/-nen] poet; writer
der/die Diener/in [-/-nen] servant
das Dienstmädchen [-] maid
der/die Dolmetscher/in [-/-nen] interpreter
der/die Dozent/in [-en/-nen] lecturer
der/die Drogist/in [-en/-nen] chemist
der/die Drucker/in [-/-nen] printer
der/die Effektenmakler/in [-/-nen] stockbroker
der Eisenbahner [-] railwayman
der/die Eisenwarenhändler/in [-/-nen] ironmonger
der/die Elektriker/in [-/-nen] electrician
der Empfangschef [-s]/**die Empfangsdame** [-n] receptionist
der/die Fahrer/in [-/-nen] driver
der/die Fahrschullehrer/in [-/-nen] driving-instructor
der/die Fensterputzer/in [-/-nen] window cleaner
der Feuerwehrmann [*pl* -er or -leute] fireman
der Fischer [-] fisherman
der/die Fischhändler/in [-/-nen] fishmonger
der/die Fleischer/in [-/-nen]; **der/die Metzger/in** [-/-nen] butcher
der Förster [-] forester
der/die Fotograf/in [-en/-nen] photographer
das Fotomodell [-e] photographic model
der/die Fremdenführer/in [-/-nen] tourist guide
der Friseur [-e]/**die Friseuse** [-n] hairdresser
der/die Gärtner/in [-/-nen] gardener
der Gasmann [-er] gasman (**der/die Gasinstallateur/in** [-e/-nen] gas-fitter)
der/die Geistliche *adj n* clergyman; minister
der/die Gelehrte *adj n*; **der/die Wissenschaftler/in** [-/-nen] scholar
der/die Gemüseanbauer/in [-/-nen] market gardener

28. Jobs Arbeit

Wie man sich ernährt What you do

Feminine forms are given where these are in everyday

der/die Abgeordnete *adj n* MP
der/die Ansager/in [-/-nen] announcer
der/die Anstreicher/in [-/-nen] painter; decorator
der/die Apotheker/in [-/-nen] chemist; pharmacist
der/die Architekt/in [-en/-nen] architect
der Arzt [≈e]/**die Ärztin** [-nen] doctor
der/die Astronaut/in [-en/-nen] astronaut
der/die Astronom/in [-en/-nen] astronomer
der/die Ausbilder/in [-/-nen] instructor
der Autor [G -s *pl* -en]/**die Autorin** [-nen] author
der/die Bäcker/in [-/-nen] baker
der/die Bankangestellte *adj n* bank clerk
der/die Bauarbeiter/in [-/-nen] builder
der Bauer [-n]/**die Bäuerin** [-nen] countryman/-woman; farmer
der Bauunternehmer [-] building contractor
der Beamte *adj n*/**die Beamtin** [-nen] official; civil servant; police
  officer
der/die Berater/in [-/-nen] counsellor (**der/die Eheberater/in**
  marriage guidance counsellor; **der/die Berufsberater/in** careers
  advisor)
der Bergarbeiter [-]; **der Bergmann** [*pl* Bergleute] miner
der/die Bergführer/in [-/-nen] mountain guide
der/die Bettler/in [-/-nen] beggar
der/die Bibliothekar/in [-e/-nen] librarian
der/die Bildhauer/in [-/-nen] sculptor
der/die Blumenhändler/in [-/-nen] florist
der Brauer [-] brewer
der/die Briefträger/in [-/-nen] postman/-woman
der/die Buchhalter/in [-/-nen] bookkeeper
der/die Buchhändler/in [-/-nen] bookseller

der **Geschäftsinhaber/in** [-/-nen] shopkeeper

der **Geselle** [-n]/die **Gesellin** [-nen] journeyman/-woman (der **Maurergeselle** journeyman bricklayer)

der/die **Goldschmied/in** [-e/-nen] goldsmith

der/die **Großhändler/in** [-/-nen] wholesaler

der/die **Grundschullehrer/in** [-/-nen] primary-school teacher

der/die **Handelsvertreter/in** [-/-nen] sales rep(resentative)

der/die **Hausierer/in** [-/-nen] hawker

der/die **Hausmeister/in** [-/-nen] caretaker

die **Hebamme** [-n] midwife

der **Hirte** [-n] (*obsolete f* die **Hirtin** [-nen]); der/die **Schäfer/in** [-/-nen] shepherd

der/die **Hochschullehrer/in** [-/-nen] university teacher

der/die **Ingenieur/in** [-e/-nen] engineer

der/die **Innenausstatter/in** [-/-nen] interior decorator

der/die **Installateur/in** [-e/-nen]; der/die **Klempner/in** [-/-nen] plumber

der/die **Journalist/in** [-en/-nen] journalist

der **Juwelier** [-e] jeweller

der **Kameramann** [-er] cameraman

der **Kaufmann** [*pl* -leute]/die **Kauffrau** [-en] businessman/ -woman; grocer

der **Kellner** [-] waiter (die **Kellnerin** [-nen] waitress)

der/die **Kindergärtner/in** [-/-nen] nursery-school teacher

das **Kindermädchen** [-] nanny

der **Koch** [-e]/die **Köchin** [-nen] cook (der/die **Küchenchef/in** [-s/-nen] chef)

der/die **Kohlenhändler/in** [-/-nen] coal-merchant

der/die **Komiker/in** [-/-nen] comedian

der **Konditor** [G -s *pl* -en]/die **Konditorin** [-nen] pastry-cook

die **Krankenschwester** [-n] nurse (der **Krankenpfleger** [-] male nurse)

der/die **Künstler/in** [-/-nen] artist

der/die **Kurzwarenhändler/in** [-/-nen] haberdasher

der/die **Ladenbesitzer/in** [-/-nen] shopkeeper

der/die **Landarbeiter/in** [-/-nen] farm worker

der/die **Landstreicher/in** [-/-nen] tramp

der/die Lebensmittelhändler/in [-/-nen] grocer

der/die Lehrer/in [-/-nen] teacher

der/die Lieferant/in [-en/-nen] delivery man/woman

der/die LKW-/Lkw-Fahrer/in [-/-nen] lorry driver

der Lokführer [-] engine driver

der Lumpensammler [-] rag-and-bone man

der/die Maler/in [-/-nen] painter

das Mannequin [-s]; **das Model** [-s] fashion model (**der Dressman** [pl -men] male model)

der Matrose [-n] sailor

der Maurer [-] bricklayer

der/die Mechaniker/in [-/-nen] mechanic

der Messerschmied [-e] cutler

der/die Metallarbeiter/in [-/-nen] metalworker

der/die Militärangehörige adj n serviceman/-woman

der/die Minister/in [-/-nen] (cabinet) minister (**der/die Premier-minister/in** prime minister)

der Möbelpacker [-] removal man

der Moderator [G -s pl -en]/**die Moderatorin** [-nen] (radio, TV) presenter

der/die Modeschöpfer/in [-/-nen] fashion designer

der/die Modist/in [-en/-nen]; **der Putzmacher/in** [-/-nen] milliner

der Mönch [-e] monk

der/die Müller/in [-/-nen] miller

der Müllmann [=er] dustman

der/die Musiker/in [-/-nen] musician

die Nonne [-n] nun

der/die Notar/in [-e/-nen] notary

der Ober [-] waiter

der/die Obst- und Gemüsehändler/in [-/-nen] greengrocer

der Offizier [-e] officer (**bei der Armee/der Luftwaffe/der Marine** in the army/air force/navy; **der/die Offiziersanwärter/in** [-/-nen] officer cadet)

der/die Optiker/in [-/-nen] optician (**der/die Augenoptiker/in** ophthalmic optician)

der/die Pfarrer/in [-/-nen] [protestant] minister; [catholic] parish priest

der/die Physiker/in [-/-nen] physicist

der/die Pilot/in [-en/-nen] pilot

der Platzanweiser [-] usher (**die Platzanweiserin** [-nen] usherette)

der/die Politiker/in [-/-nen] politician

der/die Polizist/in [-en/-nen] policeman/-woman

der Postbeamte *adj n*/**die Postbeamtin** [-nen] post-office clerk

der Priester [-] priest (**die Priesterin** [-nen] priestess)

der/die Produzent/in [-en/-nen] producer

der/die Programmierer/in [-/-nen] computer programmer

der/die Psychiater/in [-/-nen] psychiatrist

der Psychologe [-n]/**die Psychologin** [-nen] psychologist

die Putzfrau [-en]; **der/die Raumpfleger/in** [-/-nen] cleaner

das Ratsmitglied [-er] councillor (**der Stadtrat** [ǝe]/**die Stadträtin** [-nen] town councillor)

der/die Raumgestalter/in [-/-nen] interior decorator

der Rechtsanwalt [ǝe]/**die Rechtsanwältin** [-nen] lawyer

der/die Rennfahrer/in [-/-nen] racing river

der/die Reporter/in [-/-nen] reporter

der/die Richter/in [-/-nen] judge

der/die Sänger/in [-/-nen] singer

der/die Sanitäter/in [-/-nen] ambulance man/woman

der/die Schaffner/in [-/-nen] ticket inspector; guard

der Schauspieler [-] actor (**die Schauspielerin** [-nen] actress)

der Schiff(s)bauer [-] shipbuilder

der/die Schlosser/in [-/-nen] locksmith

der Schmied [-e] blacksmith

der/die Schneider/in [-/-nen] tailor/dressmaker

der/die Schornsteinfeger/in [-/-nen] chimney-sweep

die Schreibkraft [ǝe] typist [male or female] (**der/die Phonotypist/in** [-en/-nen] audio typist; **der/die Stenotypist/in** shorthand typist)

der/die Schreibwarenhändler/in [-/-nen] stationer

der/die Schriftsteller/in [-/-nen] writer

der Schuster [-]; **der Schuhmacher** [-] cobbler

der Seemann [*pl* Seeleute] seaman

der/die Sekretär/in [-e/-nen] secretary

der/die Silberschmied/in [-e/-nen] silversmith

der/die Soldat/in [-en/-nen] soldier

der/die **Sozialarbeiter/in** [-/-nen] social worker

der/die **Spion/in** [-e/-nen] spy

die **Sprechstundenhilfe** [-n] (medical/dental) receptionist

der **Staatsbeamte** *adj n*/die **Staatsbeamtin** [-nen] civil servant

der **Star** [-s] star [male or female]

der **Steinmetz** [-en] stonemason

der **Steward** [-s] steward (die **Stewardeß** [-ssen] stewardess; air hostess)

der/die **Straßenfeger/in** [-/-nen] street-sweeper

der/die **Straßenhändler/in** [-/-nen] costermonger; street-trader

der/die **Stricker/in** [-/-nen] knitter

der/die **Student/in** [-en/-nen] student

der **Studienrat** [¨e]/die **Studienrätin** [-nen] secondary-school teacher

der/die **Taxifahrer/in** [-/-nen] taxi-driver

der/die **Telefonist/in** [-en/-nen] switchboard operator

der **Tierarzt** [¨e]/die **Tierärztin** [-nen] vet

der **Tischler** [-] joiner (der **Kunst-/Möbeltischler** cabinet-maker)

der/die **Töpfer/in** [-/-nen] potter

der/die **Übersetzer/in** [-/-nen] translator

der/die **Uhrmacher/in** [-/-nen] watch/clockmaker

der/die **Verkäufer/in** [-/-nen] sales assistant

der/die **Verleger/in** [-/-nen] publisher

der/die **Vertreter/in** [-/-nen] representative; agent (der/die **Versicherungsvertreter/in** insurance agent)

der **Wäschemann** [¨er]/die **Wäschefrau** [-en] laundryman/-woman

der/die **Weber/in** [-/-nen] weaver

der/die **Weinhändler/in** [-/-nen] wine-merchant

der/die **Winzer/in** [-/-nen] winegrower

der/die **Wirtschaftsprüfer/in** [-/-nen] chartered accountant

der/die **Wissenschaftler/in** [-/-nen]/**Naturwissenschaftler/in** scientist

der **Zahnarzt** [¨e]/die **Zahnärztin** [-nen] dentist

der/die **Zeichner/in** [-/-nen] draughtsman/-woman; graphic artist

der/die **Zeitungshändler/in** [-/-nen] newsagent

das **Zimmermädchen** [-] chambermaid

der **Zimmermann** [*pl* -leute]; der **Zimmerer** [-] carpenter

der **Zollbeamte** *adj n*/die **Zollbeamtin** [-nen] customs officer

Was man ist What you are

der/die Angestellte *adj n* employee; white-collar worker (**der/die leitende Angestellte** *adj n* executive; **leiten** manage)

der/die Arbeiter/in [-/-nen] worker

der/die Arbeitgeber/in [-/-nen] employer

der/die Arbeitnehmer/in [-/-nen] employee

der/die Arbeitslose *adj n* unemployed person

der/die Arbeitssuchende *adj n* job-seeker

der/die Aufseher/in [-/-nen] overseer; supervisor

der/die Azubi [-s] [= **Auszubildende**]; **der Lehrling** [-e]/**das Lehrmädchen** [-] apprentice; trainee (**die Lehrstelle** [-n] apprenticeship [= place]; **die Lehre** apprenticeship [= training]; **die Lehrzeit** [-en] apprenticeship [= training period])

der/die Betriebsleiter/in [-/-nen]; **der/die Geschäftsführer/in** [-/-nen]; **der/die Geschäftsleiter/in** [-/-nen] manager; managing director

der/die Büroangestellte *adj n* office worker

der/die Chef/in [-s/-nen] boss

der Direktor [G -s *pl* -en]/**die Direktorin** [-nen] director; manager; headmaster/-mistress

der Fachmann [*pl* -leute]/**die Fachfrau** [-en] expert

der Geschäftsmann [*pl* -leute]/**die Geschäftsfrau** [-en] businessman/-woman

der/die Gewerkschaft(l)er/in [-/-nen] trade-unionist

das Gewerkschaftsmitglied [-er] union member

der Handwerker [-] tradesman; craftsman

der/die Hersteller/in [-/-nen] manufacturer

der/die Hilfsarbeiter/in [-/-nen] unskilled worker; labourer

der/die Industrielle *adj n* industrialist

der Kollege [-n]/**die Kollegin** [-nen] colleague

der/die Lohnempfänger/in [-/-nen] wage-earner

der/die Manager/in [-/-nen] manager

der Profi [-s] professional

der/die Rentner/in [-/-nen]; **der/die Ruheständler/in** [-/-nen] retired person; pensioner

der/die Spezialist/in [-en/-nen] specialist

der/die Streikbrecher/in [-/-nen] blackleg

der/die Streikende *adj n* striker
der/die Techniker/in [-/-nen] technician
der Verwaltungsbeamte *adj n*/**die Verwaltungsbeamtin** [-nen]
   administrator
der/die Vorarbeiter/in [-/-nen]; **der/die Werkmeister/in** [-/-nen]
   foreman/-woman; charge-hand
die Zeitarbeits-/-Aushilfskraft [ˮe]; **die Aushilfe** [-n] temporary
   worker; temp (**Zeitarbeit** *f* **machen** to temp)

Wo man arbeitet Where you work

die Baustelle [-n] building site
das Büro [-s] office
die Fabrik [-en]; **das Werk** [-e] factory; works
die Firma [*pl* Firmen]; **der Betrieb** [-e] firm
das Geschäft [-e] business; shop (**die Geschäftsreise** [-n] business
   trip; **die Geschäftswelt** business world)
die Gesellschaft [-en] company (Co. [**Compagnie**] co.; **GmbH**
   [**Gesellschaft mit beschränkter Haftung**] = plc; **beschränkt**
   limited; **die Haftung** liability)
der Handel trade; commerce (**die Hotelbranche** [-n] the hotel
   trade; **der Groß-/Einzelhandel** wholesale/retail trade)
die Hauptverwaltung; [banking] **die Hauptgeschäftsstelle**;
   [commerce] **das Hauptbüro** head office
die Industrie [-n] industry (**die Schwer-/Leichtindustrie** heavy/
   light industry)
das Labor [*pl* -s or -e] laboratory (**die Forschung** research)
der Laden [ˮ] shop
das Lagerhaus [ˮer] warehouse
die Landwirtschaft agriculture (**auf dem Feld** *n* **arbeiten** work in
   the fields)
die Leitung management
das Unternehmen [-] company
die Werkstatt [ˮen]; **die Werkstätte** [-n] workshop
die Zweigstelle [-n]; **die Filiale** [-n] branch

Was man tut What you do

sich ab|arbeiten toil; slog
arbeiten work
arbeitslos *sein be unemployed
Arbeit *f* **suchen/*finden** look for/find work
***aus|scheiden (aus** + D); **in Rente/in den Ruhestand *gehen** retire (from)
sich *be'werben für + A (**bei** + D) apply for (with)
ein|stellen take on
***ent'lassen** sack; make redundant; dismiss
führen run
kündigen (bei + D) give in one's notice (to) (**kündigen** + D give sb notice)
leiten manage
eine Stelle [-n] *an|nehmen/ab|lehnen accept/refuse a job
streiken strike
ver'dienen earn (**sich er'nähren von** + D; **seinen Lebensunterhalt verdienen mit** + D earn a/one's living by)
ver'walten administer
***zurück|treten** resign

Die Arbeitswelt Industrial life

der Abschluß [=sse] qualification
die Akkordarbeit piece-work
der Antrag [≈e] application
die Arbeit [-en] work; job
die Arbeiterschaft; die Arbeitskräfte *f pl* labour (**ungelernt** unskilled; **angelernt** semi-skilled; **ausgebildet** skilled)
das Arbeitslosengeld unemployment benefit
der Arbeitsplatz [≈e] place of work; job (**den Arbeitsplatz *ver'lieren/wechseln** be made redundant/change jobs)
der Arbeitsvertrag [≈e] contract of employment
die Ausbildung training
die Aussperrung [-en] lock-out

der Beruf [-e] profession; job (**von Beruf** by profession; **die Berufsberatung** careers advice)

die Beschäftigung employment (**die Ganztagsbeschäftigung** full-time work; **die Halbtagsbeschäftigung**: **die Teilzeit-/Halbtags-arbeit** part-time work; **die Kurzarbeit** short time)

die Betriebsferien *pl* company holidays

der Betriebsrat [ˉe] works committee

die Bewerbung [-en] (**um** + A) application (for)

die Bezahlung payment; pay

die Branche [-n] industry; branch of industry

die Demonstration [-en] demonstration

die Einstellung appointing; taking on

die Entlassung [-en] dismissal

die Erfahrung [-en] experience

der Feierabend end of work [for the day] (**nach Feierabend** after work; **Feierabend machen** knock off)

die Fort-/Weiterbildung further training

das Gehalt [ˉer] salary (**die Gehaltserhöhung** [-en] pay rise)

die Geschäftsleitung management

die Gewerkschaft [-en] trade union

die Gleitzeit flexitime (**gleitende Arbeitszeit *haben** be on flexitime)

das Handwerk [-e] craft

das Interview [-s]; **das Vorstellungsgespräch** [-e] job interview

die Laufbahn [-en] career

der Lebenslauf [ˉe] curiculum vitae; CV

der Lehrgang [ˉe] training course (**einen Lehrgang machen** go on a course)

der Lohn [ˉe] wage (**die Lohnsteuer** income tax; **die Lohnerhö-hung** [-en] pay increase; **der Lohnstopp** [-s] pay freeze)

die Mittagspause [-n] lunch-break

die Pensionskasse [-n] pension fund

das Personal staff

die Rente [-n] pension (**die Invalidenrente** disability pension)

der Ruhestand retirement

die 36-Stunden-Woche 36-hour week

die soziale Sicherheit social security (**die Sozialhilfe** social security benefit)

die Stelle [-n]; die Stellung [-en]; *colloq* **der Job [-s]** job; post (**fest** permanent; **vorübergehend** temporary; **die freie Stelle** vacancy; **die Stellenangebote** *n pl* situations vacant; **eine ruhige Kugel *schieben** have a soft job)

der Streik [-s] strike (**in den Streik/einen Bummelstreik *treten** come out on strike/go on a go-slow; **zum Streik *auf|rufen** call out on strike; **mit Streik drohen** threaten to strike; **der wilde Streik** wildcat strike; **der Dienst nach Vorschrift** work-to-rule)

der Streit [-e] dispute

die Überstunden *pl* overtime

die Verwaltung [-en] administration

der Vorstand [≃e] board

*an|treten start [a job] (**zur Arbeit antreten** report for work)

sich *be'werben um + A apply for

krank gemeldet *sein be off sick (**sich krank melden** report sick)

Überstunden machen work overtime

SEE ALSO: **Describing People; Education; Identity; Tools**

29. Justice and Law
Gerechtigkeit und Gesetz

Verfolgung des Verbrechers
Pursuit of the criminal

die Anzeige [-n] report (**gegen jn Anzeige er'statten** report sb to the police)
der Ausbruch [ˆe] escape
die Auskunft [ˆe] (piece of) information
die Aussage [-n] statement (**eine Aussage machen** make a statement)
der Ausweis [-e] identity card
die Belohnung [-en] reward
der Bericht [-e] report; account
die Beschreibung [-en] description (**der Beschreibung [D] *ent'sprechen** fit the description)
die Beschwerde [-n] complaint
die Beute loot
der Bulle [-n]; der Polyp [-en] *both colloq* cop
der/die Detektiv/in [-e/-nen] (private) detective
der/die Entflohene *adj n* escaped prisoner
der/die Ermittler/in [-/-nen] investigator
die Festnahme [-n] capture; arrest
der Fingerabdruck [ˆe] fingerprint
die Flucht [-en] escape (**die Flucht *er'greifen** take flight)
der/die Flüchtige *adj n* fugitive
die Gefahr [-en] danger
der/die Gefangene *adj n* prisoner
der/die Geheimagent/in [-en/-nen] secret agent
das Geständnis [-se] confession
die grüne Minna [-s] Black Maria
der Haftbefehl [-e] warrant [for arrest] (**der Durchsuchungsbefehl** search-warrant)

die **Handgreiflichkeiten** *f pl* scuffle

die **Handschellen** *f pl* handcuffs (**jm Handschellen an|legen** handcuff sb)

der **Helm** [-e] helmet

der/die **Informant/in** [-en/-nen] informer (**der Spitzel** [-] *colloq* grass)

die **Klage** [-n] complaint (**eine Klage führen** make a complaint)

der **Kriminalbeamte** *adj n*/die **Kriminalbeamtin** [-nen] detective

die **Kripo** [= die Kriminalpolizei] CID

das **Lösegeld** [-er] ransom

die **Nachforschung** [-en] investigation

der **Nachtwächter** [-] night-watchman

das **Opfer** [-] victim

die **Pistole** [-n] pistol

die **Polizei** police (**die Bereitschaftspolizei** riot police)

der **Polizeibeamte** *adj n*/die **Polizeibeamtin** [-nen] police-officer

der **Polizeihund** [-e] police dog

der **Polizeiinspektor** [G -s *pl* -en] police inspector

der **Polizeikommissar** [-e] police superintendent

das **Polizeipräsidium** police headquarters

die **Polizeiwache** [-n] police station

der **Polizeiwagen** [-]; das **Polizeiauto** [-s] police car

der/die **Polizist/in** [-en/-nen] policeman/woman (**der/die Polizist/in in Zivil** plain-clothes policeman/woman)

die **Razzia** [*pl* Razzien] (in + D) raid (on)

der/die **Retter/in** [-/-nen] rescuer

die **Rettung** [-en]; die **Befreiung** [-en] rescue

der **Schild** [-e] shield

die **Schlägerei** [-en]; die **Rauferei** [-en] fight; brawl

der **Schlagstock** [ẹ]; der **Knüppel** [-] truncheon

die **Spur** [-en] track (**jm auf der Spur *sein** be on sb's track)

der **Strafzettel** [-] parking-ticket

der **Streifenwagen** [-] patrol car

der **Streit** [-e] dispute

das **Tränengas** tear-gas

die **Überwachung** surveillance

die **Untersuchung** [-en] enquiry; examination

das Verbrechen [-] crime
der Verdacht [-] suspicion (**verdächtig** suspicious; **der/die Verdächtige** *adj n* suspect)
die Verhaftung [-en] arrest
die Verkehrspolizei traffic police
der Versuch [-e] attempt
die Wache [-n] guard [group] (**der Wachtposten** [-] guard [person]; **der/die Wächter/in** [-/-nen] security guard; warder)
der Wacht(haupt)meister [-] constable

*ab|fangen; [conversation] **ab|hören** intercept
an|klagen wegen + G charge with
*an|rufen challenge
be'freien free (***frei|lassen** set free)
be'gehen commit
be'lohnen reward
be'schlagnahmen; **konfiszieren** confiscate
*be'stechen bribe
durch'suchen search
*ein|ge'stehen; ***zu|geben** admit
ein|sperren imprison
*ent'kommen escape
ent'waffnen disarm
er'tappen catch (**auf frischer Tat** red-handed)
*fest|nehmen arrest (**festgenommen** under arrest)
*gefangen|nehmen take prisoner
holen *lassen send for
melden report
retten rescue
stören disturb
über'wachen watch
über'wältigen overpower
unter'suchen investigate
ver'hören interrogate
*ver'nehmen question
*zurück|weisen deny

*zusammen|schlagen beat up
zusammen|stellen compile

Prozeß und Strafe Trial and punishment

das Alibi [-s] alibi

der/die Angeklagte *adj n* accused

die Anklage [-n] charge; prosecution

die Anklagebank dock

der Anwalt [-e]/die Anwältin [-nen]; der Rechtsanwalt [-e]/die Rechtsanwältin [-nen] lawyer

die Begnadigung pardon

der Beweis [-e] proof; piece of evidence (**das Beweismaterial** evidence)

das Delikt [-e]; die Straftat [-en] offence

der Eid [-e] oath (**unter Eid** on oath; **vereidigt *werden** take the oath)

der Einspruch [ːe] (gegen + A) appeal; objection (to) (**die Berufung [-en]** appeal [to a higher court]; **das Berufungsgericht** Court of Appeal)

die Einzelhaft solitary confinement

der Fall [ːe] case

das Fallbeil [-e] guillotine

der Freispruch [ːe] acquittal

der/die Gefangene *adj n* prisoner

die Gefangenschaft imprisonment

das Gefängnis [-se] prison; imprisonment

der/die Gefängniswärter/in [-/-nen] prison officer

die Geldstrafe [-n] fine (**jn mit einer Geldstrafe be'legen** fine sb)

die Gerechtigkeit justice (**um der Gerechtigkeit willen** in order that justice be done)

das Gericht [-e] court (**jn vor Gericht stellen wegen + G** try sb for; **das Zivilgericht** civil court)

der Gerichtsdiener [-] usher

der Gerichtshof [ːe] law court

die Gerichtskosten *pl* costs

der Gerichtssaal [*pl* -säle] courtroom

der/die Geschworene *adj n* juror (**die Geschworenen** *pl* jury)

das Gesetz [-e] law (**ein Gesetz** a law; **das Gesetz** *no pl*; **das Recht** *no pl* the law)

die Haft; **die Gefangenschaft** imprisonment

der Henker [-] hangman; executioner

die Hinrichtung [-en] execution

die Jugendkriminalität juvenile delinquency

der Justizirrtum [¨er] miscarriage of justice

die Kaution bail

der Kerker [-] dungeon

die Klage [-n] accusation; complaint

die Körperstrafe corporal punishment

der/die Notar/in [-e/-nen] notary

der Prozeß [-sse]; **der Fall** [¨e] trial; case (**jm den Prozeß machen** take sb to court)

der Randalierer [-] delinquent

das Recht [-e] right; law (**das Zivilrecht** civil law; **das Strafgesetz** penal law)

der/die Richter/in [-/-nen] judge

der Schaden(s)ersatz damages

das Schafott [-e] gallows; scaffold

der Scharfrichter [-] executioner

der/die Schiedsrichter/in [-/-nen] arbitrator; magistrate (**das Schiedsgericht** [-e] = magistrates' court)

der Schöffe [-n]/**die Schöffin** [-nen] [in Germany] lay judge [= jury member]

die Schuld guilt (**schuldig** guilty)

der Staatsanwalt [¨e]/**die Staatsanwältin** [-nen] prosecutor

der Strafaufschub [¨e] reprieve

die Strafe [-n] punishment; sentence (**die Freiheitsstrafe** prison sentence; **die Strafe mit Bewährung** *f* suspended sentence; **lebenslänglich** life *adj*; **lebenslänglich *be'kommen** get life)

der/die Strafgefangene *adj n* convict

die Todesstrafe death penalty (**die Hinrichtung durch den Strang** hanging; **der elektrische Stuhl** electric chair)

die Unschuld innocence (**unschuldig** innocent)
die Untat [-en] misdeed
die Untersuchungshaft remand (**in Untersuchungshaft *be'halten**
  remand in custody)
das Urteil [-e] verdict; sentence; judgement (**mild** lenient; **die
  Verurteilung** sentencing; **das Todesurteil** death sentence)
das Verfahren/Gerichtsverfahren [-]; die Verhandlung [-en] trial
die Verteidigung defence
die Vorladung [-en] summons
der Vorsatz premeditation (**vorsätzlich** premeditated)
die Zelle [-n] cell
der Zeuge [-n]/die Zeugin [-nen] witness (**der Augenzeuge/die
  Augenzeugin** eye-witness)
die Zeugenaussage testimony
der Zeugenstand witness-box
das Zuchthaus [¨er] (long-stay) prison
die Zwangsarbeit hard labour

*ab|geben pass [judgement]
*ab|sitzen; ver'büßen serve [sentence]
an|klagen wegen + G accuse of
be'gnadigen pardon
*be'stechen bribe; suborn
*be'weisen prove
Bürge *m* ***sein (für + A)** stand bail (for)
*ent'lassen (von + D) release (from) (**auf Bewährung** *f*
  entlassen release on parole)
*frei|lassen set free
*frei|sprechen acquit
ge'horchen [+ D] obey
hin|richten execute
Jura studieren study law (**das Jus** [*pl* **Jura**] law [as subject])
plädieren plead (**sich schuldig *be'kennen** plead guilty)
schuldig/unschuldig *sein be guilty/innocent
strafen punish
strafrechtlich ver'folgen (wegen + G) prosecute (for)
ver'haften imprison

ver'handeln try [case]
*ver'stoßen gegen + A contravene
ver'teidigen defend
ver'urteilen (**zu** + D) sentence (to)

SEE ALSO: **Arguments For and Against; Crimes and Criminals**

30. Leisure and Hobbies
Freizeit und Hobbys

die Begeisterung enthusiasm (**für/über** + A for)
die Einladung [-en] invitation
die Freizeit leisure; free time (**in der Freizeit** in one's free time;
  die Freizeitbeschäftigung [-en] leisure pursuit)
der Gast [ːe] guest [male or female] (**der ungebetene Gast**
  gatecrasher; **der/die Gastgeber/in** [-/-nen] host/hostess)
das Hobby [-s] hobby
das Interesse [-n] interest
das Mitglied [-er] member (**der Mitgliedsbeitrag** [ːe] subscription)
das Taschengeld pocket-money
das Treffen [-] meeting
der Treffpunkt [-e] meeting-place
das Verein [-e]; **der Klub** [-s] club
die Versammlung [-en] meeting
der Zeitvertreib [-e] pastime

sich amüsieren enjoy oneself
an|ge'hören + D belong to [club]
*aus|gehen go out
be'gleiten accompany; go with
be'suchen visit
*ein|laden invite
faulenzen laze about
et gern *tun enjoy doing sth
sich interessieren für + A be interested in (**interessiert an** + D
  interested in)
sich langweilen be bored (**die Langeweile** boredom)
*mit|bringen bring (along)
Spaß *m* **machen** be fun
*teil|nehmen an + D take part in
vorbei|schauen (**auf** + A) come round/over (for + *time*)

wild *sein auf + A be keen on
Zeit *f* ***ver'bringen mit** + D spend time on
*zusammen|kommen meet [club, group]

faszinierend fascinating
interessant interesting
langweilig boring
spannend exciting

Freizeitbeschäftigungen Leisure-time activities

der Ausflug [¨e]; [longer] **die Reise** [-n] trip
die Ausstellung [-en] exhibition (**der Eintritt** admission; **die Ermäßigung** [-en] reduced rate)
die Autofahrt [-en] drive
das Ballett [-e] ballet (**der/die Tänzer/in** [-/-nen] dancer)
die Bar [-s] bar; night-club
die Blaskapelle [-n] brass band
der botanische Garten [¨] botanical garden(s)
die Bowlingbahn [-en] (ten-pin) bowling-alley
das Café [-s] café
die Diskothek [-en] disco (**der Diskjockey** [-s] DJ; **der Diskotanz** disco dancing; **die Juke-/Musikbox** [-en] juke-box)
die Eisbahn [-en] ice-rink (**Schlittschuh** ***laufen** skate)
die Ferienkolonie [-n]; **das Ferienlager** [-] vacation camp
das Fernsehen television (***fern|sehen** watch TV; **im Fernsehen** on television; **der Kanal** [¨e] channel; **um|schalten** change channels; **der Videorecorder** [-] video recorder)
das Feuerwerk [-e] firework display (**der Feuerwerkskörper** [-] firework)
der Freund [-e] boyfriend (**die Freundin** [-nen] girlfriend; **der/die Brieffreund/in** pen-friend)
die Gemäldegalerie [-n] art gallery (**die Sammlung** [-en] collection)
der Jahrmarkt [¨e] fun-fair (**die Messe** [-n] trade fair)
der Jazzklub [-s] jazz club (**der Jazz** jazz; **die Jazzband** [-s] jazz band)

der Jugendklub [-s] youth club

das Kasino/Spielkasino [-s] casino

die Kegelbahn [-en] bowling-alley [for skittles]

das Kino [-s] cinema (**ins Kino *gehen** go to the cinema; **der Film [-e]** film)

das Konzert [-e] concert

das Kreuzworträtsel [-] crossword

das Minigolf minigolf(-course)

das Museum [*pl* Museen] museum

der Nachtklub [-s]; das Nachtlokal [-e] night-club (**der Rausschmeißer [-]** bouncer)

die Oper [-n] opera

der Park [-s] park (**der Vergnügungspark** amusement park)

die Party [-s]; die Fete [-n] party (**die Geburtstagsfeier [-n]; die Geburtstagsparty** birthday party; **die Einladung [-en]** invitation; **das Geschenk [-e]** present; **das Betriebsfest [-e]** office party; ***geben/feiern** throw)

der Pfadfinder [-] scout (**die Pfadfinderin [-nen]** guide)

das Picknick [*pl* -e or -s] picnic (**Picknick machen/*halten** have a picnic)

der Plattenspieler [-] record-player (**die Box [-en]** speaker; **die CD-Platte [-n]** CD; **eine Platte auf|legen** put a record on; **hören** listen to)

das Popkonzert [-e] pop concert (**der/die Popsänger/in [-/-nen]** pop singer; **der Schlager [-]** pop song; hit; **der Fan [-s]** fan; **die Hitparade [-n]** hit parade)

das Radfahren cycling (**das Fahrrad [¨er]** bicycle; ***rad|fahren** cycle; **eine Radtour [-en] machen** go for a cycle ride/a cycling tour)

das Radio [-s] radio (set) (**das Radio/der Rundfunk/der Hörfunk** radio [sound broadcasting]; **im Radio/Rundfunk** on the radio; **der Transistor [G -s *pl* -en]** transistor; **Radio hören** listen to the radio)

die Rennbahn [-en] racecourse (**das Pferd [-e]** horse; **der/die Rennbesucher/in [-/-nen]** racegoer; **das (Pferde)rennen [-]** horse-race)

das Restaurant [-s] restaurant

die Rollschuhbahn [-en] roller-skating rink (**Rollschuh *laufen** roller-skate)

das Schwimmbad [ˉer] swimming-pool (**das Frei-/Hallenbad** open-air/indoor pool)

die Show [-s]; **die Schau** [-en] show (**der Showmaster** [-] compère)

der Spaziergang [ˉe] walk (***spazieren|gehen/einen Spaziergang machen** go for a walk)

das Spiel [-e]; [football, tennis, also] **das/der Match** [pl -s or -e]; [boxing] **der Kampf** [ˉe] match

der Spielautomat [-en] gaming-machine

der Sport [pl Sportarten] sport (**Sport *treiben** do sport; play games; **der Wintersport** winter sports)

das Sportstadion [pl -stadien] sports stadium

der Tanzabend [-e] dance (**tanzen** dance; **tanzen *gehen** go dancing; **der Tanzsaal** [pl -säle] ballroom; dance-hall; **die Tanzfläche** [-n] dance-floor; **ein Tanz** m a dance; **zum Tanz auf|fordern** ask for a dance)

das Theater [-] theatre (**das Stück** [-e]; **das Schauspiel** [-e] play; **im/ins Theater** at/to the theatre)

das Varieté [-s] variety theatre

das Wandern hiking (**eine Wanderung** [-en] a hike)

der Zirkus [-se] circus (**der Clown** [-s] clown)

der Zoo [-s] zoo (**im/in den Zoo** at/to the zoo)

ab|setzen drop off

be'suchen visit

***ein|laden** invite

***gehen in** + A go to (**gehen mit** + D go out with; **nach Hause gehen** go home)

***mit|gehen** go with

(sich) *treffen meet (one another)

verabredet *sein mit + D be meeting; have a date with

sich/einander *wieder|sehen meet again

Hobbys Hobbies

das Amateurtheater amateur theatre (**die Theatergruppe [-n]**, drama group; **der/die Amateur-/Laienschauspieler/in [-/-nen]** amateur actor/actress)

das Angeln fishing

der Ausflug [⁼e] outing; trip

die Band/Rockband [-s] band (**die Gruppe [-n]** group; **der/die Sänger/in [-/-nen]** singer; **das (Demo)band [⁼er]** (demo) tape)

das Basteln model-making; handicraft (**das Modell [-e]** model; **der/die Bastler/in [-/-nen]** handicraft enthusiast)

der Bildteppich [-e] tapestry (***weben** weave)

das Bingo bingo

das Briefmarkensammeln stamp-collecting

der Chor [⁼e] choir

die Computertechnik computing (**der (Mikro)computer [-]** (micro)computer; **das Computerspiel [-e]** computer game; **programmieren** program)

der Drachen [-] kite (**steigen *lassen** fly)

die Fahrt/Autofahrt [-en] drive

die Fotografie photography (**der Fotoapparat [-e]**; **die Kamera [-s]** camera; **die Filmkamera** ciné-camera; **der Film [-e]** film; **das Foto [-s]** photo; **der Abzug [⁼e]** print; **das Dia [-s]** slide)

die Gartenarbeit gardening (**der Kleingarten [⁼]** allotment; **das Gartencenter [-]** garden centre)

das Heimwerken; das Do-it-yourself DIY; do-it-yourself

das Kartenspielen card-playing (**das Kartenspiel [-e]** card-game; **ein Spiel Karten** *f pl* a pack of cards)

das Kochen cooking

die Kunst art

das Lesen reading (**der Roman [-e]** novel; **die Zeitschrift [-en]**; **die Illustrierte [-n]** magazine; **der Krimi [-s]** thriller; **das Taschenbuch [⁼er]** paperback)

die Malerei painting (**das Gemälde [-]** picture; **die Farbe [-n]** paint; **der Pinsel [-]** brush)

der Modellbau model-making

die Musik music

die Pfadfinderei scouting (**der/die Pfadfinder/in** [-/-nen] scout/guide)

das Puzzle [-s]; **das Puzzlespiel** [-e] jigsaw

das Reiten/Pferdereiten horse-riding

das Sammeln collecting (**die Sammlung** [-en] collection; **das Album** [pl Alben] album)

das Schneidern dressmaking (**die Nadel** [-n] needle; **der Faden** [ⁱⁱ] thread; **die Nähmaschine** [-n] sewing-machine)

das Segeln sailing; yachting

das Singen singing (**das Lied** [-er] song; **der Chor** [ⁱⁱe] choir)

das Spazierengehen walking

das Spiel [-e] game (**das Gesellschaftsspiel** party game)

die Stickerei embroidery

das Stricken knitting (**die Stricknadel** [-n] knitting-needle)

die Töpferei pottery (**der/die Töpfer/in** [-/-nen] potter)

das/der Toto/Fußballtoto pools (**im Toto spielen** do the pools)

das Video video (**die Videokamera** [-s] camcorder; **das Videoband** [ⁱⁱer] videotape)

die Vogelkunde; **die Vogelbeobachtung** bird-watching

das Wandern rambling

der Wettbewerb [-e]; [in magazine] **das Preisausschreiben** [-] competition

das Zeichnen [the activity]; **die Zeichnung** [-en] [the product] drawing

angeln fish

basteln make things

bauen build

fotografieren take photos; photograph (sb)

gärtnern garden

kochen cook

***lesen** read

malen paint

nähen sew

***rad|fahren** cycle

***reiten** ride [horse]

sammeln collect (**tauschen** swap)

*schreiben write
segeln sail
*singen sing
*spazieren|gehen walk
spielen play; act
sticken embroider
stricken knit
zeichnen draw

SEE ALSO: **Art and Architecture; Cinema and Photography; Cooking and Eating; Holidays; The Media; Music; Nature; Reading and Writing; Sports and Games; Theatre; Tools; Transport**

31. Liking, Dislike, Comparing
Vorliebe, Abneigung, Vergleichen

Vorliebe Liking

die Anhänglichkeit [an + A) attachment (to)
das Bedürfnis [-se] (nach + D) need (for)
die Freundschaft [-en] friendship
der Geschmack [ᴇe] taste **(nach meinem Geschmack** to my taste)
das Interesse [-n] interest
die Kameradschaft comradeship
die Leidenschaft [-en] passion
die Liebe [-n] love **(auf den ersten Blick** at first sight)
die Liebenswürdigkeit kindness
das Mitgefühl sympathy
die Neigung [-en] inclination
die Sehnsucht [ᴇe] longing; desire
das Vergnügen [-]; die Vergnügung [-en] pleasure **(mit Vergnügen** with pleasure)
die Vertraulichkeit familiarity
die Vorliebe (für + A) (special) liking (for); partiality
der Wunsch [ᴇe] wish
die Zärtlichkeit tenderness; fondness
die Zuneigung affection

be'nötigen require
be'wundern admire **(bewundernswert** admirable)
brauchen need
freuen please **(es freut mich** I'm pleased; **erfreulich** agreeable)
***ge'fallen + D** please **(es gefällt mir** I like it)
gern *haben like **(gern *essen/*trinken** like [eating/drinking])
hegen cherish
hoffen hope
lieben love **(innig/abgöttisch lieben** adore/dote on; **sich ver'lieben in + A** fall in love with; **bis über beide Ohren** head over heels)

Lust *f* ***haben (auf + A/et zu tun)** feel like (sth/doing sth)
*mögen like; be fond of **(ich möchte (gern)** I should like)
schätzen value **(richtig ein|schätzen** appreciate)
schwärmen für + A be mad about
ver'göttern idolize
*vor|haben intend
*vor|ziehen; lieber *haben/*mögen prefer
*wollen want **(wohlwollend** benevolent)
sich [D] wünschen wish for **(wünschenswert** [thing]/**begehrenswert** [person] desirable)

angenehm pleasant
freundlich friendly
großartig great
herrlich magnificent
köstlich delicious; delightful
nett; liebenswürdig kind
prima *inv;* **toll** *both colloq* fantastic; terrific
reizend charming
sagenhaft; fabelhaft fabulous
schön lovely
unwahrscheinlich incredible
verliebt (in + A) in love (with)
wohlgesinnt (+ D) well-disposed (towards)
wunderbar marvellous
wundervoll wonderful

Abneigung Dislike

die Abneigung [-en] (gegen + A) aversion (to); dislike (of)
der Abscheu revulsion
die Antipathie antipathy
die Beanstandung [-en]; die Beschwerde [-n]; die Klage [-n]
   complaint
die Boshaftigkeit spite
die Böswilligkeit ill will
der Ekel disgust

die Feindschaft hostility; enmity

die Feindseligkeit animosity

die Gleichgültigkeit indifference

der Groll resentment (**jm grollen** bear a grudge against sb)

der Haß hate

der Horror horror (**einen Horror *haben vor** + D have a horror of)

die Unzufriedenheit dissatisfaction

die Verachtung scorn

die Verärgerung annoyance

ab|lehnen reject

sich be'klagen/sich be'schweren über + A complain about

hassen hate (**wie die Pest** like the plague)

miß'billigen (+ A) disapprove of (sth)

nicht *er'tragen; nicht *aus|halten not stand (**das kann ich nicht ertragen/aushalten** I can't stand it)

nicht *mögen; nicht leiden *können dislike

sich schämen wegen + G be ashamed of

ver'abscheuen detest (**verabscheuenswert** detestable)

ver'achten despise

widerstrebend/ungern *tun do reluctantly

abscheulich hateful; abominable

ärgerlich annoying

boshaft; bösartig spiteful; malicious

entrüstet (**über** + A) indignant (at)

gleichgültig indifferent

langweilig boring

nachtragend vindictive

scheußlich dreadful

übelgesinnt (+ D) ill-disposed (towards)

übelnehmerisch resentful

unerwünscht undesirable

unzufrieden (**mit** + D) dissatisfied (with)

widerwärtig repulsive

Vergleichen Comparing

die Ähnlichkeit [-en] similarity

das Gegenteil contrary; opposite (**im Gegenteil** on the contrary)

der Kontrast [-e] contrast

der Unterschied [-e] difference

das Urteil [-e] judgement

der Vergleich [-e] comparison (**im Vergleich zu/mit** + D in comparison with/to)

die Vorliebe [-n] (für + A) preference (for)

die Wahl [-en] choice; election

*ab|wägen weigh [ideas]

*be'schließen decide

sich *ent'scheiden (zwischen + D) decide (between)

sich *ent'schließen make up one's mind

neigen zu + D incline towards

über'legen consider

*ver'gleichen compare (**vergleichbar mit** + D comparable with/to)

*vor'ziehen; lieber *haben prefer (**vorzuziehen;** [before noun] **vorzuziehend-** preferable)

wählen choose

zögern hesitate

ähnlich (+ preceding D) similar (to)

anders als different from

besser als better than

gleich equal(ly); same (**der/die/das gleiche; der-/die-/dasselbe** the same; **wie als**)

identisch (mit + D) identical (to)

in bezug auf + A concerning

lieber rather (**ich gehe lieber** I'd rather go)

Lieblings- favourite (**meine Lieblingsfarbe [-n]** my favourite colour)

mehr als more than

schlimmer als worse than

soviel . . . wie as much . . . as (**genau-/ebensoviel . . . wie** just as much . . . as; **(nicht) so viel wie** (not) as much as; **ebensoviel** just as much)

so . . . wie as . . . as (**genau-/ebenso . . . wie** just as . . . as)

verschieden; [before noun] **ander-**; [after verb] **anders** different (**als** from)

viel much; a lot (of); *pl* many

weniger als less than

SEE ALSO: **Arguments For and Against; Describing People; Feelings**

32. Materials Materialien

die Flüssigkeit [-en] liquid
das Gas [-e] gas (das Erdgas natural gas)
der Körper/feste Körper [-] solid
der Kristall [-e] crystal
das Material [*pl* Materialien] material (das Rohmaterial; der Rohstoff [-e] raw material)
das Metall [-e] metal
das Mineral [*pl* -e or Mineralien] mineral
das Produkt [-e] product
der Stoff [-e] fabric; material; substance
die Zusammensetzung composition

dicht dense
echt real
farbecht colour-fast
fest firm
flüssig liquid; runny
gasförmig gaseous
geschnitzt [from wood]; gemeißelt [from stone] carved
glatt smooth
handgearbeitet handmade
hart hard
kompakt compact
künstlich artificial
leicht light
natürlich natural
plastisch plastic; malleable
porös porous
rauh rough
schwer heavy
solide solid
stabil sturdy
steinartig stony

synthetisch synthetic
versteinert petrified
weich soft
zerbrechlich fragile

Names of materials Namen von Materialien

das Aluminium; das Alu *colloq* aluminium
der Asphalt asphalt
der Backstein [-e]; der Ziegelstein [-e] brick
der Bambus [-se] bamboo
der Beton concrete
der Bindfaden string (**die Schnur [ᵆe]** piece of string)
das Bitumen bitumen
das Blech sheet metal
das Blei lead (**bleiern** leaden; lead *adj*)
die Bronze bronze (**bronzen** bronze *adj*)
der Draht [ᵆe] wire
das Eisen iron (**das Schmiedeeisen** wrought iron;
  (schmiede)eisern (wrought) iron *adj*)
die Erde earth (**irden** earthen; earthenware *adj*)
das Erz [-e] ore
der Faden [ᵆ] (piece of) thread
der Fels [-en] rock
der Feuerstein [-e] flint
der Filz felt
der Gips plaster
das Glas [ᵆer] glass (**gläsern** glass *adj*)
der Glimmer mica
das Gold gold (**golden** golden; gold *adj*)
der Granit granite
das/der Gummi rubber (**das/der Kreppgummi** crêpe)
das Holz [ᵆer] wood (**hölzern** wooden; **das Sperrholz** plywood;
  dreilagig three-ply)
der Kalk lime (**der Kalkstein** limestone)
das Kaolin kaolin
die Keramik [-en]; die Töpferware [-n] (piece of) pottery

der Kies gravel
der Kitt putty
der Klebstoff; der Leim glue
die Kohle coal (**die Steinkohle** (hard) coal; **die Braunkohle** brown
  coal; lignite)
der Koks coke
das Korbgeflecht wickerwork
das Kristall crystal [glass] (**kristallen** crystalline)
das Kupfer copper (**kupfern** copper *adj*)
die Lava lava
der Lehm clay; loam (**lehmig** clayey)
die Luft air
der Marmor marble (**marmoriert** marbled)
das Messing brass
der Mörtel mortar
das Öl [-e] oil
das Papier [-e] paper
die Pappe; der Karton/Pappkarton cardboard
das Petroleum paraffin
der Pewter; das Zinn/Hartzinn pewter (**das Zinn** [also] tin)
das Plastik; der Kunststoff plastic
das Porzellan [-e] (piece of) porcelain/china (**die Porzellanerde**
  china clay)
das Rohr cane
der Sand sand; grit (**sandig** sandy; **der Sandstein** sand-/gritstone)
das Seil [-e]; das Tau [-e] rope
das Silber silver (**silbern** silver *adj*; **das Silberpapier** silver paper)
der Stahl steel (**stählern** steel *adj*)
der Stein [-e] stone (**steinern** stone *adj*; **der Edelstein** precious
  stone)
das Steingut earthenware
das Stroh straw
der Teer tar (**der Makadam** tar macadam)
der Ton [-e] clay (**tönern** clay *adj*; **die Tonwaren** *f pl* earthenware)
der Torf peat
das Wachs wax (**wächsern** waxen)
das Wasser [≈] water (**wäßrig** watery)

das Weißblech tin-plate
der Zement cement

SEE ALSO: **Adornment** (for jewels); **Clothing** (for textiles); **Plants**
(for woods); **Science** (for gases and chemicals)

33. The Media Die Medien

Fernsehen, Funk und Video
Television, radio, and video

die Antenne [-n] aerial
die Aufnahme [-n] recording
der Bericht [-e] report
das Bild [-er] vision; picture (**der (Bild)schirm [-e]** screen)
der Decoder [-] decoder (**das Abonnement [-s]** subscription; **der/die Abonnent/in [-en/-nen]** subscriber)
der Empfang reception (**der Empfänger [-]** receiver)
die Fernbedienung remote control
das Fernsehen television (**der Fernseher [-]; das Fernsehgerät [-e]** television [set]; **im/beim Fernsehen** on/in television; **das Werbe-/Farb-/Schwarzweiß-/Kabel-/Satellitenfernsehen** commercial/colour/black-and-white/cable/satellite television)
der Fernsehfilm [-e] television film
die Fernsehserie [-n] television series
der Funk broadcasting; radio (**der Kinderfunk** children's programmes; **der Schulfunk** schools' broadcasting; **der Werbefunk** commercial radio)
der/die Hörer/in [-/-nen] listener
das Hörspiel [-e] radio play (**das Fernsehspiel [-e]** TV play)
das Interview [-s] interview
der Kanal [≈e] channel
die Kassette [-n] cassette
der/die Korrespondent/in [-en/-nen] correspondent
das Magazin [-e] magazine (programme)
die Medien n pl media (**die Massenmedien** mass media)
das Mikrofon [-e] microphone
der Moderator [G -s pl -en]/die Moderatorin [-nen] presenter
die Nachrichten f pl; [television only] **die Tagesschau** news (**die Nachrichten *kommen um + A** the news is at . . .)
der/die Produzent/in [-en/-nen] producer

das Programm [-e] channel; *sing* programmes

das Radio; der Rundfunk; der Hörfunk radio [broadcasting] (**das Radio [-s]** radio [set]; **das Transistorradio** transistor; **im Radio** on the radio)

der/die Regisseur/in [-e/-nen] director

die Satellitenschüssel [-n] satellite dish

die Seifenoper [-n] soap opera

der Sender [-] (radio/TV) station (**das (Sender)netz** network; **die Sendepanne [-n]** breakdown; **die Sendepause [-n]** intermission; **die Sendezeit** air-time)

die Sendung [-en] broadcast; programme (**die Dokumentarsendung** documentary; **die Live-Sendung** live/outside broadcast; **die Wiederholungssendung; die Wiederholung [-en]** repeat)

der/die Sprecher/in [-/-nen]; der/die Ansager/in [-/-nen] announcer (**der/die Nachrichtensprecher/in** newscaster)

die Störung interference

das Studio [-s] studio

der Ton sound

der Transistor [G -s pl -en] transistor

der Videoclip [-s] video; video clip (**der Videorecorder [-]** video recorder; **die Videokamera [-s]** camcorder)

der Vorspann front credits (**der Nachspann** end credits)

der Walkman [-s] walkman®

die Welle [-n] wave(band) (**auf Kurz-/Lang-/Mittelwelle** on short/long/medium wave; **UKW [= die Ultrakurzwelle]** VHF; FM)

der Werbespot [-s] commercial (**die Werbung** advertising; commercial(s); **der/die Auftraggeber/in [-/-nen]** advertiser)

der/die Zuschauer/in [-/-nen] viewer

ab|spielen play [video, cassette]

***auf|nehmen** record

aus|schalten; aus|machen switch off

ein|schalten; an|machen switch on

ein|stellen tune in

***fern|sehen** watch television

hören listen to

lauter stellen turn up (**leiser stellen** turn down)

löschen wipe
schalten auf + A tune to
***sehen** watch
senden broadcast (**live** live)
***über'tragen** (**im Fernsehen/Radio**) televise/broadcast
um|schalten switch over; change channels/stations

Die Presse The press

der Artikel [-] article
die Auflage [-n] circulation
die Beilage [-n] supplement
die Briefkastentante [-n] agony aunt
der Druckfehler [-] misprint (**drucken** print)
der/die Herausgeber/in [-/-nen]; **der/die Verleger/in** [-/-nen] publisher (***heraus|bringen**; **ver'legen** publish)
die Illustrierte [-n] photo-magazine
das Inserat [-e] [newspaper] advertisement (**der Inseratenteil** [-e] advertising section; **die Kleinanzeige** [-n] small ad)
der/die Journalist/in [-en/-nen] journalist
der/die Kritiker/in [-/-nen] critic
der Leitartikel [-] leading article
der/die Leser/in [-/-nen] reader (**der Leserbrief** [-e] letter to the editor; ***lesen** read)
der/die Mitarbeiter/in [-/-nen] contributor
die Nachricht [-en] (piece of) news (**das Neueste** the latest news; **die Nachrichten-/Presseagentur** [-en] news agency)
die Presse press (**die Sensationspresse** gutter press; **eine gute/ schlechte Presse *haben/*be'kommen** have/get a good/bad press)
die Presseabteilung [-en] publicity department
der/die Pressefotograf/in [-en/-nen] newspaper photographer
die Pressekonferenz [-en] press conference
der/die Redakteur/in [-e/-nen] editor (**der Redakteur für Politik** political editor; **der/die Chefredakteur/in** managing editor)
die Reportage [-n] report
der/die Reporter/in [-/-nen] reporter

die Rubrik [-en] column; section

die Schlagzeile [-n] headline (**Schlagzeilen machen** make headlines)

die Titelseite [-n] front page

die Zeitschrift [-en]; [newspaper supplement] **das Magazin** [-e] magazine (**die Wochen-/Monatsschrift** weekly/monthly)

die Zeitung [-en] newspaper (**die Tages-/Abend-/Sonntags-/Wochenzeitung** daily/evening/Sunday/weekly paper)

SEE ALSO: **Cinema and Photography; Music; Politics; Theatre**

34. Money Geld

der Abzug [⁼e] deduction
die Aktie [-n] share [in company]
die Ausgabe [-n] item of expenditure; *pl* expenses
der Besitz [-e] property (**mein persönlicher Besitz** my assets)
der Betrag [⁼e] amount (due)
die Bezahlung [-en] payment
die Bilanz [-en] balance sheet
die Brieftasche [-n] wallet
das Budget [-s]; der Etat [-s] budget (**der Haushaltsplan [⁼e]**
personal budget)
das Darlehen [-] loan (**auf|nehmen* raise)
das Depot [-s] safe-deposit
die Ersparnis [-se] saving(s)
der/die Fälscher/in [-/-nen] counterfeiter
der Gewinn [-e] profit
die Hypothek [-en] mortgage
die Inflation inflation (**mit Inflationsausgleich** inflation-proof)
die Investition [-en]; die Anlage [-n] investment
das Kapital capital
der Kauf [⁼e] purchase
der Kredit [-e] credit; loan (**jm einen Kredit ge'währen** grant sb a
loan)
die Lebensunterhaltungskosten *pl* cost of living (**der Lebens-
standard** standard of living)
der Lieferschein [-e] invoice
die Lotterie [-n] lottery
der/die Millionär/in [-e/-nen] millionaire
das Portemonnaie [-s] purse
der Preis [-e] price (**hoch** high; **niedrig** low; **der Selbstkostenpreis**
cost price; **die Preiserhöhung [-en]** price increase; **die
Preisermäßigung [-en]** price reduction)
der Prozentsatz [⁼e] percentage

die Quittung [-en] receipt

die Rate [-n] instalment (**auf Raten kaufen** buy on hire-purchase)

die Rechnung [-en] bill

die Schuld [-en] debt (**Schulden machen** get into debt; **1 000 Mark Schulden *haben** have debts of 1,000 marks)

die Schwankung [-en] fluctuation

die Steuer [-n] tax (**die Mehrwertsteuer** value added tax)

die Summe [-n] sum

der Verkauf [ːe] sale

der Verlust [-e] loss

die Währung [-en] currency

der Wert value

der Wertverlust depreciation (**die Abschreibung** allowance for depreciation; write-down)

die Zahlung [-en] payment (**in Zahlung *nehmen** take in part-exchange; **die Barzahlung** cash payment)

*ab|heben withdraw

akzeptieren; *nehmen take [e.g. credit cards]

*aus|geben spend

*aus|kommen mit + D/ohne + A manage on/without

be'rechnen (+ D) charge (sb)

ein|lösen cash [cheque]

*ein|werfen insert [money in slot]

ein|zahlen pay in

sich [D] gönnen; sich [D] leisten treat oneself to

in Umlauf *m* ***bringen** put into circulation

kaufen buy

kosten cost

*leihen lend ((**sich [D]) *leihen** borrow)

machen come to (**das macht 30 Mark zusammen** that comes to DM 30 all together)

schulden owe

sparen save

ver'dienen earn

ver'kaufen sell

wechseln; um|tauschen (in + A) change (into)

wert *sein be worth (**soviel ist es nicht wert** it's not worth that much)

zahlen [money]; **be'zahlen** [person, debt, bill] pay (**bar/mit Scheck/mit Kreditkarte zahlen** pay cash/by cheque/by credit card)

arm poor
billig cheap
gefälscht forged
gültig valid
knapp bei Kasse short of cash
Kopf oder Zahl heads or tails
kostenlos free
pleite broke
preiswert good value
reich rich
teuer dear
wertvoll valuable

Währungen Currency

die Blüte [-n] dud/forged note
die Devisen *pl*; **die Valuta [*pl* Valuten]**; **die Sorten** *pl* foreign currency
die (D-)Mark; die deutsche Mark [-] (German) mark
der Dollar [*pl* - or -s] dollar
der Franken [-] (Swiss) franc (**der Franc [-s]** (French) franc)
das Geld [-er] money (**das Taschengeld** pocket money; **das Bargeld** cash)
der Groschen [-] (German) ten-pfennig coin; (Austrian) groschen [1/100 of a schilling]
der Hundertmarkschein [-e] hundred-mark note
das Markstück [-e] one-mark coin
die Münze [-n] coin; mint
der Pfennig [*pl* - or -e] pfennig [1/100 of a mark]
das Pfund [*pl* - or -e] pound
der Rappen [-] (Swiss) centime

der Schein/Geldschein [-e]; die Banknote [-n] banknote

der Schilling [*pl* - or -e] (Austrian) shilling

die Währung [-en] currency

das Wechselgeld change (given back) (**das Kleingeld** small change)

Finanzanstalten Financial institutions

die Bank [-en] bank (**auf der Bank** in the bank; **der Schalter [-]** counter; position; **die Kasse [-n]** cash counter; **der/die Kassierer/in** [-/-nen] cashier; **der Geldautomat [-en]** cash dispenser)

die Börse [-n] stock exchange

die Sparkasse [-n] savings bank (**das Sparkassenbuch [ër]** savings book)

die Versicherungsgesellschaft [-en] insurance company (**die Versicherung** insurance; **die Police [-n]** policy; **die Prämie [-n]** premium)

die Wechselstube [-n] bureau de change (**der Wechselkurs [-e]** rate of exchange)

Ihr Bankkonto Your bank account

die Abhebung [-en] withdrawal

das Darlehen [-]; der Kredit [-e] loan (**ge'währen** grant; **kündigen** call in)

die Einzahlung [-en] deposit

die Ersparnisse *f pl* savings

die Gebühr [-en] commission

das Giro [-s] giro

die Hypothek [-en] mortgage (**die Anzahlung [-en]** payment)

das Konto [*pl* Konten or Konti] account (**das Giro-/Spar-/Postgirokonto** current/deposit/Girobank® account; **gemeinsam** joint; **er'öffnen** open)

der Kontoauszug [ë] statement

die Kontoführungskosten *pl* bank charges

der Kontostand [ë] balance (**das Guthaben [-]** credit balance)

die Kontoüberziehung overdraft

die Überweisung *no pl* (**an** + A/**auf** + A) transfer (to)
die Zinsen *m pl* (**auf** + A) interest (on) (**zu 10% Zinsen** at 10%
   interest; **der Zinssatz** [¨e] interest rate)

ab|be'zahlen pay off
*ab|heben withdraw
ein|lösen cash
ein|zahlen pay in; deposit (**auf ein Konto** into an account)
*gut|schreiben credit (**einem Konto** to an account)
in den roten/schwarzen Zahlen *sein be in the red/black
*leihen + D lend to ((**sich** [D]) ***leihen von** + D borrow from)
sparen save (**sparen für** + A/**auf** + A save up for)
*über'weisen transfer
*über'ziehen overdraw (**um DM 30 überzogen *sein** be over-
   drawn by DM 30)
zurück|zahlen pay back

Karten und Schecks Cards and cheques

der Ausweis [-e] identity card
die Debetkarte [-n] debit card
der Eurocheque [-s] Eurocheque
der Giroscheck [-s] giro check
die Kontokarte [-n] bank card
die Kreditkarte [-n] credit card
die Postanweisung [-en] = postal order
der Reisescheck [-s] traveller's cheque
der Scheck [-s] cheque (**über DM 30** for DM 30; **mit Scheck** by
   cheque; **faul** dud; **der Verrechnungs-/Blanko-/Barscheck**
   crossed/blank/open cheque)
das Scheckheft [-e] cheque-book
die Scheckkarte [-n] cheque card

SEE ALSO: **Crimes and Criminals; Numbers and Quantities; Shops
   and Shopping**

35. Music Musik

der Dirigentenstab [ːe] baton
die Disco [-s] disco (**die rollende Disco** travelling disco)
der Gesang singing
das Instrument [-e] instrument
die Juke-/Musikbox [-en] juke-box
die Kassette [-n] cassette
der Kassettenrecorder [-] cassette recorder
das Konzert [-e] concert (**das Sinfonie-/Rock-/Solistenkonzert**
symphony concert/rock concert/recital)
die Konzerthalle [-n] concert hall
das Opernhaus [ːer]; **die Oper** [-n] opera house
die Platte [-n] record (**die CD-/Langspielplatte** CD/LP)
der Plattenspieler [-] record-player
die Saite [-n] string
der Schlüssel [-] clef
die Taste [-n] key [of instrument]
der Videorecorder [-] video recorder (**die Videokassette** [-n] video
cassette)
die Zugabe [-n] encore (**Zugabe!** encore!)
der/die Zuhörer/in [-/-nen] listener (**die Zuhörer** *pl* audience)

Musiker Musicians

der Alt [-e] alto [singer]; contralto/alto [voice, part]; the
contralto/alto section (**die Altistin** [-nen] contralto [singer])
der Bariton [-e] baritone; the baritone section (**die Baritonstimme**
[-n] baritone [voice, part])
der Baß [ːsse] bass; the bass section
der/die Begleiter/in [-/-nen] accompanist
der Contratenor [-s] counter-tenor
der/die Dirigent/in [-en/-nen] conductor
der/die Komponist/in [-en/-nen] composer
der/die Konzertmeister/in [-/-nen] leader [of orchestra]

der/die Musiker/in [-/-nen] musician
der/die Sänger/in [-/-nen] singer
die Sinfoniker *m pl* symphony orchestra
der/die Solist/in [-en/-nen] soloist
der Sopran [-e] soprano [singer, voice, part]; the soprano section
 (**die Sopranistin** [-nen] [also] soprano [singer])
der/die Spieler/in [-/-nen] player
der Tenor [¨e] tenor [singer, voice, part]; the tenor section

Musikkapellen Bands

der Chor [¨e] choir; chorus
das Duett [-e] [voices]; **das Duo** [-s] [instruments] duet
die Gruppe [-n] group (**die Rock-/Poppgruppe** rock/pop group)
die Kapelle/Musikkapelle [-n] band (**die Blaskapelle** brass band)
das Orchester [-] orchestra
das Quartett [-e] quartet (**das Streichquartett** string quartet)
das Streichorchester [-] string orchestra
das Trio [-s] trio

Was sie spielen What they play

der Akkord [-e] chord
die Arie [-n] aria
die Dissonanz [-en] discord
die Harmonie [-n] harmony
die Hitparade [-n] hit parade
der Jazz jazz
das Lied [-er] song
die Melodie [-n] tune; melody
die Musik musik (**die Pop-/Volks-/Kammermusik** pop/folk/
 chamber music; **klassisch** classical)
die Note [-n] note [= the printed symbol] (**die Noten** *pl* sheet
 music)
die Oper [-n] opera
die Operette [-n] operetta
die Ouvertüre [-n] (+ G) overture (to)

die Partitur [-en] score
der Rock rock
der Schlager [-] hit; pop-song
die Sinfonie [-n] symphony
die Sonate [-n] sonata
das Stück [-e] piece
der Ton [≃e] note [sound]; (die Taste [-n] [key of piano] note (der Mißton wrong note)
die Tonleiter [-n] scale

Was sie tun What they do

auf|legen put on [record]
*blasen blow
dirigieren conduct
interpretieren interpret
*schlagen beat
*singen sing (richtig/falsch in/out of tune)
spielen play
üben practise

Instrumente Instruments

Where not otherwise indicated the player of the instrument is der/die [instrument]spieler/in [-/-nen]

das Akkordeon [-s]; die Ziehharmonika [-s] accordeon (der/die Akkordeonist/in [-en/-nen] accordeon player)
die Becken n pl cymbals (ein Beckenteller m a cymbal)
das Blechinstrument [-e] brass instrument (die Blechbläser m pl the brass section)
die Blockflöte [-n] recorder (der/die Blockflötenspieler/in [-/-nen] recorder player)
das Bügelhorn [≃er] bugle
das Cello [pl -s or Celli] cello (der/die Cellist/in [-en/-nen] cellist)
das Cembalo [pl Cembali] harpsichord (der/die Cembalist/in [-en/-nen] harpsichordist)

der **Dudelsack** [=e] (set of) bagpipes

das **Euphonium** [*pl* **Euphonien**] euphonium

das **Fagott** [-e] bassoon (**der/die Fagottist/in** [-en/-nen] bassoonist)

die **Flöte** [-n] flute (**der/die Flötist/in** [-en/-nen] flautist)

die **Geige** [-n] fiddle (**der/die Geigenspieler/in** [-/-nen] fiddler)

die **Gitarre** [-n] guitar (**der/die Gitarrist/in** [-en/-nen] guitarist)

die **Harfe** [-n] harp (**der/die Harfenist/in** [-en/-nen] harpist)

das **Harmonium** [*pl* **Harmonien**] harmonium

das **Holzblasinstrument** [-e] woodwind [instrument] (**die Holzbläser** *m pl* the woodwind section)

die **Kesselpauken** *f pl* timpani (**der/die Paukist/in** [-en/-nen] timpanist)

das **Horn/Waldhorn** [=er] French horn (**das Jagdhorn** hunting horn; **das Englischhorn** cor anglais)

die **Klarinette** [-n] clarinet (**der/die Klarinettist/in** [-en/-nen] clarinettist)

die **Klaviatur** [-en] keyboard

das **Klavier** [-e]; [grand] **der Flügel** [-] piano (**der/die Pianist/in** [-en/-nen] pianist)

der **Kontrabaß** [=sse] double bass (**der/die Bassist/in** [-en/-nen] double-bass player)

die **Mundharmonika** [-s] mouth organ

die **Oboe** [-n] oboe (**der/die Oboist/in** [-en/-nen] oboist)

die **Orgel** [-n] organ (**der/die Organist/in** [-en/-nen] organist)

die **Posaune** [-n] trombone (**der/die Posaunist/in** [-en/-nen] trombonist)

das **Saxophon** [-e] saxophone (**der/die Saxophonist/in** [-en/-nen] saxophonist)

das **Schlagzeug** [-e] drums; drum-kit; the percussion section (**der/die Schlagzeuger/in** [-/-nen] percussionist)

die **Streichinstrumente** *n pl* strings (**die Streicher** *m pl* the string section)

das **Tamburin** [-e] tambourine

der **Triangel** [-] triangle

die **Trommel** [-n] drum (**die große Trommel** bass drum)

die **Trompete** [-n] trumpet (**der/die Trompeter/in** [-/-nen] trumpeter)

die Violine [-n] violin (**der/die Violinist/in [-en/-nen]** violinist)
das Xylophon [-e] xylophone

Die Tonleiter The scale

das As A flat
das A A
das Ais A sharp
das B B flat
das H B
das C C
das Cis C sharp
das Des D flat
das D D
das Dis D sharp
das Es E flat
das E E
das F F
das Fis F sharp
das Ges G flat
das G G
das Gis G sharp

Die Tonarten The keys

A; **A-Dur** A major
a; **a-Moll** A minor
As; **As-Dur** A♭ minor
ais; **ais-Moll** A♭ minor etc.

SEE ALSO: **Leisure and Hobbies; The Media; The Senses; Theatre**

36. Nature Natur

Der Weltraum Space

der **Asteroid** [-en] asteroid

die **Eklipse** [-n] eclipse (**die Sonnen-/Mondfinsternis** [-se] eclipse of the sun/moon)

die **Erde** Earth (**die Erdkugel** [-n] terrestrial globe)

die **Ewigkeit** eternity

das **Fernrohr** [-e]; das **Teleskop** [-e] telescope

die **Galaxie** [-n] galaxy (**die Galaxis** the [= our] Galaxy)

der **Himmel** sky (**unter freiem Himmel; im Freien** in the open air)

der **Horizont** [-e] horizon

der **Komet** [-en] comet

der **Kontinent** [-e]; der **Erdteil** [-e] continent

die **Luft** air

die **Milchstraße** Milky Way

der **Mond** [-e] moon (**der Voll-/Neumond** full/new moon; **das Mondlicht** moonlight)

der **Nebel** [-] nebula

das **Observatorium** [pl -torien]; die **Sternwarte** [-n] observatory

der **Planet** [-en] planet

der **Raum** space (**der Weltraum** outer space; **das Raumschiff** [-e] space ship; **die Raumfähre** [-n] space shuttle; **der/die Raumfahrer/in** [-/-nen] spaceman/-woman)

der **Satellit** [-en] satellite

die **Sonne** [-n] sun (**der Sonnenaufgang/Sonnenuntergang** [⸚e] sunrise/sunset; **die Morgen-/Abenddämmerung** dawn/dusk)

der **Stern** [-e] star (**das Sternbild** [-er] constellation)

die **Welt** [-en] world (**die Weltkarte** [-n] map of the world)

das **Weltall**; das **Universum** universe

blitzen twinkle

*****zu|nehmen** wax (*****ab|nehmen** wane)

*****auf|gehen** rise (*****unter|gehen** set)

sich drehen um + A revolve around

funkeln sparkle
***scheinen** shine

Die Landschaft The countryside

der Abgrund [¨e] precipice; abyss
der Abhang [¨e] slope; incline
die Abkürzung [-en] short-cut
die Anhöhe [-n] knoll
der Bach [¨e] stream (**der Sturzbach** torrent)
der Bauernhof [¨e] farm (**das Bauernhaus** [¨er] farmhouse; **der Bauer** [-n]/**die Bäuerin** [-nen]; **der/die Landwirt/in** [-e/-nen] farmer/farmer's wife)
der Baum [¨e] tree (**der Wipfel** [-] tree-top)
der Berg [-e] hill; mountain (**die Bergkette** [-n] mountain chain; **der Gipfel** [-] mountain top; **die Spitze** [-n] summit)
der Boden [¨] land; soil
die Brücke [-n] bridge (**die Hänge-/Drehbrücke** suspension/swing bridge; **der Steg** [-e] foot-bridge)
der Brunnen [-] well
der Busch [¨e] bush
das Buschwerk no pl scrub (**das Buschland** [¨er] scrubland)
das Delta [pl -s or **Delten**] delta
das Dorf [¨er] village
der Dschungel [-] jungle
die Düne [-n] dune
die Ebene [-n] plain
die Erde soil (**der Erdboden** earth; face of the earth)
das Feld [-er]; **der Acker** [¨] (cultivated) field (**pflügen** plough; **den Acker be'stellen** till the field; **die Furche** [-n] furrow; **das Eisfeld** ice-field)
das Festland [¨er] mainland; continent
das Flachland no pl lowlands
der Fluß [¨sse]; [larger] **der Strom** [¨e] river (**das Ufer** [-] bank; **das Bett** [-en] bed; **flußaufwärts/flußabwärts** upriver/downriver; **die Furt** [-en] ford; **der Damm/Staudamm** [¨e] dam)

das Gebirge [-] (range of) mountains (**der Gebirgszug** [=e]; **die Gebirgskette** [-n] mountain range)

der Gletscher [-] glacier

der Graben [=] ditch

das Grasland [=er]; **die Prärie** [-n] prairie

der Grund ground

das Gut [=er] estate

der Hang [=e] slope; hillside

die Hecke [-n] hedge

die Heide [-n] heath

der Heuschober [-]; **die Heudieme** [-n] haystack

die Hochebene [-n]; **das Plateau** [-s] plateau

das Hochland [=er] highlands

die Höhle [-n] cave

der Hügel [-] hill

der Kanal [=e] canal

die Klamm [-en]; **die Schlucht** [-en] ravine; gorge

das Land country (**auf dem Lande** in the country; **auf das Land** to the country; **über Land *fahren** go across country; **die Landschaft** [-en] countryside; landscape; region; **die Landwirtschaft** agriculture)

das Landsträßchen [-] (country) lane

die Lichtung [-en] clearing

der Mast [G -(e)s, *pl* -en or -e] pylon

das Moor/Hochmoor [-e] moor (**das Moorland** [=er] moorland)

die Mühle [-n] mill (**die Windmühle** windmill)

die Mündung [-en] estuary; river mouth

der Nationalpark [-s] national park

der Nebenfluß [=sse] tributary

die Niederung [-en] hollow

die Oase [-n] oasis

der Obstgarten [=] orchard

der Paß [=sse] pass

der Pfad [-e]; **der Weg/Fußweg** [-e] path (**der Wegweiser** [-] signpost)

die Quelle [-n] spring

die Scheune [-n] barn

der **Schlamm** mud
der **Schuppen** [-] shed
der **See** [-n] lake
der **Stein** [-e] stone; rock
der **Steinbruch** [≃e] quarry
die **Steppe** [-n] steppe
die **Straße** [-n] road (die **Haupt-/Landstraße** main/country road)
der **Sumpf** [≃e] marsh; swamp
das **Tal** [≃er] valley
der **Teich** [-e] pond
das **Tor** [-e]; das **Gatter** [-] gate
der **Tümpel** [-] pool
die **Vogelscheuche** [-n] scarecrow
der **Vulkan** [-e] volcano (der **Vulkanausbruch** [≃e] eruption; die
  Lava lava; der **Krater** [-] crater; **tätig** active; **untätig** dormant)
der **Wald** [≃er] wood; forest (der **Forst** commercially
  cultivated forest; der **Urwald** primeval forest; der **tropische**
  Urwald tropical rainforest)
der **Wasserfall** [≃e] waterfall
der **Wasserlauf** [≃e] watercourse
die **Weide** [-n] pasture; meadow
der **Weiler** [-] hamlet
der **Weinberg** [-e] vineyard
die **Wiese** [-n] meadow (die **Salzwiese** salt meadow)
die **Wüste** [-n] desert
der **Zaun** [≃e] fence

auf|ragen rise [mountain]
durch'waten ford
ein|dämmen dam
sich er'strecken stretch
***fließen** flow
grenzen/an|grenzen an + A border
***liegen** lie; be situated
***stehen** stand
***über|laufen** overflow
***über'schwemmen** flood

um'ringen (mit + D) surround (with)

bergig mountainous
eben/uneben even/uneven
flach flat
fruchtbar/unfruchtbar fertile/infertile
glatt smooth
hüg(e)lig hilly
nackt bare
rauh rough
saftig lush
sandig sandy
schiffbar navigable
schroff precipitous
senkrecht vertical
staubig dusty
steil steep
steinig stony
üppig luxuriant
zackig jagged

Das Meer und die Küste The sea and the coast

die Boje [-n] buoy
die Brandung surf (**surfen** surf)
die Bucht [-en] bay
die Dünung swell
der Felsen [-] rock; cliff (**der Fels [G -en;** *no pl*] rock [the material])
das Festland continent [as opposed to island]
das Gewässer [-] stretch of water
die Gezeiten *no sing* tides (**die Flut [-en]** (high) tide; **die Ebbe [-n]** low tide)
der Golf [-e] gulf
der Hafen [ʺ] port; harbour
der Horizont [-e] horizon

die Insel [-n] island (**die Halbinsel [-n]** peninsula; **die Landenge [-n]** isthmus; **die Inselgruppe [-n]** archipelago)

der Kai [-s] quay

das Kap [-s] cape

der Kies shingle

der Kiesel [-]; der Kieselstein [-e] pebble

die Klippe [-n] cliff

die Korallenbank [¨e]; das Korallenriff [-e] reef

die Küste [-n] coast; seaside

die Landungsbrücke [-n] jetty

der Landungssteg [-e] landing-stage

der Leuchtturm [¨e] lighthouse

die Marina [-s]; der Jachthafen [¨e] marina

das Meer [-e]; die See sea (**ans Meer/an die See *fahren** go to the seaside; **das offene Meer; die offene See** the open sea; **aufgewühlt** rough; **ruhig** calm; **bewegt** choppy; **stürmisch** stormy; **der Meeresboden; der Meeresgrund** sea bed; **der Meeresspiegel [-]** sea-level)

die Mole/Hafenmole [-n] mole

die Mündung [-en] river-mouth; estuary

die Muschel [-n]; die Muschelschale [-n] sea shell

der Ozean [-e] ocean

der Pier [-s] pier; jetty

der Sand sand (**die Sandburg [-en]** sand-castle; **die Sandbank [¨e]** sandbank)

der Schaum foam

das Seebad [¨er] seaside resort

der Sprühnebel spray

der Stein [-e] stone; rock

der Strand [¨e] beach (**die Strandpromenade [-n]** promenade; **der/ die Rettungsschwimmer/in [-/-nen]** life-guard; **der Liegestuhl [¨e]** deck-chair; **der Strandkorb [¨e]** beach basket-chair)

die Straße/Wasserstraße [-n] strait

die Strömung [-en]; der Strom [¨e] current (**gegen den Strom** against the current)

das Ufer/Seeufer [-] shore

die Untiefe [-n] shoal; shallows

das Vorgebirge [-] promontory
die Welle [-n] wave

Die Welt der Menschen The world of men

die Antarktis the Antarctic (der südliche Polarkreis [-e] Antarctic
  Circle)
der Äquator equator
die Arktis the Arctic (der nördliche Polarkreis [-e] Arctic Circle)
das Ausland foreign parts (im/ins Ausland abroad)
der Bezirk [-e] (larger) administrative district
die Breite [-n] latitude
das Dorf [¨er] village
das Gebiet [-e] region; territory
die Gegend [-en] district
die Gemeinde [-n] municipality; parish; community
der Globus [G - or -ses; pl -se or Globen] globe
die Grafschaft [-en] (British) county
die Grenze [-n] frontier; border
die Halbkugel [-n] hemisphere (nördlich northern; südlich
  southern)
die Heimat [-en] home (country/town/village) (das Heimatland
  [¨er] native land)
die Karte/Landkarte [-n] map
der Kontinent [-e]; der Erdteil [-e] continent
der Kreis [-e] (smaller) administrative district
das Land [¨er] country; (German) state (das Entwicklungsland
  [¨er] developing country)
die Länge [-n] longitude
die Nation [-en] nation
der Pol [-e] pole (der Nord-/Südpol North/South Pole)
die Provinz [-en] province (aus der Provinz [pejorative]
  provincial)
der Staat [-en] state (die Staatsangehörigkeit [-en] nationality)
die Stadt [¨e] town (die Groß-/Hauptstadt city/capital)
die Tropen pl the Tropics (der Wendekreis [-e] des Krebses/
  Steinbocks Tropic of Cancer/Capricorn)

das Volk [∺er] people
der Wahlkreis [-e] (electoral) ward
der Weiler [-] hamlet

SEE ALSO: **Animals; Disasters; Places, People, and Languages; Plants; Science; The Weather**

37. Numbers and Quantities
Zahlen und Mengen

---

der Bruch [ᵉe]; die Bruchzahl [-en] fraction
der Durchschnitt [-e] average
die Einheit [-en]; [maths] **der Einer [-]** unit
das Ganze *adj n* the whole
die Nummer [-n] [in series, street, telephone]; **die Zahl [-en]** [numeral]; **die Anzahl** [quantity] number **(eine gerade/ungerade/ganze Zahl** an even/odd/whole number)
das Rechnen; die Arithmetik arithmetic
der Rechner [-] calculator
der Teil [-e] part
die unendliche Menge infinity
der Unterschied [-e] difference
die Ziffer [-n] figure **(die arabischen/römischen Ziffern** arabic/roman numbers)

*ab|ziehen; subtrahieren (von + D from) subtract
auf|teilen share out
ge'nügen be enough
gleich *sein (eins und eins sind gleich zwei one and one are/is/equals two)
leeren empty
*mal|nehmen; multiplizieren (mit + D) multiply (by)
*messen measure
rechnen calculate
schätzen estimate
teilen; dividieren (durch + A) divide (by)
ver'doppeln double
ver'dreifachen triple
ver'teilen distribute
*wiegen weigh **(schwer** heavy; a lot)
zählen count
zusammen|zählen; addieren add

etwa about
fast almost
genau exactly; just
höchstens at most (**allerhöchstens** at the very most)
kaum scarcely
mehr oder weniger more or less
mindestens at least
nur only
ungefähr; zirka; circa approximately (**ca.** approx.)
völlig completely
wieder again

einzig only; sole
genau/ungenau exact/inexact
genug *inv*; **genügend** enough
gleich/ungleich equal/unequal
selten infrequent; rare
überflüssig superfluous
übermäßig excessive
sicher/unsicher definite/indefinite
zahllos; unzählig countless
zahlreich numerous

durch divided by
mal times
minus minus
plus plus
Prozent *n* per cent (**zehn Prozent** 10%; **in Prozenten aus|drücken** give as a percentage)
quadrieren square (**drei hoch zwei** three squared)

Die Kardinalzahlen The cardinal numbers

0 null	5 fünf
1 ein; eins	6 sechs
2 zwei; *colloq* zwo	7 sieben
3 drei	8 acht
4 vier	9 neun

10 zehn	28 achtundzwanzig
11 elf	29 neunundzwanzig
12 zwölf	30 dreißig
13 dreizehn	31 einunddreißig
14 vierzehn	40 vierzig
15 fünfzehn	50 fünfzig
16 sechzehn	60 sechzig
17 siebzehn	70 siebzig
18 achtzehn	80 achtzig
19 neunzehn	90 neunzig
20 zwanzig	100 (ein)hundert
21 einundzwanzig	101 (ein)hundert(und)eins
22 zweiundzwanzig	200 zweihundert
23 dreiundzwanzig	201 zweihundert(und)eins
24 vierundzwanzig	1000 (ein)tausend
25 fünfundzwanzig	1001 tausendeins
26 sechundzwanzig	1002 tausendzwei
27 siebenundzwanzig	2000 zweitausend

1 000 000 eine Million
1 200 000 eine Million zweihunderttausend
2 000 000 zwei Millionen
1 000 000 000 eine Milliarde
2 000 000 000 zwei Milliarden
1 000 000 000 000 eine Billion

Ein has an **-s** when counting, in arithmetic, and when used after a noun (**Zimmer eins**, *room one*); otherwise it declines like the indefinite article. Unlike the indefinite article, **ein** = *one* is stressed in spoken German.

As well as their numerical-adjective forms above, **das Hundert** and **das Tausend** are also nouns (**viele Tausende von Menschen**, *many thousands of people*). **Die Million** and **die Milliarde** have only noun forms. Both take plural (**-(e)n**); this plural form is also used when counting.

Die Ordinalzahlen The ordinal numbers

erst- first
zweit-; *colloq* **zwot-** second
dritt- third
viert- fourth
fünft- fifth
sechst- sixth
siebt- seventh
acht- eighth
neunt- ninth
zehnt- tenth
elft- eleventh
zwölft- twelfth
dreizehnt- thirteenth
vierzehnt- fourteenth
fünfzehnt- fifteenth
sechzehnt- sixteenth
siebzehnt- seventeenth
achtzehnt- eighteenth

neunzehnt- nineteenth
zwanzigst- twentieth
einundzwanzigst- twenty-first
dreißigst- thirtieth
vierzigst- fortieth
fünfzigst- fiftieth
sechzigst- sixtieth
siebzigst- seventieth
achtzigst- eightieth
neunzigst- ninetieth
(ein)hundertst- hundredth
(ein)hundert(und)erst- hundred
  and first
zweihundertst- two hundredth
(ein)tausendst- thousandth
zweitausendst- two thousandth
millionst- millionth
milliardst- thousand millionth
billionst- billionth

letzt- last

erstens firstly
zweitens secondly
drittens thirdly
viertens fourthly

einmal once
zweimal twice
dreimal three times; thrice
viermal four times
x-mal umpteen times

einfach simple
zweifach; doppelt double
dreifach triple
vierfach fourfold
mehrfach multiple

Brüche Fractions

halb *adj*; **die Hälfte** half
ein drittel one/a third
ein viertel one/a quarter (**ein Viertel** *n* **Leberwurst** a quarter
  (pound) of liver sausage; **Viertel vor eins** a quarter to one;
  dreiviertel *inv adj and adv* three-quarters)
ein fünftel one/a fifth
drei siebtel three sevenths
ein achtel one/an eighth (**ein achtel Liter** an eighth of a litre)
ein zehntel one/a tenth
ein zwanzigstel one/a twentieth
ein hundertstel one/a hundredth

eineinviertel one and a quarter
anderthalb; **ein(und)einhalb** one and a half
zweieinhalb two and a half

eins Komma sieben null vier; **einskommasiebennullvier (1,704)**
  one point seven o four (1.704)

Mengenausdrücke Expressions of quantity

die meisten *pl* most
ein bißchen a bit (of)
eine Menge a lot (of) (**die Menge** [-n] crowd; **jede Menge** any
  amount)
einige some; a few
ein paar a few
ein wenig a little
etwas a little; some (**etwas Kleines** something small; **etwa** about)
genug enough
kein no
mehr more (**die meisten** most)
mehrere several
nichts nothing
viel much; a lot of (**viele** *pl* many; **zu viel/zu viele** too much/too
  many; **wieviel/wie viele** how much?/how many?; **so viel** as
  much; **recht viele** a fair number)

wenig little (**wenige** few; **weniger** less; fewer)

der Becher [-] (plastic) pot; [ice-cream] tub; glass
der Bissen [-] mouthful [food] (**der Schluck** [*pl* -e or ¨e] mouthful [drink])
die Büchse [-n]; **die Dose** [-n] tin; can
das Faß [¨sser] barrel; drum
die Flasche [-n] bottle
das Glas [¨er] glass; jar
die Handvoll [-] handful
der Haufen [-] heap (**ein Haufen** . . . a pile of; loads of)
die Herde [-n] herd; flock
die Kanne [-n] [coffee, tea] pot
der/das Knäuel [-] [wool, string] ball
der Löffel [-] spoon(ful)
das Paar [-e] pair (**ein paar** a few)
das Päckchen [-]; **das Paket** [-e] packet
die Packung [-en] [cigarettes] pack; [chocolates] box
die Portion [-en] portion; helping; serving
der Riegel [-]; [larger] **die Tafel** [-n] (chocolate) bar
die Rolle [-n] roll
die Schachtel [-n] box
die Scheibe [-n] slice
die Schüssel [-n] bowl; dish
der Stapel [-] pile; stack
das Stück [-e] piece; item (**zwei Stück, bitte** two of those, please)
die Tasse [-n] cup(ful)
der Teller [-] plate(ful)
die Tube [-n] tube
die Tüte [-n] bag

Maße und Gewichte Weights and measures

das Ampere [-] amp
das Gramm [*pl* - or -e] gram
der/das Hektar [*pl* - or -e] hectare

die Kalorie [-n] calorie
das Kilogramm [*pl* - or -e] kilogram (**das Kilo [*pl* - or -s]** kilo)
der Kilometer [-] kilometre
der/das Liter [-] litre
die Meile [-n] mile
der/das Meter [-] metre
der/das Millimeter [-] millimetre
das Pfund [*pl* - or -e] pound [half a kilo]
die Tonne [-n] (metric) ton; tonne [1,000 kg.]
die Unze [-n] ounce
das Volt [-] volt (**die Netzspannung** voltage)
das Watt [-] watt
der/das Zentimeter [-] centimetre
der Zentner [-] (metric) hundredweight [50 kg.]

Kubik- cubic
Quadrat- square

die Breite [-n] breadth; width
die Dicke; die Stärke thickness
die Dimension [-en]; die Abmessung [-en] dimension
die Entfernung [-en] distance
die Fläche [-n] (surface) area
das Gewicht [-e] weight
die Größe [-n] size; [person, animal, building] height
die Höhe [-n] height
die Länge [-n] length
das Maß [-e] measurement (**bei jm Maß/die Maße *nehmen** take
 sb's measurements)
der Rauminhalt [-e]; das Volumen [-] volume
die Tiefe [-n] depth

breit broad; wide
eng narrow
flach flat
groß large; tall
hoch; hoh- high
hohl hollow

klein small
kurz short
lang long
leicht light
niedrig low
schwer heavy
seicht shallow
sperrig bulky
tief deep

Dimensionen Dimensions

wie groß/breit/lang/hoch/tief ist es? how big/wide/long/high/deep
is it?

es ist drei Meter breit/lang/hoch/tief it's three metres wide/long/
high/deep

zwei (Meter) mal fünf Meter two metres by five

die Größe [-n] size in clothes (**welche Größe *haben/*tragen Sie?**
what size do you take?; **in Größe 40** in size 40; **wie groß sind
Sie?** what is your height?)

die Hüftweite/der Hüftumfang hip size (**die Hüfte [-n]** hip)

die Kragenweite collar size (**der Kragen [-]** collar)

die Oberweite bust size (**sie hat Oberweite 90** she has a 34-inch
bust)

die Schuhgröße; die Schuhnummer shoe size (**welche Schuhgröße/
Schuhnummer hast du?** what size shoes do you take?)

die Taillenweite waist measurement (**die Taille [-n]** waist)

die Weite [-n] width [clothing]

SEE ALSO: **Money; Post and Telephone; Time**

38. Places, People, and Languages
Orte, Völker und Sprachen

Ozeane, Meere, Seen Oceans, seas, lakes

die Adria Adriatic
der Atlantik/der Atlantische Ozean Atlantic
der Bodensee Lake Constance
der Genfer See Lake Geneva
der Indische Ozean Indian Ocean
die Irische See Irish Sea
der Kanal/Ärmelkanal English Channel
die Karibik Caribbean
das Mittelmeer Mediterranean
die Nordsee North Sea
die Ostsee Baltic
der Pazifik; der Pazifische Ozean; der Stille Ozean Pacific

Erdteile und ihre Einwohner
Continents and their inhabitants

(das) Afrika Africa **afrikanisch; der/die Afrikaner/in [-/-nen]** African
(das) Amerika America **(Süd-/Mittel-/Nord-** South/Central/North) **amerikanisch; der/die Amerikaner/in [-/-nen]** American
die Antarktis Antarctica **antarktisch** antarctic
(das) Asien Asia **(Kleinasien** Asia Minor) **asiatisch; der/die Asiat/in [-en/-nen]** Asian
(das) Australien Australia **australisch; der/die Australier/in [-/-nen]** Australian
(das) Europa Europe **europäisch; der/die Europäer/in [-/-nen]** European

Flüsse und Berge Rivers and mountains

die **Alpen** Alps (**alpin**; **Alpen-** alpine)
die **Donau** Danube
die **Mosel** Moselle
die **Pyrenäen** *pl* Pyrenees
der **Rhein** Rhine (**rheinisch**; **Rhein-** Rhineland *adj*)
die **Themse** Thames
der **Vesuv** Vesuvius
die **Vogesen** *pl* Vosges
die **Wolga** Volga

Städte, Inseln, Gebiete Towns, islands, regions

Algier Algiers
die **Antillen** Antilles; West Indies
Antwerpen Antwerp
(das) **Arabien** Arabia (**arabisch** Arabian; **der/die Araber/in** [-/-nen] Arab)
Athen Athens
der **Balkan** the Balkans (**auf dem Balkan** in the Balkans)
Basel Basle (**der/die Bas(e)ler/in** [-/-nen] inhabitant of Basle)
(das) **Bayern** Bavaria (**bay(e)risch** Bavarian; **der/die Bayer/in** [-/-nen] Bavarian)
(das) **Böhmen** Bohemia (**böhmisch** Bohemian; **der Böhme** [-n]/**die Böhmin** [-nen] Bohemian)
die **Bretagne** Brittany
die **Britischen Inseln** *f pl* the British Isles (**Großbritannien** *n* Great Britain; **britisch** British; **der Brite** [-n]/**die Britin** [-nen] Briton; **Brit**; *pl* the British)
Brügge Bruges
Brüssel Brussels
das **Burgund** Burgundy
die **dritte Welt** the Third World
(das) **Den Haag** [also (das) **Haag** and der **Haag**] The Hague
Edinburg Edinburgh

(das) Elsaß Alsace (**elsässisch** Alsatian; **der/die Elsässer/in** [-/-nen] Alsatian)

die Europäische Gemeinschaft (EG) the European Community (EC)

die Ex-DDR [= **Deutsche Demokratische Republik**] former GDR [= German Democratic Republic]; eastern Germany

der Ferne Osten the Far East (**der Nahe Osten** the Middle East; **fernöstlich** Far Eastern; **nahöstlich** Middle Eastern)

(das) Flandern Flanders (**flämisch** Flemish; **der Flame** [-n]/**die Flamin/Flämin** [-nen] Fleming)

Genf Geneva

Gent Ghent

Genua Genoa

Hannover Hanover (**hannoversch**; **der/die Hannoveraner/in** [-/-nen] Hanoverian)

die Hebriden the Hebrides

(das) Helgoland Heligoland

(das) Hessen Hesse (**hessisch** Hessian; **der Hesse** [-n]/**die Hessin** [-nen] Hessian)

Kairo Cairo

die Kanalinseln the Channel Islands

Köln Cologne

Kopenhagen Copenhagen

(das) Korsika Corsica

(das) Kreta Crete

die Krim Crimea

Lissabon Lisbon

(das) Lothringen Lorraine

Lüttich Liège

Mailand Milan

(das) Mallorca Majorca

Mekka Mecca

Moskau Moscow

München Munich (**der/die Münch(e)ner/in** [-/-nen] inhabitant of Munich)

Neapel Naples (**der/die Neapolitaner/in** [-/-nen] Neapolitan)

(das) Ostfriesland East Friesland (**ostfriesisch** East Frisian; **der Ostfriese** [-n]/**die Ostfriesin** [-nen] East Frisian)

der Orient Middle East and S.W. Asia (**der Orientale** [-n]/**die Orientalin** [-nen] Middle Easterner; **orientalisch** oriental)

Prag Prague

(das) Preußen Prussia (**preußisch** Prussian; **der Preuße** [-n]/**die Preußin** [-nen] Prussian)

das Rheinland Rhineland (**rheinisch** Rhenish; Rhineland *adj*; **der/die Rheinländer/in** [-/-nen] Rhinelander)

Rom Rome (**römisch** Roman; **der/die Römer/in** [-/-nen] Roman)

(das) Sachsen Saxony (**sächsisch** Saxon; **der Sachse** [-n]/**die Sächsin** [-nen] Saxon)

die Sahara Sahara

(das) Sardinien Sardinia

(das) Schwaben Swabia (**schwäbisch** Swabian; **der Schwabe** [-n]/**die Schwäbin** [-nen] Swabian)

der Schwarzwald the Black Forest (**Schwarzwälder** Black Forest [*as adj*])

(das) Sizilien Sicily (**sizilianisch** Sicilian)

(das) Skandinavien Scandinavia (**skandinavisch** Scandinavian; **der/die Skandinavier/in** [-/-nen] Scandinavian)

Tanger Tangiers

(das) Thüringen Thuringia (**thüringisch** Thuringian; **der/die Thüringer/in** [-/-nen] Thuringian)

(das) Tirol the Tyrol (**Tiroler** Tyrolean; **der/die Tiroler/in** [-/-nen] Tyrolean)

Tokio Tokyo

Venedig Venice (**venezianisch** Venetian; **der/die Venezianer/in** [-/-nen] Venetian)

die Vereinten Nationen United Nations

Wallonien Wallonia (**wallonisch** Walloon)

Warschau Warsaw

Westfalen Westphalia (**westfälisch** Westphalian; **der Westfale** [-n]/**die Westfälin** [-nen] Westphalian)

Wien Vienna (**wienerisch**; **Wiener** Viennese; **der/die Wiener/in** [-/-nen] Viennese)

Länder und ihre Einwohner
Countries and their inhabitants

(das) **Ägypten** Egypt **ägyptisch; der/die Ägypter/in** [-/-nen]
Egyptian

(das) **Algerien** Algeria **algerisch; der/die Algerier/in** [-/-nen]
Algerian

(das) **Bangladesch** Bangladesh **bangalisch; der/die Bangali** [-s]
Bangladeshi

(das) **Belgien** Belgium **belgisch; der/die Belgier/in** [-/-nen]
Belgian

(das) **Brasilien** Brazil **brasilianisch; der/die Brasilianer/in** [-/-nen]
Brazilian

(das) **Bulgarien** Bulgaria **bulgarisch; der Bulgare** [-n]/die
Bulgarin [-nen] Bulgarian

(das) **Chile** Chile **chilenisch; der Chilene** [-n]/die Chilenin [-nen]
Chilean

(das) **China** China **chinesisch; der Chinese** [-n]/die Chinesin [-nen]
Chinese

(das) **Dänemark** Denmark **dänisch** Danish; **der Däne** [-n]/die
Dänin [-nen] Dane

(das) **Deutschland** Germany (**die Bundesrepublik** Federal
Republic) **deutsch; der/die Deutsche** *adj n* German

(das) **England** England **englisch** English; **der/die Engländer/in**
[-/-nen] Englishman/-woman

(das) **Finnland** Finland **finnisch** Finnish; **der Finne** [-n]/die
Finnin [-nen] Finn

(das) **Frankreich** France **französisch** French; **der Franzose** [-n]/
die **Französin** [-nen] Frenchman/-woman

(das) **Griechenland** Greece **griechisch; der Grieche** [-n]/die
Griechin [-nen] Greek

(das) **Holland** Holland (**die Niederlande** *pl* the Netherlands) **holländisch** Dutch; **der/die Holländer/in** [-/-nen]
Dutchman/-woman (**niederländisch** Netherlands [*as adj*]; **der/
die Niederländer/in** [-/-nen] Netherlander)

(das) **Indien** India **indisch; der/die Inder/in** [-/-nen] Indian

(das) Irland Ireland **(Nordirland** Northern Ireland) **irisch** Irish;
der Ire [-n]/**die Irin** [-nen] Irishman/-woman

(das) Island Iceland **isländisch** Icelandic; **der/die Isländer/in**
[-/-nen] Icelander

(das) Israel Israel **israelisch; der/die Israeli** [*pl* - or **-s**] Israeli
(jüdisch Jewish; **der Jude** [-n]/**die Jüdin** [-nen] Jew)

(das) Italien Italy **italienisch; der/die Italiener/in** [-/-nen] Italian

(das) Japan Japan **japanisch; der/die Japaner/in** [-/-nen]
Japanese

(das) Kanada Canada **kanadisch; der/die Kanadier/in** [-/-nen]
Canadian

(das) Korea Korea **koreanisch; der/die Koreaner/in** [-/-nen]
Korean

(das) Kroatien Croatia **kroatisch; der Kroate** [-n]/**die Kroatin**
[-nen] Croat

(das) Kuba Cuba **kubanisch; der/die Kubaner/in** [-/-nen] Cuban

(das) Libyen Libya **libysch; der/die Libyer/in** [-/-nen] Lybian

(das) Luxemburg Luxemburg **luxemburgisch** Luxemburg [*as
adj*]; **der/die Luxemburger/in** [-/-nen] Luxemburger

(das) Malta Malta **maltesisch; der/die Malteser/in** [-/-nen]
Maltese

(das) Marokko Morocco **marokkanisch; der/die Marokkaner/in**
[-/-nen] Moroccan **(maurisch** Moorish; **der Maure** [-n]/**die Maurin**
[-nen] Moor)

(das) Mexiko Mexico **mexikanisch; der/die Mexikaner/in** [-/-nen]
Mexican

(das) Neuseeland New Zealand **neuseeländisch** New Zealand
[*as adj*]; **der/die Neuseeländer/in** [-/-nen] New Zealander

(das) Norwegen Norway **norwegisch; der/die Norweger/in** [-/-nen]
Norwegian

(das) Österreich Austria **österreichisch; der/die Österreicher/in**
[-/-nen] Austrian

(das) Pakistan Pakistan **pakistanisch; der/die Pakistaner/in**
[-/-nen]; **der/die Pakistani** [*pl* - or **-s**] Pakistani

(das) Palästina Palestine **palästinensisch; der/die Palästinenser/in**
[-/-nen] Palestinian

(das) Peru Peru **peruanisch; der/die Peruaner/in** [-/-nen] Peruvian

(das) Polen Poland **polnisch** Polish; **der Pole** [-n]/**die Polin** [-nen] Pole

(das) Portugal Portugal **portugiesisch; der Portugiese** [-n]/**die Portugiesin** [-nen] Portuguese

(das) Rumänien Romania **rumänisch; der Rumäne** [-n]/**die Rumänin** [-nen] Romanian

(das) Rußland Russia **(die ehemalige Sowjetunion** former Soviet Union) **russisch; der Russe** [-n]/**die Russin** [-nen] Russian

(das) Schottland Scotland **schottisch** Scottish; **der Schotte** [-n]/**die Schottin** [-nen] Scotsman/-woman; Scot

(das) Schweden Sweden **schwedisch** Swedish; **der Schwede** [-n]/**die Schwedin** [-nen] Swede

die Schweiz Switzerland **schweizerisch; der/die Schweizer/in** [-/-nen] Swiss

(das) Serbien Serbia **serbisch; der Serbe** [-n]/**die Serbin** [-nen] Serbian; Serb

die Slowakei Slovakia **slowakisch; der Slowake** [-n]/**die Slowakin** [-nen] Slovak

(das) Slowenien Slovenia **slowenisch; der Slowene** [-n]/**die Slowenin** [-nen] Slovenian

(das) Spanien Spain **spanisch** Spanish; **der/die Spanier/in** [-/-nen] Spaniard

(das) Südafrika South Africa **südafrikanisch; der/die Südafrikaner/in** [-/-nen] South African

die Tschechische Republik the Czech Republic **tschechisch; der Tscheche** [-n]/**die Tschechin** [-nen] Czech

die Türkei Turkey **türkisch** Turkish; **der Türke** [-n]/**die Türkin** [-nen] Turk

(das) Ungarn Hungary **ungarisch; der/die Ungar/in** [-n/-nen] Hungarian

das Vereinigte Königreich United Kingdom

die Vereinigten Staaten *m pl* **(von Amerika)** (the) United States (of America) **(die USA** *pl* the USA) **amerikanisch; der/die Amerikaner/in** [-/-nen] American

(das) Vietnam Vietnam **vietnamesisch; der Vietnamese [-n]/die Vietnamesin [-nen]** Vietnamese

(das) Wales Wales **walisisch** Welsh; **der/die Waliser/in [-/-nen]** Welshman/-woman

die Westindischen Inseln West Indies **westindisch; der/die Westinder/in [-/-nen]** West Indian

Sprachen Languages

(das) Deutsch German (**auf deutsch** in German; **ins Deutsche** into German)

[and similarly all other languages that correspond to adjectives in the 'Countries' list above]

der Akzent [-e] accent

(das) Altgriechisch classical Greek

die Aussprache [-n] pronunciation; accent

der/die Deutschsprachige *adj n* German speaker

der Dialekt [-e]; die Mundart [-en] dialect

(das) Gälisch Gaelic

die Grammatik grammar

(das) Latein(isch) Latin

die Linguistik; die Sprachwissenschaft linguistics

die Phonetik phonetics

(das) Schweizerdeutsch Swiss German

die Sprache [-n] language (**die Muttersprache** mother tongue; **die Fremdsprache** foreign language; **neuere/tote Sprachen** modern/ dead languages; **das Sprachgefühl** feeling for languages)

der Wortschatz [ːe]; das Vokabular [-e] vocabulary

sich aus|drücken express oneself

*aus|sprechen pronounce

lernen learn

meinen [= intend to convey]; **be'deuten** [= signify] mean (**was willst du damit sagen?** what do you mean by that?)

*sprechen speak **(fließend** fluently)
über'setzen translate
*ver'stehen understand

SEE ALSO: **Identity; Nature; Towns**

39. Plants Pflanzen

die Abholzung; die Entwaldung deforestation (**die Wiederaufforstung** reafforestation)

der Ast [⸚e] (large) branch (**der Zweig [-e]** small branch; twig)

der Baum [⸚e] tree (**der Weihnachts-/Christbaum** Christmas tree; **der Obstbaum** fruit tree; **der Laubbaum** broad-leafed/deciduous tree; **der Nadelbaum** conifer)

die Baumschule [-n] tree nursery

die Beere [-n] berry

das Blatt [⸚er] leaf

die Blume [-n] flower (**das Blumenbeet [-e]** flower-bed; **der (Blumen)strauß [⸚e]** bunch of flowers; bouquet)

die Blüte [-n] blossom (**in voller Blüte** in full flower)

das Blütenblatt [⸚er] petal

die Borke; die Rinde bark

der Busch [⸚e] bush

das Dickicht [-e] thicket

der Dorn [-en]; der Stachel [-] thorn

der Duft [⸚e] scent

die Ernte [-n] harvest

der Forst [-e] forest

die Frucht [⸚e] fruit

die Gärtnerei [-en] nursery; gardening

das Geäst no pl branches

das Gebüsch [-e] bushes; clump of bushes

das Gemüse [-] vegetable(s)

die Girlande [-n] garland

der Halm [-e]; der Stiel [-e] stalk

die Hecke [-n] hedge

der Kern [-e] pip

die Knospe [-n] bud

der Kranz [⸚e] wreath

das Laub no pl leaves; foliage

die Lichtung [-en] clearing

der Obstgarten [¨] orchard
die Pflanze [-n] plant (**wildwachsend** wild)
die Plantage [-n] plantation
der Pollen [-]; **der Blütenstaub** *no pl* pollen
der Rasen [-] lawn; turf
der Saft [¨e] sap
der Samen [-]; **das Samenkorn** [¨er] seed
der Stamm [¨e] trunk
der Stein [-e] stone [of fruit]
der Strauch [¨er] shrub
der Stumpf [¨e] tree-stump
der Trieb [-e]; **der Sproß** [-ssen] shoot
das Unkraut weed(s)
das Unterholz undergrowth
der Wald [¨er] wood; forest (**der Urwald** primeval forest)
das Wäldchen [-] copse
der Weinberg [-e]; **der Weingarten** [¨] vineyard
der Wipfel [-] tree-top
die Wurzel [-n] root

aus|dünnen thin out
*aus|reißen uproot
*aus|treiben shoot
*be'gießen water
blühen blossom
ernten harvest
fällen fell
*graben [hole]; ***um|graben** [garden] dig
harken rake
jäten weed
klettern auf + A climb
kultivieren; be'bauen cultivate
pflanzen; an|bauen plant
pflücken pick
pflügen plough
pfropfen graft
reifen ripen (**reif** ripe)

roden clear
säen; aus|säen sow
***schneiden** trim
um|pflanzen transplant
um'zäunen fence in (**der Zaun** [¨e] fence)
ver'faulen rot
ver'welken fade; wither
***wachsen**; [flowers, crops] **züchten/an|pflanzen** grow
***zurück|schneiden** prune

Wald- und Zierbäume, Sträucher
Forest and ornamental trees, shrubs

der Ahorn [-e] maple
der Bambus [-se] bamboo
die Birke [-n] birch (**die Weißbirke** silver birch)
die Buche [-n] beech (**die Blutbuche** copper beech)
der Buchsbaum [¨e] box (tree)
die Eibe [-n] yew
die Eiche [-n] oak (**die Eichel** [-n] acorn)
die Erle [-n] alder
die Esche [-n] ash
die Espe [-n] aspen
die Fichte [-n] spruce
der Flieder [-] lilac [also its flower]
das Geißblatt no pl; **das Jelängerjelieber** [-] honeysuckle
der Goldregen [-] laburnum
die Hainbuche [-n]; **der Hornbaum** [¨e] hornbeam
der Holunder [-] elder
die Hortensie [-n] hydrangea
der Jasmin [-e] jasmine
die Kamelie [-n] camellia
die Kiefer [-n] pine (**der Kiefernzapfen** [-] pine-cone; **die Kiefernnadel** [-n] pine-needle)
der Lavendel [-] lavender
der Liguster [-] privet

die Linde [-n] lime
die Lorbeerkirsche [-n] laurel
die Magnolie [-n] magnolia
der Mahagonibaum [¨e] mahogany tree (**das Mahagoni** mahogany [wood])
die Myrte [-n] myrtle
die Pappel [-n] poplar
die Pinie [-n] (umbrella) pine
die Platane [-n] plane tree
der/das Rhododendron [*pl* -dren] rhododendron
die Roßkastanie [-n] horse-chestnut
die Stechpalme [-n] holly
die Tanne [-n]; **der Tannenbaum** [¨e] fir
die Ulme [-n] elm
die Weide [-n] willow (**die Trauerweide** weeping willow)
der Weißdorn [-e] hawthorn (**der Rotdorn** red hawthorn)
die Zeder [-n] cedar
die Zypresse [-n] cypress

Obst- und Nußbäume Fruit and nut trees

der Apfelbaum [¨e] apple tree
die Aprikose [-n] apricot tree
die Bananenstaude [-n] banana palm
der Birnbaum [¨e] pear tree
der Brombeerstrauch [¨er] blackberry bush
die Dattelpalme [-n] date palm
der Feigenbaum [¨e] fig tree
der Granat(apfel)baum [¨e] pomegranate tree
der Hazelnußstrauch [¨er] hazel
die Kastanie/Edelkastanie [-n] (sweet) chestnut
der Kirschbaum [¨e] cherry tree
die Kokospalme [-n] coconut palm
der Mandelbaum [¨e] almond tree
der Nußbaum/Walnußbaum [¨e] walnut tree
der Ölbaum [¨e]; **der Olivenbaum** [¨e] olive tree

der Orangenbaum [¨e] orange tree
der Pfirsichbaum [¨e] peach tree
der Pflaumenbaum [¨e] plum tree
die Weinrebe [-n]; **der Weinstock** [¨e] vine
der Zitronenbaum [¨e] lemon tree

Blumen Flowers

die Anemone [-n] anemone
die Aster [-n] aster
die Butterblume [-n] buttercup
die Chrysantheme [-n] chrysanthemum
die Dahlie [-n] dahlia
das Edelweiß [-e] edelweiss
der Fingerhut [¨e] foxglove
das Gänseblümchen [-] daisy
die Geranie [-n] geranium
der Goldlack wallflower(s)
die Hyazinthe [-n] hyacinth (**die Sternhyazinthe** bluebell)
das Immergrün [-] periwinkle
die Iris [-] iris
der Jasmin [-e] jasmine
die Kornblume [-n] cornflower
der Krokus [*pl* -se or -] crocus
die Levkoje [-n] stock
die Lilie [-n] lily
der Löwenzahn dandelion(s)
das Maiglöckchen [-] lily of the valley
die Margerite [-n] ox-eye daisy
der Mohn [plant]; **die Mohnblume** [-n] [flower] poppy
die Narzisse [-n] narcissus (**die gelbe Narzisse**; **die Osterglocke** [-n] daffodil)
die Nelke [-n] carnation
die Orchidee [-n] orchid
die Petunie [-n] petunia
die Pfingstrose [-n] peony

die Primel [-n] primrose
die Rose [-n] rose (**der Rosenstrauch** [ˑer] rose-bush)
die Schlüsselblume [-n] cowslip
das Schneeglöckchen [-] snowdrop
die Seerose [-n] water-lily
die Sonnenblume [-n] sunflower
das Stiefmütterchen [-] pansy
die Tulpe [-n] tulip
das Veilchen [-] violet
das Vergißmeinnicht [*pl* -e or -] forget-me-not
die Wicke [-n] sweet pea

Wildwachsende Pflanzen Wild plants

die Distel [-n] thistle
der Efeu *no pl* ivy
der Farn [-e] fern
der Ginster [-] broom (**der Stechginster** gorse)
das Gras [ˑer] grass (**die Quecke** couch-grass)
das Heidekraut *no pl* heather
der Klee *no pl* clover
die Mistel [-n] mistletoe (**der Mistelzweig** piece of mistletoe)
das Moos [-e] moss
die Nessel/Brennessel [-n] nettle (**die Taubnessel** dead nettle)
das Schilf [-e] reed(s)
der Tang/Seetang [-e] seaweed
das Unkraut [ˑer] weed(s)

Getreidearten Grains

die Gerste barley
das Getreide *no pl* grain; cereals
der Hafer *no pl* oats
das Heu hay
das Korn [ˑer] corn; grain of corn
der Mais maize

der Roggen rye
der Weizen wheat

SEE ALSO: **Cooking and Eating** (for herbs); **Food** (for fruits, vegetables, nuts); **Nature**

40. Politics Politik

die Abstimmung [-en] poll
der Adel nobility
die Arbeiterklasse *no pl* working class (**an|ge'hören** + D be a member of)
die Aristokratie aristocracy
der Aufstand [ˆe] riot; rebellion
die Barrikade [-n] barricade
die Brüderlichkeit fraternity
das Budget [-s]; der Etat [-s] budget
der Coup [-s] coup (**der Staatsstreich [-e]** *coup d'état*)
die Debatte [-n] debate
die Demonstration [-en] demonstration
die Diskussion [-en] discussion
die Einheit unity
der Erlaß [-sse] decree
die Fahne [-n]; [national] die Flagge [-n] flag
der Fortschritt [-e] step forward; [*often pl*] progress
die Freiheit [-en] freedom; liberty
das Gesetz [-e] law; act (**der Gesetzentwurf [ˆe]** bill; **die Debatte [-n]** debate)
die Gleichheit equality
die Heimat [-en] homeland
die Inflation inflation
die Krise [-n] crisis
die Krönung [-en] coronation (**die Krone [-n]** crown)
das Land [ˆer] country (**das Land; das Bundesland** (German) Federal Land)
die Linke the left (**die Rechte** the right)
die Macht [ˆe] power (**an die Macht *kommen** take power)
die Mehrheit [-en] majority (**knapp** narrow; **überwiegend** great)
die Meinungsumfrage [-n] opinion poll (**die Meinung [-en]** opinion; **die öffentliche Meinung** public opinion)
die Menge [-n] crowd

das Menschenrecht [-e] human right

die Minderheit [-en] minority

die Mitte the centre (**rechts von der Mitte** right of centre)

der Mittelstand *no pl* middle class(es)

der Mob *no pl*; **der Pöbel** *no pl* the mob

die Neutralität neutrality

die Oberschicht [-en] upper class

die Opposition opposition (**der/die Oppositionsführer/in** [-/-nen] Leader of the Opposition)

die Partei [-en] party

die Pflicht [-en] duty

die Politik [-en] politics; policy

das Recht [-e] right; law

das Referendum [*pl* **-den** or **-da**] referendum

das Regime [-] regime

die Revolution [-en] revolution

der Sitz [-e]; **das Mandat** [-e] seat [in parliament]

die Solidarität solidarity

die Staatsangehörigkeit [-en] nationality

die Steuer [-n] tax (**die Besteuerung** taxation)

die Tagung [-en] conference

die Verantwortung responsibility

die Vereinigung union

die Verfassung [-en] constitution

die Versammlung [-en] rally

die Verwaltung administration

das Volk [¨er] the people

die Wahl [-en] election (**das Wahlrecht** *no pl* right to vote; franchise; **die Wählerschaft** [-en] electorate; **der Wahlkampf** [¨e] election campaign; **der Wahlkreis** [-e] constituency; **die Wahlurne** [-n] ballot-box; **die Stimme** [-n] vote; **eine Abstimmung** a vote [= act of voting]; **der Stimmzettel** [-] ballot-paper)

die Wiedervereinigung reunification (**die Wende** the turnaround [pre-unification political U-turn in E. Germany])

die Wirtschaft [-en] economy

die Zusammenarbeit co-operation

ab|lehnen reject

ab|schaffen abolish
auf|lösen dissolve
be'steuern tax
demonstrieren demonstrate
*er'nennen appoint
gültig *werden come into effect
herrschen rule
nationalisieren; ver'staatlichen nationalize
organisieren organize
privatisieren privatize
regieren govern; rule
revoltieren revolt
stimmen vote (**mit Ja/Nein stimmen** vote in favour/against)
unter'drücken repress
unter'stützen support
ver'abschieden pass [bill]
*ver'treten represent
wählen elect; choose; vote for [party]
zentralisieren centralize (**dezentralisieren** decentralize)
*zurück|treten resign

autonom autonomous
einstimmig unanimous
extremistisch extremist
gemäßigt moderate
links left(-wing) (**rechts** right(-wing))
linksextrem; links-radikal extreme left(-wing) (**rechtsextrem; rechtsradikal** extreme right(-wing))
politisch political

Die Institutionen The institutions

der Bundesrat Federal Upper House
der Bundestag Federal Lower House
die EG the EC (**die Europäische Gemeinschaft** European Community; **der Gemeinsame Markt** Common Market)
das Kabinett [-e] Cabinet

die Monarchie [-n] monarchy
die Nation [-en] nation
das Parlament [-e] parliament
die Regierung [-en] government
die Republik [-en] republic (**die Bundesrepublik (Deutschland)** (German) Federal Republic)
der Stadtrat [ᵉe] town council
der Staat [-en] state (**der Wohlfahrtsstaat** Welfare State)
die UNO the UN (**die Vereinten Nationen** United Nations)
die Verfassung [-en] constitution

Die Männer und Frauen The men and women

der/die Abgeordnete *adj n* MP (**der/die Bundesabgeordnete** Member of the Federal Parliament)
der/die Botschafter/in [-/-nen] ambassador (**die Botschaft [-en]** embassy)
der Bundeskanzler Federal Chancellor; [Swiss] Chancellor of the Federation
der/die Bundespräsident/in Federal President; [Swiss] President of the Confederation
der/die Bürger/in [-/-nen] citizen
der/die Bürgermeister/in [-/-nen] mayor
der/die Demokrat/in [-en/-nen] democrat
der Diktator [G -s *pl* **-en]** dictator
der/die Fürst/in [-en/-nen] prince/princess; ruler
der Kaiser [-] emperor (**die Kaiserin [-nen]** empress; **das Kaiserreich [-e]** empire)
der/die Kandidat/in [-en/-nen] candidate
der Kanzler [-] chancellor
der König [-e] king (**die Königin [-nen]** queen; **das Königreich [-e]** kingdom; **der Thron [-e]** throne; **die Königinmutter** queen mother)
der/die Minister/in [-/-nen] (government) minister (**der Staatsminister** minister of state; **der Außen-/Finanzminister** foreign minister/Chancellor of the Exchequer)

der/die Ministerpräsident/in [-en/-nen] prime minister; minister-president [of a German Land]

der/die Mitbürger/in [-/-nen] compatriot; fellow citizen

der/die Politiker/in [-/-nen] politician

der/die Präsident/in [-en/-nen] president

der/die Premierminister/in [-/-nen] prime minister

der Prinz [-en] prince (**die Prinzessin** [-nen] princess)

der/die Regierungschef/in [-s/-nen] head of government

der Souverän [-e] sovereign

der Staatsbeamte adj n/**die Staatsbeamtin** [-nen] civil servant

der Staatsmann [ⁿer] statesman

das Staatsoberhaupt [ⁿer] Head of State

Ideologien Ideologies

der Anarchismus anarchism (**die Anarchie** anarchy) **anarchistisch** anarchistic (**anarchisch** anarchic)

der Antisemitismus anti-Semitism **antisemitisch** anti-Semitic

der Chauvinismus chauvinism **chauvinistisch** chauvinist

die Demokratie [-n] democracy **demokratisch** democratic

die Diktatur [-en] dictatorship **diktatorisch** dictatorial

der Faschismus Fascism **faschistisch** Fascist

die Ideologie [-n] ideology **ideologisch** ideological

der Imperialismus imperialism **imperialistisch** imperialist (**kaiserlich** imperial)

der Internationalismus internationalism **international** international

der Kapitalismus capitalism **kapitalistisch** capitalist

der Kommunismus Communism (**der Marxismus** Marxism) **kommunistisch** Communist (**marxistisch** Marxist)

der Konservatismus conservatism **konservativ** conservative

der Liberalismus liberalism **liberal** liberal

der Monarchismus monarchism (**die Monarchie** monarchy) **monarchisch** monarchical (**königlich** royal)

der Nationalismus nationalism **nationalistisch** nationalistic (**national** national)

der Patriotismus patriotism **patriotisch** patriotic

der Pazifismus pacifism **pazifistisch** pacifist
der Radikalismus radicalism **radikal** radical
der Rassismus racism **rassistisch** racist
der Republikanismus republicanism **republikanisch** republican
die Sozialdemokratie social democracy **sozialdemokratisch**
social democratic
der Sozialismus socialism **sozialistisch** socialist
die Tyrannei tyranny (**der Tyrann [-en]** tyrant) **tyrannisch**
tyrannical

SEE ALSO: **Arguments For and Against; History; Justice and Law;
The Media; War, Peace, and the Armed Services**

41. Post and Telephone
Post und Telefon

Die Post The post

der/die Absender/in [-/-nen] sender (**Abs.** from [on back of envelope])

die Adresse [-n]; **die Anschrift** [-en] address

die Anlage [-n] enclosure

der Brief [-e] letter (**die Antwort** [-en] reply)

der Briefkasten [⸚] post-box (**der Schlitz** [-e] slot)

die Briefmarke [-n]; [official language] **das Postwertzeichen** [-] (postage) stamp (**eine Briefmarke zu . . .** [+ D] a . . . stamp; **der Satz** [⸚e] set; **die Sondermarke** commemorative stamp)

der Briefmarkenautomat [-en] stamp-machine

der/die Briefträger/in [-/-nen] postman/-woman (**zu|stellen** deliver; **ab|holen** collect; **die Zustelltasche** [-n] post-bag; **der Geldbriefträger** special postman for letters containing money)

der Briefwechsel [-] correspondence

die Drucksache [-n] (item of) printed matter

der Eilbrief [-e] express letter

der Einschreibebrief [-e] registered letter (**per Einschreiben** by registered post)

der/die Empfänger/in [-/-nen] addressee

das Formular [-e] form (**aus|füllen** fill in)

die Geld-/Postanweisung [-en] = postal order

die Karte [-n] card (**die Post-/Ansichts-/Geburtstags-/Weihnachtskarte** post-/picture-/birthday/Christmas card)

der Kartenbrief [-e] letter-card

die Leerung [-en] collection

die Luftpost airmail (**der Luftpostbrief** [-e] airmail letter)

das Paket [-e] parcel (**die Paketpost** parcel post; **der Inhalt** contents; **das Packpapier** brown paper)

das Porto postage (**die Nachgebühr** postage due; **die Portomarke** [-n] postage-due stamp)

die Post post (**mit der Post** by post; **mit getrennter Post** under separate cover; **postlagernd** poste restante)

das Postamt [¨er] post office (**der Schalter [-]** counter; position; **der Postbeamte** *adj n*/**die Postbeamtin [-nen]** counter clerk)

das Postfach [¨er] PO box

die Postleitzahl [-en] post-code

der Poststempel [-] postmark (**Datum *n* des Poststempels** date as postmarked)

das Siegel [-] seal

das Streifband [¨er] wrapper

das Telegramm [-e] telegram

der Umschlag/Briefumschlag [¨e] envelope

die Waage [-n] scales (**die Briefwaage** letter scales)

der Werbeprospekt [-e] (advertising) circular

die Zollerklärung [-en] customs declaration

die Zustellung [-en] (postal) delivery

adressieren address

***auf|geben**; **auf die Post *geben**; ***ab|senden**; ***ein|werfen** post

be'antworten [letter]; **antworten auf** + A [invitation, question] answer; reply to

bei|legen enclose

***ein|schreiben** register (**eingeschrieben *ver'senden** send by registered post)

***ent'halten** contain

***er'halten** receive

frei|machen; **frankieren** frank (**mit 0,50 DM freimachen** put a 50-pfennig stamp on; **(un)frankiert** (un)stamped)

kleben stick

lesbar/unlesbar *sein; **leserlich/unleserlich *sein** be legible/illegible

nach|schicken forward (**bitte nachschicken!** please forward)

schicken; ***senden** send (**ab|schicken**; ***ab|senden** send off)

siegeln [with wax]; **zu|kleben** [stick down] seal (**der Siegellack** sealing wax)

sortieren sort

***wiegen** weigh

zurück|schicken send back

abgestempelt in + D postmarked . . .
als Eilsache f express
bei . . . ; per Adresse . . . care of . . .
beigeheftet attached
dringend urgent
per Luftpost by airmail
per Post postal
postwendend by return of post
siehe Rückseite see overleaf

Das Telefon The telephone

das Amt/Fernmeldeamt [⁼er] (telephone) exchange
das Amts-/Freizeichen [-]; **der Wählton** [⁼e] dialling tone
der Anrufbeantworter [-] answering machine (**der Signalton** [⁼e] tone)
die Auskunft/Fernsprechauskunft directory enquiries
das Autotelefon [-e] car-phone
das Besetztzeichen [-] engaged tone
das Ferngespräch [-e] long-distance call
der Fernsprechkunde [-n]/**die Fernsprechkundin** [-nen] subscriber
die gelben Seiten f pl; **das Branchenverzeichnis** [-se] Yellow Pages
das Gespräch/Telefongespräch [-e]; **der Anruf** [-e] (phone) call (**ein Telefongespräch führen/*er*halten** make/receive a call; **das Gespräch mit Voranmeldung** personal call)
der Hörer [-] receiver (**den Hörer *ab*nehmen/*auf*legen** pick up/put down the receiver)
der Nebenanschluß [⁼sse] extension (**Apparat 7** extension 7)
der Notruf [-e] emergency call/number (**die Notrufsäule** [-n] emergency telephone)
die Nummer/Telefonnummer [-n]; **die Rufnummer** [-n] phone number (**die falsche Nummer** wrong number)
das Ortsgespräch [-e] local call
das R-Gespräch [-e] reverse-charge call (**an|melden** make)
das Rufzeichen [-] ringing tone

das Telefon [-e]; der Fernsprecher [-] telephone (**das Tastentelefon** push-button phone; **die Taste [-n]** button; **drahtlos** cordless; **der Münzfernsprecher** payphone)

das Telefonbuch [ˈer] telephone directory

die Telefonkarte [-n] phonecard

die Telefonleitung [-en] telephone line (**eine schlechte Verbindung** a bad line; **die Verbindung [-en]** connection)

die Telefonzelle [-n] call-box

das Telegramm [-e] telegram

die Vermittlung no pl operator (**der/die Telefonist/in [-en/-nen]** switchboard operator)

die Vorwahl [-en] dialling code

die Wählscheibe [-n] dial [of phone]

die Zeitansage speaking clock

die Zentrale [-n] switchboard

*an|rufen; telefonieren mit + D (tele)phone; call

antworten answer

auf|legen hang up

besetzt/außer Betrieb *sein be engaged/out of order

*durch|kommen get through

*ein|werfen insert

läuten; klingeln ring

sich melden answer

telefonisch er'reichen reach by phone

*ver'binden mit + D connect with (**falsch verbunden *sein** have a wrong number)

wählen dial (**durch|wählen** dial direct; **sich ver'wählen** dial the wrong number)

*zurück|rufen call back

Was man sagt und hört

What you say and hear

am Apparat! speaking!

auf Wiederhören goodbye [on phone]

bleiben Sie am Apparat! hold the line!

danke für den Anruf thanks for calling

der Anschluß/die Nummer ist besetzt/außer Betrieb/antwortet nicht the number is engaged/out of order/does not answer (**der Betrieb** operation)

es ist eine sehr schlechte Verbindung it's a very bad line

es ist jemand in der Leitung we've got a crossed line

es ist niemand da there's no one there

hallo! hello

hier (ist) X this is X; X speaking

ich habe mich verwählt I've dialled the wrong number

ich möchte (mit) X **sprechen**; [politer] **ich hätte gern mit X gesprochen** I'd like to speak to X

ich rufe (Sie) zurück I'll call (you) back

ich verbinde (Sie) (mit + D) I'm putting you through (to)

meine Nummer ist zwoundzwanzig null sieben neunundneunzig my number is 220799

Moment mal; Augenblick mal just a moment

niemand meldet sich there's no answer

Sie sind durch you're through

Sie sind/ich bin falsch verbunden you've/I've got the wrong number

soll ich/würden Sie etwas ausrichten? can I take/may I leave a message?

Vermittlung! operator!

wer ist am Apparat, bitte?; wer spricht, bitte? who's speaking please?

wir sind unterbrochen worden we've been cut off

Buchstabiertabelle Spelling Code

A **wie** [as in] **Anton**	G **wie Gustav**
Ä **wie Ärger**	H **wie Heinrich**
B **wie Berta**	I **wie Ida**
C **wie Cäsar**	J **wie Julius**
D **wie Dora**	K **wie Konrad**
E **wie Emil**	L **wie Ludwig**
F **wie Friedrich**	M **wie Martin**

N wie Nordpol	U wie Ulrich
O wie Otto	Ü wie Übel
Ö wie Ökonom	V wie Viktor
P wie Paula	W wie Wilhelm
Q wie Quelle	X wie Xanten
R wie Richard	Y (Ypsilon)
S wie Siegfried	Z wie Zeppelin
T wie Theodor	

SEE ALSO: **Greetings and Replies; Reading and Writing**

42. Reading and Writing
Lesen und Schreiben

Die Leute, die es tun People who do it

der Antiquar [-e] second-hand bookseller

der Autor [G -s *pl* -en]/die Autorin [-nen]; der/die Schriftsteller/in [-/-nen] author

der/die Biograph/in [-en/-nen] biographer

der/die Brieffreund/in [-e/-nen] pen-friend

der/die Buchhändler/in [-/-nen] bookseller (die Buchhandlung [-en] bookshop)

der/die Dichter/in [-/-nen] poet

der/die Journalist/in [-en/-nen] journalist

der/die Leser/in [-/-nen] reader

der/die Romanautor [G -s *pl* -en]/die Romanautorin [-nen] novelist

der/die Verleger/in [-/-nen] publisher

Was sie tun What they do

aus|füllen fill in

be'antworten answer

*be'schreiben describe

dichten write [especially poetry]

drucken print

*er'finden invent

faxen fax

korrespondieren correspond

kritzeln scribble

*lesen read

*nach|senden forward

notieren note down

reimen rhyme

*schaffen create

schmökern browse
*schreiben write
tippen; ***maschine|schreiben** [*inf and past part.* only] type (**mit der Maschine geschrieben; maschinegeschrieben** typed)
*unter'halten entertain
*unter'schreiben sign
*unter'streichen underline
ver'öffentlichen publish
zitieren quote

Was sie gebrauchen What they use

der Absatz [¨e] paragraph
der Aktendeckel [-] folder
die Anlage [-n] enclosure
der Ausdruck [¨e] expression
der Auszug [¨e] extract
die Beschreibung [-en] description
die Bibliothek [-en] library
der Bleistift [-e] pencil (**der Drehbleistift** propelling pencil; **der Bunt-/Filzstift** crayon/felt-tip pen)
der Bleistiftspitzer [-] pencil-sharpener
der Blockbuchstabe [-n] block capital (**in Druckschrift** *f sing* in block letters)
die Büroklammer [-n] paper-clip
der Computer [-] computer (**die Diskette** [-n] floppy disc; **die Magnet-/Festplatte** [-n] hard disc; **die Datei** [-en] file; **der Datenbestand** [¨e] database; **das Text(verarbeitungs)system** [-e] word processor; **der (Laser-/Matrix)drucker** [-] (laser/dot-matrix) printer; **die Maus** [¨e] mouse)
das Etikett [*G* -s; *pl* -en or -e] label (**selbstklebend** adhesive)
das Fax [*pl* - or -e]; **die Fernkopie** [-n] fax (**das Fax;** **der Fernkopierer** [-] fax machine; **die Faxnummer** [-n] fax number)
das Fotokopiergerät [-e] photocopier (**die Fotokopie** [-n] photocopy)
der Füller [-]; **der Füllhalter** [-] (fountain) pen

der Großbuchstabe [-n] capital letter (**der Kleinbuchstabe** small
  letter; **groß/klein geschrieben** written with a capital/small letter)
der Gummi/Radiergummi [-s] rubber; eraser
die Handlung [-en] plot
die Handschrift handwriting (**leserlich/unleserlich** legible/illegible)
das Heft [-e] exercise book
der Hefter [-] stapler (**die Heftklammer** [-n] staple)
die Illustration [-en] illustration
der Kugelschreiber [-]; **der Kuli** [-s] ball-point
der Leim; der Klebstoff glue
das Lineal [-e] ruler
die Linie [-n] line
das Notizbuch [ʺer] notebook (**die Notiz** [-en] note)
das Papier paper (**das Umweltpapier** recycled paper; **das
  Schreib-/Briefpapier** writing-paper)
die Patrone [-n] [ink] cartridge
der Rand [ʺer] margin
der Reim [-e] rhyme
die Reißzwecke [-n] drawing-pin
der Rhythmus [pl **Rhythmen**] rhythm
der Satz [ʺe] sentence
der Schreibblock [pl ʺe or -s] writing-pad
die Schreibmaschine [-n] typewriter (**das Farbband** [ʺer] ribbon)
die Schreibwarenhandlung [-en] stationer's
der Stil style
der Tesafilm® sellotape®
die Tinte [-n] ink
der Umschlag [ʺe] envelope
das Wort [pl -e = continuous words, ʺer = individual words]
  word
der Zettel note
das Zitat [-e] (**aus** + D) quotation (from)

Ihre Werke Their products

die Ausgabe [-n] edition (**die Erstausgabe** first edition)
die Autobiographie [-n] autobiography

die Ballade [-n] ballad

der Band [¨e] volume

die Biographie [-n] biography

der Brief [-e] letter (**das Briefchen [-]** note)

das Buch [¨er] book (**die Hard-cover-Ausgabe [-n]** hardback; **das Paperback [-s]; das Taschenbuch** paperback)

der Comicstrip [-s] strip cartoon

die Dichtung poetry

das Gedicht [-e] poem

die Geschichte [-n] story (**die Kurzgeschichte** short story)

die Gespenstergeschichte [-n] ghost story (**der Geist [-er]; das Gespenst [-er]** ghost; **das Skelett [-e]** skeleton; **der Vampir [-e]** vampire; **das Ungeheuer [-e]** monster; **spuken in** + D haunt)

das Handbuch [¨er] handbook

das Kapitel [-] chapter

die Karte [-n] card; map (**die Gruß-/Ansichtskarte** greetings card/ picture postcard)

der Katalog [-e] catalogue

das Konzept [-e] rough draft

der Krimi [pl - or -s] crime thriller .

das Lesen reading

das Lied [-er] song

die Literatur literature

das Märchen [-] fairytale (**die Magie; der Zauber** magic; **die Fee [-n]** fairy; **der Kobold [-e]** goblin; **die Hexe [-n]** witch; **der Zauberer [-]** magician; wizard; **der Zauberstab [¨e]** magic wand; **der Zwerg [-e]** dwarf; **der Riese [-n]** giant)

das Meisterwerk [-e] masterpiece

das Nachschlagewerk [-e] reference book

die Ode [-n] (an + A) ode (to)

die Postkarte [-n] postcard

die Prosa prose

der Reiseführer [-] guidebook

der Roman [-e] novel

die Sage [-n] myth; legend

die Sammlung [-en] collection

das Schreiben [-] (formal) letter (**Betreff** re; **in der Anlage** enclosed; **(mit Bezug) auf Ihr Schreiben . . .** in reply to your letter . . .)

die Science-fiction science fiction (**das außerirdische Wesen [-]** extra-terrestrial being; **das Raumschiff [-e]** spaceship; **das Ufo [-s]** [= **unbekanntes fliegendes Objekt**] UFO)

das Sonett [-e] sonnet

die Strophe [-n] verse

das Tagebuch [ˉer] diary

der Text [-e] text

der Titel [-] title

die Unterschrift [-en] signature

das Wörterbuch [ˉer] dictionary

die Zeitschrift [-en]; das Magazin [-e] magazine

die Zeitung [-en] newspaper

Anreden und Grußformeln

Beginnings and endings to letters

Lieber/Liebe X; Hallo X Dear X [informal]

Lieber Herr X; Liebe Frau X Dear Mr/Mrs X [moderately formal]

Sehr geehrte(r) Frau/Herr X Dear Mrs/Mr X [formal]

Sehr geehrte Damen und Herren Dear Sir or Madam [to a firm]

Alles Liebe All the best

Bis bald See you soon

Dein(e) X Yours, X

Herzliche Grüße Ever

Hochachtungsvoll Yours truly [very formal]

Mit besten Empfehlungen Yours faithfully [formal]

Mit freundlichen Grüßen Yours sincerely [moderately formal]

Mit herzlichen Grüßen Best wishes [moderately informal]

Tschüs Cheers

Viele liebe Grüße With love from

SEE ALSO: **Arguments For and Against; Education; The Media; Post and Telephone**

43. Relationships
Verwandtschaftsverhältnisse

das Au-Pair-Mädchen [-] au pair

das Baby [-s] baby (**der Säugling [-e]** infant)

der/die Bekannte *adj n* acquaintance

die Braut [¨e] bride; fiancée (**der Bräutigam [-e]** bridegroom; fiancé)

der/die Erwachsene *adj n* grown-up (**erwachsen** adult)

die Familie [-n] family (**das Familienmitglied [-er]** member of the family; **der Familienkreis** family circle; **Familie Schmidt** the Schmidt family)

der Freund [-e] boyfriend (**die Freundin [-nen]** girlfriend)

der Junggeselle [-n] bachelor (**eingefleischt** confirmed)

die Junggesellin [-nen] single girl

der/die Kamerad/in [-en/-nen] companion; comrade; friend

das Kind [-er] child (**das Einzelkind** only child)

der Kollege [-n]/die Kollegin [-nen] colleague

der Kumpel [-] pal; mate

der/die Liebhaber/in [-/-nen]; der/die Geliebte *adj n* lover

der/die Nachbar/in [-n/-nen] neighbour

der Nachkomme [-n] descendant

der Stammbaum [¨e] family tree

der/die Verwandte *adj n* relative; relation (**meine Verwandtschaft** *sing* my relatives; **nah(e)-** near; **entfernt** distant)

der Vorfahr [-en] ancestor

die Waise [-n]; das Waisenkind [-er] orphan [male or female]

die Witwe [-n] widow (**der Witwer [-]** widower)

der Zwilling [-e] twin (**der Zwillingsbruder [¨]** twin brother; **die Zwillingsschwester [-n]** twin sister)

adoptiert adopted

minderjährig under age (**der/die Minderjährige** *adj n* minor)

mütterlicherseits on mother's side (**väterlicherseits** on father's side)

verwandt mit + D related to

Die Familie The family

der Bruder [⍩] brother (**der Halbbruder** half-brother; **brüderlich** fraternal)

der/die Cousin/e [-s/-n] cousin (**der Vetter** [G -s *pl* -n] (male) cousin; **die Kusine** [-n] (female) cousin; **der/die Cousin/e zweiten Grades** second cousin)

das Ehepaar married couple (**die (Ehe)frau** [-en] wife; **der (Ehe)mann** [⍩er] husband)

die Eltern *no sing* parents (**der Elternteil** [formal] parent)

der Enkel [-] grandson (**die Enkelin** [-nen] granddaughter; **die Enkel** *pl* [also] grandchildren; **das Enkelkind** [-er] grandchild; **der/die Urenkel/in** great-grandson/-granddaughter)

das Geschwister [-] sibling; [*in pl*] brothers and sisters

die Großeltern *no sing* grandparents (**die Großmutter** [⍩] grandmother; **der Großvater** [⍩] grandfather; **die Oma** [-s] granny; **der Opa** [-s] grandpa)

das Kind [-er] child (**das Adoptivkind** adopted child)

die Mutter [⍩] mother (**Mutti** *f* mum)

der Neffe [-n] nephew (**der Großneffe** great-nephew)

die Nichte [-n] niece (**die Großnichte** great-niece)

der Onkel [-] uncle (**der Großonkel** great-uncle)

der Pate/Taufpate [-n]; **der Patenonkel** godfather (**die Patin/ Taufpatin** [-nen]; **die Patentante** [-n] godmother; **die Taufpaten** *pl* [also] godparents)

das Patenkind [-er] godchild (**der Patensohn** [⍩e] godson; **die Patentochter** [⍩] goddaughter)

der Schwager [⍩] brother-in-law (**die Schwägerin** [-nen] sister-in-law)

die Schwester [-n] sister (**die Halbschwester** half-sister)

die Schwiegereltern *no sing* parents-in-law (**die Schwiegermutter** [⍩]/**der Schwiegervater** [⍩]/**der Schwiegersohn** [⍩e]/**die Schwiegertochter** [⍩] mother-/father-/son-/daughter-in-law)

der Sohn [⍩e] son (**der Adoptivsohn** adopted son)

die Stiefmutter [⍩]/**der Stiefvater** [⍩]/**der Stiefsohn** [⍩e]/**die Stieftochter** [⍩] stepmother-/father-/son-/daughter

die Tante [-n] aunt (**die Großtante** great-aunt)

die Tochter [ː] daughter (**die Adoptivtochter** adopted daughter)
die Urgroßeltern *no sing* great-grandparents (**der/die Urgroß-
vater** [ː]/**Urgroßmutter** [ː] great-grandfather/-grandmother)
Urur- great-great-
der Vater [ː] father (**Vati** *m* dad)
der/die Verlobte *adj n* fiancé/fiancée

SEE ALSO: **Birth, Marriage, and Death**

44. Religion Religion

der Allmächtige *adj n* the Almighty
(der) Buddha Buddha
Jesus [G **Jesu**] **Christ** Jesus Christ (**der Christus** [G **Christi**] Christ; **das Christkind** the Christ-child)
(der) Mohammed Mohammed
(der) Mose(s) Moses

das Abendmahl [protestant]; **die Kommunion** [Catholic] Communion
die Absolution absolution (**er'teilen** give)
der Apostel [-] apostle
die Blasphemie [-n]; **die Gotteslästerung** [-en] blasphemy
der Dämon [G **-s** *pl* **-en**] demon
der Engel [-] angel
die Erlösung salvation
die Erschaffung; die Schöpfung creation
das Fegefeuer purgatory
der Geist [-er] spirit; ghost
der Glaube(n) [G **-ns**] (**an** + A) faith; belief (in)
der Gott [ˑer] god (**die Göttin** [-nen] goddess)
der Gottesdienst [-e] service (**der Familiengottesdienst** family service)
der Götze [-n] idol (**die Götzenverehrung** idolatry)
der Heide [-n]/**die Heidin** [-nen] heathen; pagan
der/die Heilige *adj n* saint
die Hexerei witchcraft (**die Hexe** [-n] witch; **der Hexer** [-] sorcerer)
der Himmel [-] heaven
die Hölle [-n] hell
die Hymne [-n]; **das Kirchenlied** [-er] hymn (**die Nationalhymne** national anthem)
der Jünger [-] disciple
der/die Ketzer/in [-/-nen] heretic (**die Ketzerei** [-en] heresy)

die Konversion [-en] conversion

die Lehre [-n] doctrine

die Magie magic (**der/die Magier/in** [-/-nen]; **der/die Zauberer/in** [-/-nen]) magician)

der/die Märtyrer/in [-/-nen] martyr

die Messe [-n] mass

das Paradies paradise (**auf Erden** earthly)

der/die Pilger/in [-/-nen]; **der/die Wallfahrer/in** [-/-nen] pilgrim (**die Pilger-/Wallfahrt** [-en] pilgrimage)

die Predigt [-en] sermon

der Prophet [-en] prophet (**die Prophetin** [-nen] prophetess; **die Prophezeiung** [-en] prophecy)

das Schicksal fate

die Sekte [-n] sect

die Sünde [-n] sin (**der/die Sünder/in** [-/-nen] sinner)

der Teufel [-] devil

die Versuchung [-en] [act]; **die Verlockung** [-en] [thing] temptation

die Vorsehung providence

das Wunder [-] miracle (**Wunder wirken** work miracles)

*be'gehen commit

beichten confess

be'reuen repent of

beten pray

glauben an + A believe in

konvertieren be converted

kreuzigen crucify

predigen preach

segnen bless (**der Segen** [-] blessing)

sündigen sin

ver'dammen damn

wiedergut'machen [ich mache wieder gut] atone for

Was man glaubt What you believe

abergläubisch superstitious (**der Aberglaube** [G **-ns**; *no pl*] superstition)

agnostizistisch agnostic (**der Agnostizismus** agnosticsm; **der/die Agnostiker/in** [-/-nen] agnostic)

anglikanisch Anglican; Church of England (**der Anglikanismus** Anglicanism; **der/die Anglikaner/in** [-/-nen] Anglican)

atheistisch atheist (**der Atheismus** atheism; **der/die Atheist/in** [-en/-nen] atheist)

buddhistisch Buddhist (**der Buddhismus** Buddhism; **der/die Buddhist/in** [-en/-nen] Buddhist)

christlich Christian (**das Christentum** Christianity; **der/die Christ/in** [-en/-nen] Christian; **die Bibel** the Bible; **das Alte/Neue Testament** [-e] the Old/New Testament; **das Kreuz** the Cross; **die Kreuzigung** the Crucifixion)

evangelisch; protestantisch Protestant (**der Protestantismus** Protestantism; **der/die Protestant/in** [-en/-nen]; **der/die Evangelische** *adj n* Protestant)

fromm pious (**die Frömmigkeit** piety)

heilig holy; blessèd (**die Heiligkeit** holiness)

jüdisch Jewish (**das Judentum**; **der Judaismus** Judaism; **der Jude** [-n]/**die Jüdin** [-nen] Jew)

katholisch Catholic (**der Katholizismus** Catholicism; **der/die Katholik/in** [-en/-nen] Catholic)

konvertiert converted (**der/die Konvertit/in** [-en/-nen] convert)

moslemisch; muslimisch Moslem (**der Islam** Islam; **der Moslem** [-s]/**die Moslime** [-n] Moslem; **der Koran** the Koran)

puritanisch puritanic (**der Puritanismus** Puritanism; **der/die Puritaner/in** [-/-nen] Puritan)

skeptisch sceptical (**die Skepsis**; **die Skeptizismus** scepticism; **der/die Skeptiker/in** [-/-nen] sceptic)

Bauten und Geistliche
Buildings and clergy

der Abt [≈e] abbot (**die Äbtin** [-nen] abbess)

die Abtei [-en] abbey

der Bischof [≈e] bishop (**der Erzbischof** archbishop)

der Dom [-e]; **das Münster** [-] cathedral

der/die Geistliche *adj n* minister; clergyman

der Kardinal [≈e] cardinal

die Kirche [-n] church

der Kurat [-en] curate

der Mönch [-e] monk

die Moschee [-n] mosque

der Muezzin [-s] muezzin

die Nonne [-n] nun

der Papst [≈e] Pope

der/die Pfarrer/in [-/-nen] vicar; minister

der Priester [-] priest (**die Priesterin** [-nen] priestess)

der Rabbi [*pl* **Rabbinen**]; **der Rabbiner** [-] rabbi (**der Oberrabbiner** Chief Rabbi)

die Synagoge [-n] synagogue

SEE ALSO: **Art and Architecture; Birth, Marriage, and Death; History**

45. Science Naturwissenschaften

das Ammoniak ammonia
das Atom [-e] atom
die Chemikalie [-n] chemical
das Chlor chlorine
der Druck pressure
die Elektrizität electricity (**der Strom** current)
das Element [-e]; **der Grundstoff** [-e] element
die Erfindung [-en] invention (**der/die Erfinder/in** [-/-nen] inventor; **das Patent** [-e] patent)
das Experiment [-e]; **der Versuch** [-e] (**an** + D) experiment (on)
die Formel [-n] formula
die Forschung [-en] research
der Gefrierpunkt [-e] freezing-point (**der Siedepunkt** boiling-point)
die Gleichung [-en] equation
das Jod iodine
der Kohlenstoff carbon (**das Kohlenmonoxid** carbon monoxide; **das Kohlendioxid** carbon dioxide)
die Kraft [ᵉe] force
das Labor [*pl* -s or -e]; **das Laboratorium** [*pl* **Laboratorien**] laboratory
das Licht light
der Magnetismus magnetism (**der Magnet** [-e] magnet)
das Mikroskop [-e] microscope
das Molekül [-e] molecule
die Reaktion [-en] reaction
die Reibung friction
der Sauerstoff oxygen
die Säure [-n] acid
der Schall sound
der Schwefel sulphur (**die Schwefelsäure** sulphuric acid)
die Schwerkraft; **die Gravitation** gravity (**der Schwerpunkt** [ᵉe] centre of gravity)

der Stickstoff nitrogen (**das Distickstoffmonoxid** nitrous oxide)
der Strahl [-en] ray (**der Röntgenstrahl** X-ray)
die Strahlung radiation
die Technik; die Technologie technology (**der Technologe [-n]/die Technologin [-nen]** technologist)
das Teleskop [-e] telescope (**die Linse [-n]** lens)
die Wärme heat
der Wasserstoff hydrogen
die Welle [-n] wave (**die Licht-/Schallwelle** light/sound wave)
die Wissenschaft [-en] science (**angewandt** applied; **rein** pure; **die Natur-/Sozialwissenschaften** *pl* physical/social science)
der/die Wissenschaftler/in [-/-nen] scientist

Namen von Naturwissenschaften
Names of Sciences

die Akustik acoustics
die Algebra algebra
die Anthropologie anthropology
die Archäologie archaeology
die Arithmetik arithmetic
die Astronomie astronomy
die Biologie biology (**die Molekularbiologie** molecular biology)
die Botanik botany
die Chemie chemistry (**organisch/anorganisch** organic/inorganic)
die Differentialrechnung differential calculus
die Elektronik electronics (**die Mikroelektronik** micro-electronics)
die Geologie geology
die Geometrie geometry
die Optik optics
die Mathematik mathematics
die Mechanik mechanics
die Metallurgie metallurgy
die Mineralogie mineralogy

die Physik physics (**die Atom-/Quantenphysik** atomic/quantum physics)

das Programmieren computer programming (**der Computer** [-] computer)

die Psychologie psychology

die Soziologie sociology

die Trigonometrie trigonometry

die Zoologie zoology

Naturwissenschaftler Scientists

der Anthropologe [-n]/**die Anthropologin** [-nen] anthropologist

der Archäologe [-n]/**die Archäologin** [-nen] archaeologist

der/die Astronom/in [-en/-nen] astronomer

der Biologe [-n]/**die Biologin** [-nen] biologist

der/die Botaniker/in [-/-nen] botanist

der/die Chemiker/in [-/-nen] chemist (**der/die (An)organiker/in** [-/-nen]/ (in)organic chemist)

der/die Elektroniker/in [-/-nen] electronics engineer

der Geologe [-n]/**die Geologin** [-nen] geologist

der/die Mathematiker/in [-/-nen] mathematician

der/die Metallurg/in [-en/-nen] metallurgist

der Mineraloge [-n]/**die Mineralogin** [-nen] mineralogist

der/die Physiker/in [-/-nen] physicist

der/die Programmierer/in [-/-nen] computer programmer

der Psychologe [-n]/**die Psychologin** [-nen] psychologist

der Soziologe [-n]/**die Soziologin** [-nen] sociologist

der Zoologe [-n]/**die Zoologin** [-nen] zoologist

SEE ALSO: Animals; Art and Architecture; Education; Health and Sickness; The Human Body; Materials; Nature; Numbers and Quantities; Plants; The Senses

46. The Senses Die Sinne

Gesichtssinn Sight

das Aufleuchten flash(ing)

das Auge [-n] eye (sich [D] die Augen *ver'derben spoil one's eyesight; die Augen *auf-/nieder|schlagen look up/down; aus den Augen *ver'lieren lose sight of; einäugig one-eyed)

der Blick [-e] look [glance] (der Seitenblick sidelong look; auf den ersten Blick at first sight; einen (kurzen) Blick *werfen auf + A glance at; das Aussehen look [appearance])

das Blinzeln blink

die Brille [-n] (pair of) spectacles (die Sonnenbrille sunglasses; das Monokel [-] monocle)

die Dunkelheit; die Finsternis darkness (dunkel; finster dark)

die Farbe [-n] colour

das Fernglas [¨er]; das Binokular [-e] (pair of) binoculars

der Gesichtssinn [visual faculty]; der Anblick [-e] [thing seen]; das Sehvermögen [ability to see] sight (jn vom Sehen n *kennen know sb by sight)

die Helligkeit brightness

das Licht [-er] light

die Lupe [-n]; das Vergrößerungsglas [¨er] magnifiying glass

das Mikroskop [-e] microscope

der Schein no pl gleam

der Schimmer no pl glimmer; shimmer

die Sehkraft vision (das Sehfeld field of vision; die Sichtweite range of vision)

die Sicht [-en] visibility; view (in Sicht in sight)

das Teleskop [-e] telescope

das Zwinkern wink

auf|leuchten flash

*auf|sehen look up (*nach|schlagen look up [in sth])

aus|machen make out

*aus|sehen wie look like

be'merken notice
be'obachten observe; watch
be'trachten look at; contemplate
blenden dazzle (**blendend** dazzling; **geblendet** dazzled)
blicken look (**zur Seite blicken** look away)
blinzeln blink
er'blicken catch sight of
er'leuchten illuminate
*er'scheinen appear (**wieder auf|tauchen** reappear)
glitzern sparkle
gucken peep
schielen squint
*sehen see; look (**sich um|sehen** look back; **wieder|sehen** see
  again; **nichts zu sehen** nothing to be seen)
starren auf + A stare at
suchen look for
unter'suchen (**auf** + A) examine (for)
*ver'schwinden disappear
*wahr|nehmen discern; perceive
zwinkern wink (**zu|zwinkern** + D wink at)

blind blind (**die Blindenschrift** Braille; **verblendet** blinded)
düster gloomy
farblos colourless
hell bright; light
kurzsichtig short-sighted (**weitsichtig** long-sighted)
sichtbar/unsichtbar visible/invisible

SEE ALSO: **Health and Sickness** (At the optician's)

Gehör Hearing

das Echo [-s] echo
die Explosion [-en] explosion
das Flüstern *no pl* whisper(ing)
das Gehör hearing
das Geräusch [-e] sound; noise

die Hörweite earshot (**in/außer Hörweite** within/out of earshot)

das Klingeln ring(ing)

das Knarren creak(ing)

das Knistern crackle; crackling

der Kopfhörer [-] (pair of) headphones

das Krachen crash(ing)

der Lärm *no pl* noise; din

das Läuten ringing; tolling

der Lautsprecher [-] loudspeaker (**die Lautsprecheranlage [-n]** PA system)

das Lied [-er] song

das Ohr [-en] ear (**die Ohren spitzen** prick up one's ears)

das Radio [-s]; der Rund-/Hörfunk *no pl* radio (**im Rundfunk** on the radio)

das Rascheln rustle; rustling

der Schall [-e] sound

der Schrei [-e] cry

das Singen singing

die Sirene [-n] siren

die Sprechanlage [-n] intercom

die Stimme [-n] voice

das Summen buzzing

die Taubheit deafness (**das Hörgerät [-e]** hearing-aid)

der Ton [ⁿe] tone; note; sound [film, TV]

der Walkman [-s] walkman®

brummen buzz; drone

donnern thunder

dröhnen throb

flüstern whisper

hören hear (**hörbar/unhörbar** audible/inaudible)

klingen sound

knarren creak

knistern crackle

läuten [church bell, phone]; **klingeln** [doorbell, alarm, phone] ring

*pfeifen whistle

rascheln rustle
rauschen roar [waterfall]; swish [silk]; rustle [leaves]
*schallen ring out; resound (**die Schallmauer** the sound barrier)
*singen sing
summen hum
surren whirr
wider|hallen echo
zu|hören + D listen to

durchdringend piercing
laut loud
leise soft
matt faint
ohrenbetäubend deafening
schalldicht soundproof
schrill shrill; sharp
schwach faint
schwerhörig hard of hearing
still silent
taub deaf (**taubstumm** deaf and dumb)

Tastsinn Touch

die Berührung [-en] touch (**der Tastsinn** touch [the sense])
das Gefühl [-e] feeling (**das Fingerspitzengefühl** *no pl* (**für** + A)
  special feeling (for); **die Fingerspitze** [-n] fingertip)
der Händedruck [¨e] handshake
die Hitze heat (**die Wärme** warmth; heat)
die Kälte cold
die Liebkosung [-en] caress
der Schlag [¨e] blow
der Stoß [¨e] bump; kick; punch
das Streicheln *no pl* stroke; stroking

be'fingern finger
be'rühren touch
*er'fahren experience

fühlen feel (**sich weich/hart an|fühlen** feel soft/hard; **tasten nach** + D feel for)

***greifen** grip; grab

kitzeln tickle

klopfen (an + A) knock (against)

kratzen scratch

***reiben** rub

***schlagen** hit

***stoßen (gegen** + A) bump (into)

streicheln stroke

glatt smooth

hart hard

heiß hot

kalt cold

rauh rough

warm warm

weich soft

Geruchssinn Smell

das Aroma [*pl* **Aromen**] aroma [also flavour; taste]

der Duft [⁼e] scent; [pleasant] smell

der Geruch [⁼e] **(nach** + D) smell (of) (**der Geruchssinn** smell [= sense])

der Gestank *no pl* stench

die Nase [-n] nose (**das Nasenloch** [⁼er] nostril)

das Parfüm/Parfum [-s] perfume

der Rauch smoke

auf|spüren smell out

parfümieren perfume (**parfümiert** fragrant)

***riechen (gut/schlecht/nach** + D) smell (nice/nasty/of)

schnüffeln sniff

***stinken** stink (**stinkend** stinking)

wittern scent; detect

geruchlos odourless

muffig musty

rauchig smoky; smelling of smoke
stickig stuffy
stinkend stinking
streng strong; pungent

Geschmackssinn Taste

der Geschmack [ˑe] taste [also = discernment]; flavour (**der Geschmack(ssinn)** taste [the sense]; **die Geschmacksrichtung** [-en] [individual's] taste; **die Geschmacksknospe** [-n] taste-bud)
der Mund [ˑer] mouth (**die Zunge** [-n] tongue)
der Speichel saliva (**die Speicheldrüse** [-n] salivary gland)

*essen eat
*ge'nießen enjoy; savour
kauen chew
kosten (A or **von** + D) taste; try; sample
lecken lick
pfeffern pepper (**stark gepfeffert** peppery)
probieren try; taste
salzen salt
schlucken swallow
schlürfen slurp up; sip (**nippen an** + D sip at/from)
schmecken nach + D taste of
süßen sweeten (**ungesüßt** unsweetened)
*trinken drink
*ver'schlingen gobble up
würzen spice
zuckern sugar

appetitlich; appetitanregend savoury; appetizing
bissig acid
bitter bitter
fade insipid
geschmackvoll in good taste (**geschmacklos** tasteless; in bad taste)
herb sharp; dry [wine]
köstlich delicious

lecker tasty
pikant piquant
ranzig rancid
salzig salty
sauer sour
scharf hot [= spicy]; pungent
süß sweet
zuckrig sugary

SEE ALSO: **Adornment** (for perfume); **Cooking and Eating; Drinks; Health and Sickness; The Human Body; Music; Tobacco and Drugs**

47. Shops and Shopping
Geschäfte und Einkaufen

die Abteilung [-en] department
der Artikel [-] article
die Auswahl range
die Besorgung [-en] errand (**Besorgungen machen** go shopping)
die Bestellung [-en] order
der Betrieb [-e] business (**Betriebsruhe** *f* **montags** closed on Mondays)
die Bude [-n] stall
der Einkauf [ˈe] purchase
das Einkaufen shopping
der Einkaufskorb [ˈe] shopping basket
die Einkaufstasche [-n] shopping bag
der Einkaufswagen [-] (supermarket) trolley
das Einkaufszentrum [*pl* -zentren] shopping centre
das Erzeugnis [-se] product (**deutsches Erzeugnis** made in Germany)
die Filiale [-n] branch
das Flaschenpfand [ˈer] deposit [on bottle]
die Garantie [-n] guarantee
das Geld money (**das Wechselgeld** change [returned]; **das Kleingeld** (small) change
der Gelegenheitskauf [ˈe] bargain
das Geschäft [-e] shop; business
der/die Geschäftsführer/in [-/-nen] manager (**der/die Filialleiter/in [-/-nen]** branch manager)
die Geschäftszeit(en) *f sing* or *pl* opening hours
das Geschenkpapier gift wrap(ping) (**als Geschenk** *n* **ein|packen** gift-wrap)
die Größe [-n] size
der Großmarkt [ˈe] superstore
der Gutschein [-e] coupon (**der Geschenkgutschein** gift voucher)

der Handel trade

der/die Händler/in [-/-nen] dealer; trader

die Herabsetzung [-en] reduction (**herabgesetzt** reduced; cut-price)

die Kasse [-n] till; check-out

der Kassenzettel [-] receipt

der/die Käufer/in [-/-nen] buyer

das Kaufhaus [¨er]; **das Warenhaus** [¨er] department store

der Kaufmann [*pl* **-leute**] merchant

der Kiosk [-e] kiosk

die Kreditkarte [-n] credit card (**die Debetkarte** debit card)

der Kunde [-n]/**die Kundin** [-nen] customer

der Kundendienst after-sales service

der Laden [¨]; **die Handlung** [-en] shop (**der/die Ladenbesitzer/in** [-/-nen] shopkeeper)

das Ladenfenster [-] shop window

der Ladentisch [-e] counter

die Lieferung [-en] delivery

der Markt [¨e] market (**der Flohmarkt** flea market; **der Trödelmarkt; der Wohltätigkeitsbazar** [-e] jumble sale; **die Markthalle** [-n] market hall; **der Markttag** [-e] market day; **der Stand** [¨e] stall)

die Mietung; die Pachtung rental (**der Autoverleih** car-rental)

das Mindesthaltbarkeitsdatum use-by date (**mindest haltbar bis . . .** use by . . .)

das Muster [-] sample

die Packung [-en] packet

die Plastiktüte [-en] plastic bag

der Preis [-e] price (**der Einkaufs-/Verkaufs-/Sonderpreis** whole-sale/retail/special price)

das Produkt [-e] product

die Quittung [-en] receipt

die Rechnung [-en] bill

die Rückzahlung [-en] refund

der Schalter [-] counter; service point

das Schaufenster [-] shop window (**einen Schaufensterbummel** [-] **machen** go window-shopping)

der Scheck [-s] cheque (**die Scheckkarte [-n]** cheque card)

die Schlange [-n] queue (***an|stehen** queue up)

die Selbstbedienung self-service

das Sonderangebot [-e] special offer (**im Sonderangebot** on offer)

der Supermarkt [¨e] supermarket

die Theke [-n] bar-counter

der Umtausch [-e] exchange

der/die Verbraucher/in [-/-nen]; der/die Konsument/in [-en/-nen] consumer (**die Konsumgüter** *n pl* consumer goods)

der Verkauf [¨e] sale (**der Aus-/Schluß-/Sommerschluß-/Winterschlußverkauf** clearance/end-of-season/summer/winter sale)

der/die Verkäufer/in [-/-nen] shop assistant

die Versteigerung [-en]; die Auktion [-en] auction (**der Abschlag [¨e]** Dutch auction)

die Ware [-n] article; *pl* goods

das Wechselgeld change

*an|bieten offer

*an|nehmen take delivery of

*aus|geben spend

be'stellen order

be'zahlen [bill, etc.]; **zahlen** [hand over money] pay (**bar (be)zahlen** pay cash; **mit Scheck** *m*/**Kreditkarte** *f* by cheque/ credit card)

ein|kaufen shop (**einkaufen *gehen; Einkäufe** *m pl* **machen** go shopping)

feilschen haggle

garantieren guarantee

kaufen buy

kosten cost (**drei Mark das Stück** three marks apiece)

liefern deliver

machen come to (**was macht das?** what does it come to?)

*mit|nehmen take with one (**zum Mitnehmen** to go; to take away)

reparieren *lassen have repaired

um'tauschen exchange

ver'kaufen sell

ver'steigern auction
wählen (aus|wählen choose [from a selection]) choose
***zurück|geben** return [goods]

ausverkauft sold out; out of stock
billig cheap
erhältlich (bei + D) available (at)
gebraucht second-hand; used
geöffnet; auf open
geschlossen; zu closed (**wir haben montags zu** we're closed on
  Mondays)
günstig/preisgünstig very reasonably priced
kostenlos *adj*; **gratis** *adj* free
preiswert good value
reduziert; herabgesetzt reduced
teuer dear
umsonst for nothing

Geschäfte und ihre Besitzer
Shops and shopkeepers

das Antiquariat [-e] second-hand bookshop (**das moderne
  Antiquariat** remaindered bookshop; **der Antiquar [-e]** second-
  hand book dealer)
der Antiquitätenladen antiques shop (**die Antiquität** antique; **der/
  die Antiquitätenhändler/in** [-/-nen] antique-dealer)
die Apotheke dispensing chemist's; pharmacy (**der/die Apothe-
  ker/in** [-/-nen] dispensing chemist; pharmacist)
die Bäckerei [-en] baker's (**der/die Bäcker/in** [-/-nen] baker)
die Bank [-en] bank (**die Sparkasse [-n]** savings bank; **der/die
  Bankangestellte** *adj n* bank clerk)
die Bibiothek [-en]; die Bücherei [-en] library (**der/die Bibliothe-
  kar/in** [-e/-nen] librarian)
die Blumenhandlung [-en] florist's (**der/die Blumenhändler/in**
  [-/-nen] florist)
die Boutique [-n] boutique

die Buchhandlung [-en] bookshop (**der/die Buchhändler/in** [-/-nen] bookseller)

die Drogerie chemist's (**der/die Drogist/in** [-en/-nen] chemist)

das Eisenwarengeschäft [-e] ironmonger's (**der/die Eisenwaren-händler/in** [-/-nen] ironmonger)

der Feinkostladen [¨] delicatessen

das Fischgeschäft [-e] fishmonger's (**der/die Fischhändler/in** [-/-nen] fishmonger)

die Fleischerei [-en]; **die Metzgerei** [-en] butcher's (**der/die Fleischer/in** [-/-nen]; **der/die Metzger/in** [-/-nen] butcher)

das Fotogeschäft [-e] camera shop (**der/die Fotograf/in** [-en/-nen] photographer)

der Friseursalon [-s] hairdresser's (**der Friseur** [-e]/**die Friseuse** [-n] hairdresser)

die Gemüsehandlung [-en] greengrocer's (**der/die Gemüsehänd-ler/in** [-/-nen] greengrocer)

das Haushaltswarengeschäft [-e] household-goods/hardware shop

der Herrenausstatter [-] gentlemen's outfitter

das Hutgeschäft [-e] milliner's (**der/die Putzmacher/in** [-/-nen] milliner)

das Juweliergeschäft [-e] jeweller's shop (**der Juwelier** [-e] jeweller)

die Konditorei [-en] cake shop (**der/die Konditor/in** [G -s *pl* -en/-nen] pastry-cook)

das Lebensmittelgeschäft [-e] grocer's (**der/die Lebensmittel-händler/in** [-/-nen] grocer)

die Lederwarenhandlung [-en] leather-goods shop

die Maklerfirma [*pl* -firmen] estate agency (**der/die Grund-stücksmakler/in** [-/-nen] estate agent)

das Möbelgeschäft [-e] furniture shop

das Modegeschäft [-e]; **das Modehaus** [¨er] fashion store

die Obsthandlung [-en] fruiterer's (**der/die Obsthändler/in** [-/-nen] fruiterer)

die Parfümerie [-n] perfume shop; cosmetics store

das Platten-/Schallplattengeschäft [-e] record shop (**das Musik-geschäft** music shop)

das Porzellangeschäft [-e] china shop

die Post [-en]; das Postamt [ᵉer] post office **(der Postbeamte** *adj n*/**die Postbeamtin [-nen]** counter clerk)

das Reformhaus [ᵉer] health-food shop

die Reinigung [-en] dry cleaner's; dry-cleaning

das Reisebüro [-s] travel agency **(der Reisebürokaufmann** *[pl* **-leute]/die Reisebürokauffrau [-en]** travel agent)

die Schneiderei [-en] tailor's; dressmaker's **(der/die Schneider/in [-/-nen]** tailor; dressmaker)

der Schönheitssalon [-s] beauty salon **(der/die Kosmetiker/in [-/-nen]** beautician)

das Schreibwarengeschäft [-e] stationer's **(der/die Schreibwarenhändler/in [-/-nen]** stationer)

das Schuhgeschäft [-e] shoe-shop **(der/die Schuhhändler/in [-/-nen]** shoe salesman/woman; **der/die Schuster/in [-/-nen]** shoe-repairer; cobbler)

der Selbstbedienungsladen [ᵉ] self-service shop

der Souvenirladen [ᵉ] souvenir shop

das Spielwarengeschäft [-e] toyshop

das Sportwarengeschäft [-e] sport's shop

der Supermarkt [ᵉe] supermarket **(die Kassendame [-n]/der Kassenjunge [-n]** check-out assistant)

das Süßwarengeschäft [-e] sweet-shop **(der/die Süßwarenhändler/in [-/-nen]** sweet-shop keeper)

der Tabakladen [ᵉ]; die Tabakwarenhandlung [-en] tobacconist's **(der/die Tabak(waren)händler/in [-/-nen]** tobacconist)

das Textilgeschäft [-e] draper's **(der Textilkaufmann** *[pl* **-leute]/die Textilkauffrau [-en]** draper)

die Tierhandlung [-en] pet shop **(der/die Tierhändler/in [-/-nen]** pet-shopkeeper)

das Waren-/Kaufhaus [ᵉer] department store **(der/die Verkäufer/in [-/-nen]** sales assistant)

die Wäscherei [-en] laundry **(der Waschsalon [-s]** launderette; **der/die Wäscher/in [-/-nen]** laundryman/woman)

der Wein- und Sprituosenladen [ᵉ] = off-licence **(der/die Weinhändler/in [-/-nen]** wine-merchant)

das Zeitungsgeschäft [-e]/der Zeitungskiosk [-e] newspaper shop/
kiosk (der/die Zeitungshändler/in [-/-nen]) newsagent; news-
vendor)

Was der Ladenbesitzer sagt
What the shopkeeper says

das macht zusammen . . . that comes to . . .

haben Sie Kleingeld? do you have change?

ich kann auf einen Hundertmarkschein nicht herausgeben I
haven't got change for a hundred-mark note

könnten Sie mir das Geld passend geben? could you give me the
exact money?

soll ich es als Geschenk verpacken? shall I gift-wrap it?

(und) sonst noch etwas? anything else?

was darf es sein? can I help you?

wir haben es leider nicht vorrätig I'm afraid it isn't in stock

wollen Sie es mitnehmen? will you take it with you?

Was Sie sagen What you say

darf ich es anprobieren? may I try it on?

das ist alles that's all

es gefällt mir (nicht) I (don't) like it

es ist genau/nicht das, was ich suche it's exactly/not what I'm
looking for

es ist im Schaufenster it's in the window

ich hätte gern . . . ; ich möchte . . . I should like . . .

ich möchte das umtauschen/zurückgeben I want to exchange/
return this

ich will mich nur umsehen I'm only looking

kann ich mit (einem) Scheck bezahlen? can I pay by cheque?

können Sie es mir bestellen? can you order it for me?

**können Sie mir eine Quittung/noch einen Plastikbeutel geben
bitte?** could I have a receipt/another plastic bag please?

können Sie mir helfen? can you help me?

können Sie mir mein Geld zurückerstatten? can you refund my money?

legen Sie es für mich zurück, bitte please put it aside for me

nehmen Sie Kreditkarten? do you take credit cards?

was kostet . . . ? how much does . . . cost?

wieviel macht das? what does that come to?

SEE ALSO: **Adornment; Cinema and Photography; Clothing; Drinks; Food; Hair; Health and Sickness; Leisure and Hobbies; The Media; Money; Music; Numbers and Quantities; Post and Telephone; Sport and Games; Tobacco and Drugs; Towns**

48. Sports and Games
Sport und Spiele

der Amateur [-e] amateur
der/die Anfänger/in [-/-nen] beginner
der Angriff [-e] attack (**der/die Angreifer/in** [-/-nen] attacker)
der/die Anhänger/in [-/-nen] supporter
der Anstoß [ːe] kick-off (**der Anpfiff** whistle for the start of play)
der Aufschlag [ːe] service; serve
das Aus; [rugby, also] **die Mark** touch (**im Aus** in touch)
der Einstand deuce [tennis]
das Endspiel [-e] final
das Ergebnis [-se] result (**eins zu null** one-nil)
die Etappe [-n] stage; leg
der Fan [-s] [male or female] fan
das Feld [-er] [running, cycling] pack
das Finale [pl - or -s]; **das Endspiel** [-e] final (**das Viertel-/ Halbfinale** quarter-/semi-final)
das Foul [-s] foul
der Freistoß [ːe] free kick
die Führung; **die Spitze** lead (**in Führung *gehen/*liegen** go into/ be in the lead)
das Gedränge scrum
der/die Gegner/in [-/-nen] opponent; competitor
die Halbzeit half-time; half [of match]
das Herreneinzel men's singles (**das Dameneinzel** women's singles; **das Herren-/Damendoppel** men's/women's doubles; **das gemischte Doppel** mixed doubles)
die Laufwettbewerbe *m pl* track events (**die technischen Disziplinen** field events)
die Leistung [-en] performance
der Libero [-s] sweeper [football]
die Liga [pl **Ligen**] league; division (**die Bundesliga** [German] football league)

los! go! (auf die Plätze, fertig, los! on your marks, get set, go!;
Achtung, fertig, los! ready, steady, go!)

die Mannschaft [-en]; das Team [-s]; [football, also] **die Elf [-en]**
team

der Marathonlauf [ᵉe] marathon

die Medaille [-n] medal

der/die Meister/in [-/-nen] champion

die Meisterschaft [-en] championship **(die Weltmeisterschaft**
world cup)

der/die Mittelfeldspieler/in [-/-nen] midfield player

die Niederlage [-n] defeat

die Olympischen Spiele Olympic Games

der Paß [ᵉsse]; die Abgabe [-n] pass **(der Vorpaß** forward pass)

der Pokal [-e] cup

der Profi [-s] professional

die Rallye [-s] (motor) rally

der Rechtsaußen [-] outside right **(der Linksaußen** outside left)

die Regatta [*pl* Regatten] regatta

der Rekord [-e] record **(auf|stellen** set; ***inne|haben** hold;
***brechen** break)

das Rennen [-] race **(das tote Rennen** dead heat)

der Renntag [-e] race-meeting

die Runde [-n] round; lap

der Satz [ᵉe] set [tennis]

der/die Schiedsrichter/in [-/-nen] referee; umpire **(der Ring-/
Kampfrichter** boxing/wrestling referee)

der Schuß [ᵉsse] shot **(auf + A)** shot (at)

der Sieg [-e] victory **(auf Sieg spielen** go for a win)

der/die Sieger/in [-/-nen] winner

das Spiel [-e] match; game ([football, tennis, also] **das/der Match**
[*pl* -s or -e] match; **der Kampf [ᵉe]** (boxing) match)

der/die Spieler/in [-/-nen] player

der Spielstand [ᵉe] score **(der Halbzeit-/Endstand** half-time/final
score; **die Punktzahl [-en]** (personal) score)

der Sport [*no pl: use* die Sportarten types of sport] sport

der/die Sportler/in [-] sportsman/woman

der Sprint [-s] sprint

der **Sprung** [¨e] jump (der **Hoch-/Weitsprung** high/long jump)

der **Spurt** [*pl* -s or -e] spurt (der **Endspurt** final spurt)

der **Stoß** [¨e] kick; [swimming, rowing] stroke

der **Strafstoß** [¨e]; der **Elfmeter** [-] penalty [football] (der **Straftritt** penalty [rugby]; das **Elfmeterschießen** [-] penalty shoot-out)

der/die **Stürmer/in** [-/-nen] striker

die **Tabelle** [-n] (league) table (die **Tabelle an|führen** be at the top of the table)

der/die **Titelhalter/in** [-/-nen] title holder

das **Tor** [-e] goal (der **Torpfosten** [-] goal-post; die **Querlatte** [-n] crossbar; das **Netz** [-e] net; der **Torwart** [-e] goal-keeper)

der/die **Trainer/in** [-/-nen] coach; trainer

das **Training** training (im **Training *sein** be in training)

das **Treffen** [-] meeting (das **Rennen** [-] race-meeting)

die **Tribüne** [-n] stand

die **Turnhalle** [-n] gymnasium

das **Turnier** [-e] tournament

das **Unentschieden** [-]; [chess] das **Remis** [*pl* - or -en] draw (**mit einem Unentschieden enden** end in a draw)

die **Verlängerung** injury/extra time (**nach Verlängerung** after extra time)

der/die **Verlierer/in** [-/-nen] loser

der **Versuch** [-e] try [rugby] (**er|zielen; legen** score)

die **Verteidigung** defence (der/die **Verteidiger/in** [-/-nen] defender)

der **Vorlauf** [¨e] heat

der **Wettkampf** [¨e]; der **Wettbewerb** [-e] competition (der/die **Wettkämpfer/in** [-/-nen]; der/die **Wettbewerber/in** [-/-nen] competitor)

das **Wettrennen** [-]; der **Wettlauf** [¨e] race (**einen Wettlauf machen** run a race)

das **Wettschwimmen** [-] swimming competition

der **Wintersport** no pl winter sports

der/die **Zeitnehmer/in** [-/-nen] timekeeper (die **Stoppuhr** [-en] stop-watch)

das **Ziel** [-e] finish (der **Zielpfosten** [-] winning-post)

die **Ziel-/Schießscheibe** [-n] target

der/die Zuschauer/in [-/-nen] spectator

*ab|geben pass
*auf|schlagen serve (*zurück|schlagen return)
aus|buhen boo (sb)
*aus|gehen end; result
er'zielen score (**einen Punkt erzielen** score a point)
führen lead; be ahead (**nach Punkten** on points; **in Führung**
  *liegen be in the lead; **die Führung *über'nehmen** take the lead)
galoppieren gallop
*ge'winnen; siegen win
jagen hunt
*schießen shoot
*schlagen beat
spielen play
Sport *m* *treiben go in for sport
*springen bounce
*teil|nehmen an + D take part in
traben trot
trainieren train
sich trimmen get into shape
üben practise
*ver'lieren lose
wetten (auf + A) bet (on) (**die Odds** *pl* odds)
zählen keep score
zischen hiss
zu|jubeln (+ D) cheer (sb)

Sportarten Sports

das Aerobic aerobics
das Angeln fishing
der Autorennsport motor racing
der Basketball basketball
das Bergsteigen mountaineering
das Bogenschießen archery
das Bowling (ten-pin) bowling

das Boxen boxing
der Crosslauf; der Querfeldeinlauf cross-country running
das Diskuswerfen discus-throwing
das Drachenfliegen hang-gliding (**das Ultraleichtflugzeug [-e]** microlight)
das Eishockey ice hockey
der Eiskunstlauf figure-skating
das Fallschirmspringen parachuting
das Fechten fencing
der Federball badminton
der Fußball football
das Gewichtheben weight-lifting
das Golf golf
der Handball handball
das Hockey hockey
das Jagen; die Jagd shooting; hunting (**die Fuchsjagd** fox-hunting)
das Jogging jogging
das Judo judo
der Kanusport canoeing
das Karate karate
das Kegelschieben skittles; ninepins
das Klettern/Felsklettern (rock-)climbing
das Kricket cricket
das Krocket croquet
das Kugelstoßen shot-putting
das Laufen running; walking
die Leichtathletik (track and field) athletics
der Netzball netball
der Radsport cycling
der Reitsport; das Reiten (horse-)riding
das Rennen running; racing; race (**das Kirchturmrennen** point-to-point)
der Rennsport racing (**die Wette [-n]** bet; **wetten** bet)
das Ringen wrestling (**das Freistilringen** all-in wrestling)
das Rodeln tobogganing
das Rollschuhlaufen roller-skating

der **Rudersport**; das **Rudern** rowing
das **Rugby** rugby
das **Schießen** shooting
das **Schlittschuhlaufen** skating
das **Schwimmen** swimming (das **Kraulen** crawl; das **Brust-
schwimmen** breast-stroke; das **Kunstspringen** diving)
das **Segelbootrennen** yacht racing
das **Segelfliegen** gliding
das **Segeln** sailing
das **Skateboardfahren** skateboarding
der **Skilauf**; das **Skilaufen**; der **Skisport** skiing (der **(Ski)langlauf**
cross-country skiing)
das **Spazierengehen** walking
das **Speerwerfen** javelin-throwing
das **Squash** squash
der **Stabhochsprung** pole-vaulting
die **Stierkämpfe** *m pl* bull-fighting (der **Stierkampf** bullfight)
das **Strandsegeln** sand-yachting
das **Surfbrettfahren** surf-boarding (das **Surfen** surfing)
das **Tauchen** (skin-)diving
das **Tauziehen** tug-of-war
das **Trabrennen** trotting
das **Tennis** tennis (das **Tischtennis** table tennis)
das **Tontaubenschießen** clay-pigeon shooting
das **Turnen**; die **Gymnastik** gymnastics
der **Volleyball** volley ball
das **Wandern** hiking
der **Wasserball** water polo
das **Wasserskilaufen** water-skiing
das **Windhundrennen** greyhound-racing
das **Windsurfen** windsurfing; sailboarding
der **Wintersport** winter sports

Sportsleute Sportspeople

der/die **Angler/in** [-/-nen] angler
der/die **Athlet/in** [-en/-nen]; der/die **Sportler/in** [-/-nen] athlete

der/die Bergsteiger/in [-/-nen] mountaineer

der Bogenschütze [-n] archer

der Boxer [-] boxer

der/die Drachenflieger/in [-/-nen] hang-glider

der/die Eisläufer/in [-/-nen] skater (**der/die Rollschuhläufer/in** roller-skater; **der/die Eiskunstläufer/in** figure skater)

der/die Fallschirmspringer/in [-/-nen] parachutist

der/die Fechter/in [-/-nen] fencer

der/die Fußballspieler/in [-/-nen] footballer

der/die Gewichtheber/in [-/-nen] weight-lifter

der/die Golfer/in [-/-nen] golfer

der/die Hochspringer/in [-/-nen] high-jumper

der/die Jäger/in [-/-nen] hunter; marksman

der Jockey [-s]; der Jockei [-s] jockey

der/die Jogger/in [-/-nen] jogger

der/die Kletterer/in [-/-nen] climber

der/die Läufer/in [-/-nen] runner

der/die Leichtathlet/in [-en/-nen] athlete

der/die Radfahrer/in [-/-nen] cyclist (**der/die Radrennfahrer/in** racing cyclist)

der/die Reiter/in [-/-nen] rider

der/die Ringer/in [-/-nen] wrestler

der/die Rodler/in [-/-nen] tobogganer; luger

der Ruderer [-] oarsman (**die Ruderin [-nen]** oarswoman)

der/die Schlittschuhläufer/in [-/-nen] skater

der/die Schwimmer/in [-/-nen] swimmer

der/die Skiläufer/in [-/-nen] skier

der/die Spaziergänger/in [-/-nen] walker (**der/die Geher/in [-/-nen]** walker [in race])

der/die Sportler/in [-/-nen] sportsman/-woman

der/die Surfer/in [-/-nen] surfer

der/die Taucher/in [-/-nen] diver

der/die Tennisspieler/in [-/-nen] tennis-player

der/die Turner/in [-/-nen] gymnast

der/die Windsurfer/in [-/-nen] windsurfer

Was sie tun What they do

angeln fish
***berg|steigen** [*inf and past part. only*] go mountaineering/
  mountain climbing
boxen box
***gehen; *spazieren|gehen** walk
***heben** lift
***hoch|springen** [*inf and past part. only*] do the high jump
jagen hunt; shoot (**auf die Jagd *gehen** go hunting/shooting)
joggen jog
klettern climb
***laufen** run
***rad|fahren** cycle (**ich fahre Rad** I cycle)
***reiten** ride [horseback] (**traben** trot; **galoppieren** gallop)
***ringen** wrestle
rodeln toboggan
Rollschuh *m* ***laufen** roller-skate
rudern row
***schießen** shoot (**ein Tor schießen** score a goal)
Schlittschuh *laufen/*fahren skate
schwimmen** swim (treiben** float)
segeln sail
Ski *laufen/*fahren ski
***springen** jump
surfen surf
tauchen dive
Wasserski *laufen water-ski
***weit|springen** [*inf and past part. only*] do the long jump
***werfen** throw

Ausrüstung Equipment

die Angel [-n]; **die Angelrute** [-n] fishing-rod (**die Schnur** [ᴂe] line;
  der Köder [-] bait; **der Schwimmer** [-] float)
der Badeanzug [ᴂe] swimsuit
die Bahn [-en] track (**die Renn-/Radrennbahn** race-/cycle-track)

der Ball [≈e] ball (**die Kugel** [-n] ball [croquet, billiards]; bowl; bullet)

der Barren *sing* parallel bars

der Billiardstock [≈e]; **das Queue** [-s] cue

der Bogen [-] bow (**der Pfeil** [-e] arrow)

die Bowlingbahn [-en] (tenpin) bowling alley

der Boxhandschuh [-e] boxing-glove

die Eisbahn [-en] ice-rink

das Fahrrad [≈er] bicycle

der Federball [≈e] shuttlecock

das Gewehr [-e] gun

der Golfschläger [-] golf-club

der Hockeystock [≈e] hockey stick

die Kegelbahn [-en] skittle alley

das Kanu [-s] canoe

das Netz [-e] net

der Platz [≈e] court; ground (**der Tennis-/Golf-/Sportplatz** tennis-court/golf course/playing-field)

die Rennstrecke [-n] race-track; (race) distance

der Ring [-e] ring

der Rodelschlitten [-] toboggan

der Rollschuh [-e] roller-skate

das Ruderboot [-e] rowing-boat

der Sattel [-] saddle (**die Zügel** *m pl* reins)

der Schläger [-] racket; bat (**der Golfschläger** club)

der Schlitten [-] sledge

der Schlittschuh [-e] skate

die Schlittschuhbahn [-en] ice-rink

der Schnorchel [-] snorkel

das Schwimmbad [≈er] swimming-pool (**das Frei-/Hallenbad** open-air/indoor pool; **das Sprungbrett** [-er] diving-board)

die Schwimmflosse [-n] flipper

das Segelboot [-e] sailing-boat (**das Ding(h)i** [-s] dinghy)

das Skateboard [-s] skateboard

der Ski [*pl* -e or -] ski (**der Skistock** [≈e] ski pole; **der Skistiefel** [-] ski boot; **der Skilift** [*pl* -e or -s] ski-lift; **die Skipiste** [-n] ski-run; **der Wasserski** water-ski) der **Speer** [-e] javelin

das **Spielfeld** [-er] field; pitch

das **Sportfeld** [-er]; das **Sportplatz** [ᵂe] sports ground; sports stadium

das **Stadion** [*pl* Stadien] stadium (die **Tribüne** [-n] stand; der **Umkleideraum** [ᵂe] dressing-room)

die **Stoppuhr** [-en] stop-watch

der **Sturzhelm** [-e] crash-helmet

das **Surfbrett** [-er] surf-board

der **Tauch-/Naßanzug** [ᵂe] wetsuit

die **Taucherbrille** [-n] (pair of) diving-goggles

der **Tennisschläger** [-] tennis-racket

das **Trikot** [-s]; das **Jersey** [-s] jersey

Spiele Games

das **Billiard(spiel)** billiards (eine **Partie Billiard** a game of billiards)

das **Bingo** bingo

das **Bowlspiel**; das **Bowls** bowls

das **Brettspiel** [-e] board game (der **Würfel** [-] die [*pl* dice]; der **Stein** [-e] piece; das **Feld** [-er] square)

das **Computerspiel** [-e] computer game

die **Dame** *f sing* draughts (**Dame spielen** play draughts; der **Stein** [-e] draughtsman)

das **Domino** dominoes (**Domino spielen** play dominoes; der **Stein** [-e] domino [the piece])

der **Flipperautomat** [-en] pinball machine

das **Kartenspielen** card-playing (die **(Spiel)karte** [-n] playing-card; das **Kartenspiel** [-e] pack of cards; der **Kartentisch** [-e] card-table; **Karten spielen** play cards; das **Bridge** bridge; der **Skat** skat)

das **Kreuzworträtsel** [-] crossword

das **Puzzle** [-s]; das **Puzzlespiel** [-e] jigsaw (der **Teil** [-e] piece)

das **Quartett** happy families

das **Schach** chess (**Schach spielen** play chess; das **Schachbrett** [-er] chessboard; die **Schachfigur** [-en] chessman)

(das) **Schnippschnapp(schnurr)** snap
das **Spiel** [-e] game; pack (das **Glücksspiel** game of chance; **das Gesellschaftsspiel** party game)

SEE ALSO: **Leisure and Hobbies**; **Nature**

49. Theatre Theater

der Abgang [⸚e] (actor's) exit
die Arie [-n] aria
die Aufführung [-en] performance; production (**zur Aufführung
*bringen** put on)
der Auftritt [-e] entrance; scene (**seinen Auftritt *haben** make
one's entrance; **2. Auftritt** scene 2)
der Beifall applause
die Karte/Theaterkarte [-n] ticket
die Kartenvorverkaufsstelle [-n] ticket agency
die Kritik [-en] review (**der/die Kritiker/in** [-/-nen] reviewer)
das Laientheater amateur dramatics
das Lampenfieber stage fright
die Nachmittagsvorstellung [-en] matinée
die Nummer [-n] number; turn
das Opernglas [⸚er] (pair of) opera-glasses
die Pause [-n] interval
das Programm [-e]; **das Programmheft** [-e] programme
die Reservierung [-en] reservation; booking
die Show [-s] show
die Szene [-n] scene (**hinter der Szene** backstage; **in Szene setzen**
stage)
der Text [-e] script
das Theater [-] theatre (**beim Theater *sein** work in the theatre;
zum Theater *gehen go on the stage; **ins Theater *gehen** go to
the theatre; **Theater spielen** act; **theatralisch** theatrical)
das Theaterplakat [-e] playbill; poster
die Tournee [pl -s or -n] tour (**auf Tournee** on tour)
die Vorstellung [-en] (actor's) performance; performance of play
(**schwach** weak; **stark** strong; **die zweite Vorstellung** second
house)
die Zugabe [-n] encore (**Zugabe!** encore!)

*ab|gehen exit (**Faust ab** exit Faust)

applaudieren applaud

auf|führen put on; stage; perform

*auf|treten enter (**Auftritt Faust** enter Faust)

aus|ver'kaufen sell out (**ausverkauft** house full)

buhen boo (**aus|buhen** boo (at sb))

inszenieren put on

klatschen; **Beifall klatschen** clap

proben rehearse

reservieren *lassen; vor|be'stellen book (in advance)

spielen act (**eine Rolle spielen** play a part)

tanzen dance

sich ver'beugen bow

zischen hiss

zurück|zahlen refund (**das Eintrittsgeld zurückzahlen** refund
  entrance)

Shows Shows

das Ballett [-e] ballet (**das Ballettabend [-e]** (evening of) ballet)

das Drama [*pl* Dramen] drama

die Komödie [-n]; **das Lustspiel [-e]** comedy

das Melodram(a) [*pl* Melodramen] melodrama

das Musical [-s] musical

die Oper [-n] opera [also, opera house]

die Operette [-n] operetta

die Posse [-n]; **die Farce [-n]** farce

das Puppen-/Marionettenspiel [-e] puppet-show

das Stück/Theaterstück [-e]; **das Schauspiel [-e]** play (**der Akt [-e]**
  act; **der Einakter [-]** one-act play; *geben put on)

der Tanz [ᵉe] dance

der Thriller [-] thriller

die Tragödie [-n]; **das Trauerspiel [-e]** tragedy

das Varieté [-s] variety-show

der Zirkus [-se] circus

Theaterleute Theatre people

die Besetzung [-en] cast (**die zweite Besetzung** understudy)
der/die Bühnenarbeiter/in [-/-nen] scene-shifter
der/die Bühnenbildner/in [-/-nen] designer
der Dramatiker [-] dramatist
der/die Dramaturg/in [-en/-nen] literary and artistic director
der Gewandmeister [-] wardrobe-master (**die Gewandmeisterin** [-nen] wardrobe-mistress)
der/die Inspizient/in [-en/-nen] stage-manager
der/die Intendant/in [-en/-nen] theatre director
die Platzanweiserin [-nen] usherette (**der Platzanweiser** [-] usher; attendant)
das Publikum audience
der/die Regisseur/in [-e/-nen] director
der Schauspieler [-] actor (**die Schauspielerin** [-nen] actress; ***auf|treten als** appear as)
der Souffleur [-e]/**die Souffleuse** [-n] prompter (**der Souffleurkasten** prompt-box)
der Star [-s] star [male or female]
der/die Tänzer/in [-/-nen] dancer
der/die Theaterbesucher/in [-/-nen] theatre-goer
die Truppe [-n] troupe; company
der/die Verfasser/in [-/-nen] author
der/die Zuschauer/in [-/-nen] member of the audience (**die Zuschauer** *pl* audience)

Das Haus The theatre building

der Ausgang [⸚e] exit (door) (**der Notausgang** emergency exit)
der Balkon [*pl* -s or -e]; **der Rang** [⸚e] circle (**erster/zweiter/dritter Rang** dress circle/upper circle/gallery; **der Olymp** the gods)
die Bühne [-n] stage
der Eingang [⸚e] entrance (door)
das Foyer [-s] foyer
die Garderobe [-n] cloakroom
die Kasse [-n] box-office (**an der Kasse** at the box-office)

die Kulisse [-n] wing; flat; *pl* scenery (**der Kulissenwechsel** [-] scene-change; **hinter den Kulissen** behind the scenes)

das Haus [ˈer] theatre; house (**ausverkauftes Haus** full house)

die Loge [-n] box

der Orchestergraben [ˈ] orchestra pit

das Parkett stalls

der Platz [ˈe] seat [place] (**der Sitz** [-e] seat [the physical object])

das Rampenlicht [-er] footlight; (light from the) footlights

die Reihe [-n] row

der Saal [*pl* Säle] auditorium

der Scheinwerfer [-] spotlight

die Vorführung [-en] performance; house

der Vorhang [ˈe] curtain (**der eiserne Vorhang** safety curtain; **eisern** iron; ***auf|gehen** rise; ***fallen** fall)

die Vorverkaufskasse [-n] advance-booking office (**der Vorverkauf** advance booking; **Karten im Vorverkauf be'sorgen** book tickets in advance)

Das Schauspiel The play

die Beleuchtung lighting (**an|strahlen** light)

das Bühnenbild [-er] set

die Dekoration [-en] scenery

die Handlung [-en] plot

die Inszenierung [-en] staging; production

das Kostüm [-e] costume

die Maske (theatrical) make-up

die Personen *f pl* cast; dramatis personae

die Premiere [-n] first night

die Probe [-n] rehearsal (**die Generalprobe** dress rehearsal)

die Regie direction (**Regie führen bei** + D direct)

das Requisit [G -s *pl* -en] prop(erty)

die Rolle [-n] role; part (**die Haupt-/Nebenrolle** leading/ supporting role)

das Spiel acting (**tragisch** tragic; **komisch** comic; **dramatisch** dramatic)
der Text [-e] text; script; lines

SEE ALSO: **Adornment; Cinema and Photography; Leisure and Hobbies; The Media; Music**

50. Time Zeit

das Datum [*pl* **Daten**] date
die Dauer duration
die Ewigkeit eternity
der Geburtstag [**-e**] birthday
die Hundertjahrfeier [**-n**] centenary
der Kalender [**-**] calendar
der Namenstag [**-e**] name-day; saint's day
die Periode [**-n**]; **das Zeitalter** [**-**] period
die Uhr clock time; time o'clock
die Verspätung [**-en**] delay
die Zeit [**-en**] time (**die Sommerzeit** Summer Time; **die Zeit
*ver'bringen/ver'schwenden/ver'geuden/*tot'schlagen** spend/
waste/fritter away/kill time)
die Zeitzone [**-n**] time zone (**der Zeitunterschied** [**-e**] time
difference)

Die Uhr The clock

die Armbanduhr [**-en**] watch
die Glocke [**-n**] bell (**der Glockenturm** [**≈e**] belfry)
das Pendel [**-**] pendulum
die Uhr [**-en**] clock; watch (**die Quarz-/Digitaluhr** quartz/digital
clock/watch; **die Stoppuhr** stop-watch; **die Sonnenuhr** sundial;
die Schaltuhr timer; **die Stand-/Kuckucksuhr** grandfather/
cuckoo clock; **die Sanduhr** hourglass; **die Eieruhr** egg-timer)
der Wecker [**-**] alarm clock (**der Reise-/Küchenwecker** travel
alarm/kitchen timer)
der Zeiger [**-**] hand [of clock] (**der Sekunden-/Minuten-/
Stundenzeiger** second/minute/hour hand)
die Zeitansage speaking clock
das Zifferblatt [**≈er**] dial; face

*auf|ziehen wind up
*schlagen strike
stellen nach + D set by
*vor|gehen be fast (*nach|gehen be slow; richtig *gehen be right)

Uhrzeit Clock time

wieviel Uhr ist es?; wie spät ist es? what time is it?
haben Sie die richtige Uhrzeit? do you have the right time?

es ist . . .
  ein Uhr one o'clock
  zwei Uhr two o'clock
  fünf (Minuten) nach drei five past three
  Viertel nach vier quarter past four
  halb fünf half past four
  fünfundzwanzig (Minuten) vor sechs; fünf nach halb sechs
    twenty-five to six
  Viertel vor sieben quarter to seven
  Mittag/Mitternacht twelve o'clock (der Mittag [-e] noon; die
    Mitternacht no pl midnight)

  zwölf Uhr 12.00
  dreizehn Uhr zehn 13.10
  vierzehn Uhr fünfzehn 14.15
  fünfzehn Uhr dreißig 15.30
  vierundzwanzig Uhr 24.00
  null Uhr eins 00.01

abends in the evening [= p.m.]
morgens; vormittags in the morning [= a.m.]
nachmittags in the afternoon [= p.m.]
nachts at night [= a.m.]

erst um + A not until
gegen + A; etwa um + A at about
nach + D after
um + A at (um wieviel Uhr . . . ? at what time . . . ?; genau
  um . . . at exactly . . .)

vor + D before
während + G during

bei Einbruch *m* **der Dunkelheit** at nightfall
bei Sonnenaufgang *m* at sunrise (**bei Sonnenuntergang** *m* at sunset)
bei Tagesanbruch *m* at daybreak
im Morgengrauen *n* at dawn
in der Abenddämmerung at dusk
mittags at noon (**mitternachts** at midnight)

Zeiteinheiten Units of time

der Abend [-e] evening
der Augenblick [-e]; **der Moment** [-e] moment
die Epoche [-n] epoch
das Jahr [-e] year (**im Jahr X** in X; **das Schaltjahr** leap year; **das Halbjahr** (school) term)
die Jahreszeit [-en] season
das Jahrhundert [-e] century
das Jahrtausend [-e] millennium; thousand years
das Jahrzehnt [-e] decade
das Mal [-e] time [occasion] (**zum zweiten Mal** for the second time)
die Minute [-n] minute
der Monat [-e] month
der Morgen [-]; **der Vormittag** [-e] morning
der Nachmittag [-e] afternoon
die Nacht [¨e] night (**letzte/diese Nacht** last night/tonight)
die Sekunde [-n] second
die Stunde [-n] hour (**eine halbe Stunde** half an hour; **eine Viertelstunde** quarter of an hour; **eine Dreiviertelstunde** three-quarters of an hour; **anderthalb Stunden** an hour and a half)
der Tag [-e] day (**vierzehn Tage** a fortnight)
die Woche [-n] week (**das Wochenende** [-n] weekend; **heute in/vor einer Woche** a week today/a week ago today; **diese/nächste Woche** this/next week; **letzte/vorige Woche** last week)

jährlich yearly
monatlich monthly
täglich daily
wöchentlich weekly (**zweiwöchentlich** fortnightly)

Das Datum The date

der Wievielte ist heute?; was für ein Datum/welches Datum/den Wievielten haben wir heute? what is the date?

heute ist der erste/zweite/dritte Mai neunzehnhundertneunund-neunzig; heute ist der 1./2./3. Mai 1999 today is the first/second/third of May 1999

am 1. Mai on the first of May
stammen aus + D date from

Die Tage der Woche The days of the week

was ist heute für ein Tag?; welchen Tag haben wir heute? what day is it today?

heute ist Sonntag today's Sunday

der Sonntag [-e] Sunday (**am Sonntag; sonntags** on Sunday(s); **sonntags morgens** on Sunday mornings; **am folgenden Sonntag** the following Sunday; **letzten/nächsten/jeden Sonntag** last/next/every Sunday; **Sonntag in/vor einer Woche** a week on/ago Sunday; **der Sonntagmorgen/der Sonntagnachmittag** Sunday morning/afternoon)
der Montag [-e] Monday
der Dienstag [-e] Tuesday
der Mittwoch [-e] Wednesday
der Donnerstag [-e] Thursday
der Freitag [-e] Friday
der Sonnabend [-e] [N. Germany, E. Germany]; **der Samstag [-e]** [S. Germany, Austria, Switzerland] Saturday

Die Jahreszeiten The seasons

der Frühling [-e]; das Frühjahr [-e] spring (**im Frühling** in spring; **(im) Frühling vergangenen/nächsten Jahres** last/next spring)
der Sommer [-] summer
der Herbst [-e] autumn
der Winter [-] winter

Die Monate The months

der Januar [-e] January (**im Januar** in January; **Anfang/Ende Januar** at the beginning/end of January; **Mitte Januar** in mid-January; **vor/nach Januar** before/after January)
der Februar [-e] February
der März [-e] March
der April [-e] (**der Aprilscherz** April-fool trick; **jn in den April schicken** make an April fool of sb)
der Mai [-e] May (**der Maibaum [ʺe]** maypole; May-tree)
der Juni [-s] June
der Juli [-s] July
der August [-e] August
der September [-] September
der Oktober [-] October
der November [-] November
der Dezember [-] December

Wann geschieht es? When does it happen?

ab und zu now and then
alle drei Tage/Stunden etc. every three days/hours etc.
am nächsten/folgenden Tag/Abend etc. (on) the next/following day/evening etc.
am übernächsten Tag two days later (**drei Tage später** three days later)
am vorigen Tag/Abend etc. (on) the previous day/evening etc.
bald soon
dann [next]; **damals** [at that time] then

dann und wann now and then

früh early (**zu früh *kommen** be too early)

früher formerly

gerade just (now)

gestern yesterday (**gestern morgen/nachmittag** yesterday morning/afternoon; **gestern abend** last night)

gleichzeitig at the same time; simultaneously

häufig frequently

heute today (**heute vormittag/morgen** this morning; **heute nachmittag** this afternoon; **heute abend** tonight; **heute nacht** last night; tonight)

heutzutage nowadays

im Jahre 1900; 1900 in 1900 (**Anfang** m/**Mitte** f/**Ende** n **1970** at the beginning/in the middle/at the end of 1970)

immer always

im Moment m/**Augenblick** m at the moment

im zwanzigsten Jahrhundert in the twentieth century

in den sechziger Jahren in the sixties

in der Zukunft in future

in der Zwischenzeit in the meantime

in zwei Tagen in two days (**innerhalb von zwei Tagen** within two days)

jährlich yearly (**halbjährlich** biannual(ly); **zweijährlich** biennial(ly))

jede Minute any minute (now)

jeden Tag every day

jetzt now

längere Zeit for a long time

manchmal sometimes

morgen tomorrow (**morgen früh/nachmittag/abend** tomorrow morning/afternoon/night)

nachts; in der Nacht at night (**diese/letzte Nacht** tonight/last night)

nie; [stronger] **niemals** never

oft often

plötzlich suddenly

Punkt . . . . . . on the dot

pünktlich punctually

rechtzeitig on time

schließlich [last in a sequence]; **endlich** [at last; after all this time]
finally)

schon already

seitdem since

selten seldom

sofort; (so)gleich immediately

spät [at an advanced hour]; **verspätet** [after the proper time] late
(**du kommst so spät heute** you're so late today; **verspätet
*an|kommen** arrive late; **X Minuten Verspätung** *f* ***haben** be X
minutes late; **spätestens** at the latest)

stündlich hourly

tagsüber; am Tag(e) during the day (**am hellichten Tag(e)** in
broad daylight)

übermorgen the day after tomorrow

um diese Tageszeit [-en] at this time of day (**zu jeder Tages- und
Nachtzeit** at any time of the day or night)

von nun an from now on

von Zeit zu Zeit from time to time (**von Stunde zu Stunde** from
hour to hour; **von morgens bis abends** from morning to night)

vor einer Woche etc. a week etc. ago

vorgestern the day before yesterday

vor kurzem; kürzlich; neulich recently; a short time ago

vor kurzer/langer Zeit a short/long time ago (**lange Zeit** for a
long time)

währenddessen meanwhile

wieder; nochmals again

zuerst first

zu meiner Zeit in my day

zur Zeit at the moment (**zu der Zeit** at that time)

Feiertage und Feste
Public holidays and festivals

feiern celebrate

(das) Allerheiligen All Saints' Day/All Hallows

(das) Allerseelen All Souls' Day

(der) Aschermittwoch Ash Wednesday (**(der)Rosenmontag** Monday before Ash Wednesday)

(der) Buß- und Bettag Penitence Day [Wednesday 11 days before Advent]

Himmelfahrt/Christi Himmelfahrt *f* Ascension Day (**Mariä Himmelfahrt** Assumption)

Dreikönige *n* Epiphany; Twelfth Night (**zu/an Dreikönige** on Twelfth Night)

der erste April April Fools' Day (**April! April!** April fool!)

der Fasching [*pl* -e or -s] (pre-Lent) Carnival

die Fasten *f pl*; **die Fastenzeit** *sing* Lent

(der) Fastnachtsdienstag; **(die) Fastnacht** Shrove Tuesday

der Feiertag [-e]; **der Festtag** [-e] holiday (**der gesetzliche/ kirchliche Feiertag** public/religious holiday)

das Fest [-e] festival; celebration

das Festival [-s] festival

der Geburtstag [-e] birthday (**ich habe Geburtstag** it's my birthday)

(der) Gründonnerstag Maundy Thursday

(der) Karfreitag Good Friday

der Maifeiertag May Day

der Namenstag [-e] saint's day

(das) Neujahr New Year's Day (**ein gutes neues Jahr!** happy New Year!)

der Nikolaus St Nicolas' day

(das) Ostern Easter (**zu Ostern** at Easter; **nächste Ostern** *pl* next Easter; **fröhliche Ostern** *pl* happy Easter)

(der) Ostersonntag Easter Day

(der) Palmsonntag Palm Sunday

(das) Pfingsten Whitsuntide (**zu Pfingsten** at Whitsun) (der) **Pfingstmontag** Whit Monday

(der/das) **Silvester**; **der Neujahrsabend** New Year's Eve (**Silvester feiern** see the New Year in)

der Tag der deutschen Einheit Day of German Unity [3 October]

der Valentinstag St Valentine's day

(das) **Weihnachten** Christmas (**zu Weihnachten** at Christmas; **frohe/fröhliche Weihnachten** *pl* Merry Christmas; **der erste/zweite Weihnachtstag** Christmas Day/Boxing Day; **der Heiligabend** Christmas Eve; **die Bescherung** distribution of presents)

SEE ALSO: **Birth; Marriage, and Death; History; Numbers and Quantities**

51. Tobacco and Drugs
Tabak und Drogen

Tabak Tobacco

der Aschenbecher [-] ashtray (**die Asche** ash)

das Feuerzeug [-e] lighter (**der Feuerstein** [-e] flint; **der Docht** [-e] wick; **die Patrone** [-n] refill)

der Lungenkrebs cancer of the lung

die Pfeife [-n] pipe (**der Pfeifenreiniger** [-] pipe-cleaner)

der Rauch smoke

der/die Raucher/in [-/nen] smoker (**der/die Nichtraucher/in** nonsmoker)

der Schnupftabak snuff (**eine Prise** [-n] **schnupfen** take a pinch of snuff)

das Streichholz [¨er] match (**die Schachtel** [-n] box)

der Tabak tobacco (**der Pfeifentabak** pipe tobacco; **der Tabak(s)beutel** [-] tobacco pouch)

das Verbot [-e] ban (**Rauchverbot; Rauchen** *n* **verboten** no smoking)

die Zigarette [-n] cigarette (**eine Schachtel** [-n] **Zigaretten** a packet of cigarettes; **die Stange** [-n] ten-packet carton; **die Filterzigarette** filter-tip cigarette; **der Filter** [-] filter-tip)

das Zigaretten-/Zigarrenetui [-s] cigarette-/cigar-case

die Zigarettenspitze [-n] cigarette-holder

der Zigarettenstummel [-] cigarette-end (**die Kippe** [-n] *colloq* fag-
)

garre [-n] cigar

*a light up
aus give up
rauc rub out
um light;

ask for a light (**jm Feuer *geben** give sb a
er? have you got a match?)

Drogen Drugs

die Behandlung cure
das Betäubungsmittel [-] narcotic
die Droge [-n]; **das Rauschgift** *no pl* drug (**unter Drogen *stehen**;
  Rauschgift *nehmen be on drugs)
die Drogeneinnahme drug taking
der Drogenhandel drug trafficking
der/die Drogenhändler/in [-/-nen]; **der/die Dealer/in** [-/-nen] drug
  trafficker
das/der Haschisch hashish (**das Hasch** hash)
das Heroin heroin
das Kokain cocaine
die Nadel [-n] needle
der/die Pusher/in [-/-nen] drug pusher
die Sucht [ˤe] (**nach** + D) addiction (to) (**süchtig** addicted; **der/
  die Süchtige** *adj n* addict)
die Überdosis overdose
die Wiedereingliederung rehabilitation [into society]

be'schlagnahmen confiscate
***nehmen** take
sich [D] **et spritzen** inject oneself with sth

SEE ALSO: **Crimes and Criminals; Drinks; Health and Sickness**

52. Tools Werkzeuge

der Bastler DIY enthusiast (**basteln** make things)
der Werkzeugkasten [=] tool-box

die Beißzange [-n] pincers ***heraus|ziehen** pull out
der Besen [-] broom **kehren** sweep
der Bohrer [-] drill **bohren** drill
das Bügel-/Plätteisen [-] iron **bügeln; plätten** iron
die Drahtzange wire-cutters (**der Draht** [=e] wire)
***durch|schneiden** cut (through)
die Drehbank [=e] lathe **drehen** turn
die Esse [-n] [hearth]; **die Schmiede** [blacksmith's shop] forge
(**der Amboß** [-sse] anvil) **schmieden** forge
die Feile [-n] file **ab|feilen** file down
die Gabel [-n] (pitch)fork **gabeln** fork
die Gießkanne [-n] watering-can ***gießen; *be'gießen** water
das Gerüst [-e] scaffolding **bauen** build
die Hacke [-n] hoe **hacken** hoe
der Hammer [=] hammer (**der Nagel** [=] nail) **hämmern/
*schlagen in** + A hammer into
die Harke [-n] rake **harken** rake (**zusammen|harken** rake up)
der Hobel [-] plane **hobeln** plane
der Holzhammer [=]; **der Schlegel** [-] mallet ***schlagen** hit
die Leiter [-n] ladder (**die Stehleiter** step-ladder) ***steigen
auf** + A climb up
der Lötkolben [-] soldering-iron (**das Lot** solder) **löten** solder
der Mähdrescher [-] combine harvester **ernten** harvest
die Maschine [-n] machine **be'nutzen** use
der Meißel [-] chisel **meißeln** chisel
die Nadel [-n] needle (**der Faden** [=] thread; **der Fingerhut** [=e]
thimble) **flicken; aus|bessern** mend; **stopfen** darn
die Nähmaschine [-n] sewing-machine (**der Stich** [-e] stitch [in
sewing]) **nähen** sew
die Pflanzkelle [-n] garden trowel ***aus|graben** dig up
der Pflug [=e] plough **pflügen** plough

der Pinsel [-] paintbrush ***an|streichen** [houses]; **malen** [pictures] paint

der Preßluftbohrer [-] pneumatic drill ***auf|brechen** break up

der Rasenmäher [-] lawn-mower **mähen** mow

die Reißzwecke [-n] drawing-pin ***an|schlagen** pin up

die Säge [-n] saw **sägen** saw (**durch|-/um|sägen** saw in two/down)

das Sandpapier sandpaper **schmirgeln** sand down

die Schaufel [-n] shovel **schaufeln** shovel

die Schere [-n] (pair of) scissors (**die Heckenschere** garden shears) ***schneiden** cut; clip

der Schlauch [ᵉe] garden hose **be'spritzen** spray

der Schraubenschlüssel [-] spanner (**die Schraube** [-n] [threaded] bolt; **die Mutter** [-n] nut) **lösen** loosen; ***an|ziehen** tighten

der Schraubenzieher [-] screwdriver (**die Schraube** [-n] screw) **schrauben** (**an** + A) screw (to) (**ab|-/los|schrauben** unscrew)

der Schraubstock [ᵉe] vice ***halten** hold

der Schubkarren [-] wheelbarrow ***tragen** carry

die Sense [-n] scythe **mähen**; **ab|mähen** mow

die Sichel [-n] sickle ***schneiden** cut; reap

der Spaten spade ***graben** dig

die Spitzhacke [-n] pick ***auf|brechen** break up

das Stemmeisen [-] (wood) chisel **stemmen** chisel [wood]

die Stricknadel [-n] knitting-needle (**die Masche** [-n] stitch [in knitting]; **der/das Knäuel** [-] ball [of wool]; **die Wolle** wool) **stricken** knit

der Trichter funnel ***aus|gießen** pour out

der Wagenheber [-] jack **auf|bocken** jack up

die Wasserwaage [-n]; **die Libelle** [-n] spirit-level **gerade machen** straighten

der Webstuhl [ᵉe] loom ***weben** weave

das Werkzeug [-e] tool **reparieren** repair

die Zange [-n] (pair of) pliers; (pair of) tongs ***biegen** bend

SEE ALSO: **Cooking and Eating** (for kitchen equipment); **Health and Sickness** (for medical equipment); **The Home** (for household equipment); **Jobs**; **Materials**

53. Towns Städte

Siedlungen Settlements

der Bezirk [-e] district; area
das Dorf [¨er] village
die Großstadt [¨e] city (**die Kleinstadt** small town)
die Hafenstadt [¨e]; **der Hafen** [¨] port
die Hauptstadt [¨e] capital
die Metropole [-n] metropolis
das Nest [-er] tiny little place
der Ort [-e] place (**der Marktort** market town)
die Stadt [¨e] town; city (**in die Stadt** to town; **in der Stadt** in town)
der Stadtteil [-e]; **das (Stadt)viertel** [-] district; part of town
die Vorstadt [¨e] suburb (**in der Vorstadt** in the suburbs)
der Weiler [-] hamlet
das Wohngebiet [-e]; **die Wohngegend** [-en] residential area (**das Industriegebiet** [-e] industrial zone)

In der Stadt In town

der Abwasserkanal [¨e] sewer
die Allee [-n] avenue
der botanische Garten [¨] botanical gardens
die Brücke [-n] bridge
der Bürgersteig [-e] pavement
die Bushaltestelle [-n] bus-stop
das Denkmal [¨er] monument (**das Kriegerdenkmal** war memorial)
die Einkaufspassage [-n] shopping arcade
das Einkaufszentrum [*pl* -zentren] shopping mall
die Fahrbahn [-en] carriageway
der Festplatz [¨e] fairground (**der Jahrmarkt** [¨e] fair)
der Flughafen [¨e] airport

der Friedhof [÷e] cemetery (**das Grab** [÷er] grave)

der Fußgängerüberweg [-e] pedestrian crossing

die Fußgängerzone [-n] pedestrian precinct

die Gasse [-n] lane; narrow street

die Geschäftsstraße [-n] shopping street

die Grünanlagen *f pl* gardens

der Hafen [÷] harbour

das Hochschulgelände [-] university campus

die Kreuzung [-en] crossroads

die Lichtreklame [-n] neon sign

der Markt [÷e] market (**der Marktplatz** [÷e] market-place; **der Stand** [÷e] stall; **die Markthalle** [-n] market hall)

das Messegelände [-] exhibition centre/site

die öffentliche Anlage [-n] public garden; park

die öffentliche Toilette [-n]; **die Bedürfnisanstalt** [-en] public convenience

der Park [-s] park

der Parkplatz [÷e] car-park; parking-space (**die Parkuhr** [-en] parking-meter; **die Parkscheibe** [-n] parking-disc; **die Parkkralle** [-n] wheel-clamp)

das Pflaster road surface (**das Kopfsteinpflaster** cobble-stones)

das Plakat [-e] poster

der Platz [÷e] square

der Radweg [-e] cycle-track

die Ringstraße [-n] ring road (**die Umgehungsstraße** bypass)

der Rinnstein [-e] gutter

die Ruinen *f pl* ruins

die Sackgasse [-n] dead-end street; cul-de-sac

das Schwimmbad [÷er] swimming-pool

die Sehenswürdigkeit [-en] place of interest; *pl* the sights

der Springbrunnen [-] fountain

die Stadtautobahn [-en] urban motorway

die Stadtbahn [-en] urban railway

die Stadtmauer [-n] town wall(s)

die Stadtmitte [-n]; **das (Stadt)zentrum** [*pl* -zentren]; **die Innenstadt**; **die City** town/city centre (**die Altstadt** the old town;

der Stadtrand *sing*; die Außenbezirke *m pl* the outskirts; die Umgebung [-en] surrounding area)

der Stadtplan [⁼e] street map

das Stadttor [-e] town gate

die Statue [-n] statue

die Straße [-n] street; road (die Hauptstraße high street; main road; die Einbahn-/Einkaufs-/Fußgängerstraße one-way/shopping/pedestrian street)

die Straßenbahnhaltestelle [-n] tram stop

die Straßenecke [-n] street corner

die Straßenlampe [-n]; die Straßenlaterne [-n] street lamp

die Straßenüberführung [-en] footbridge (die Straßenunterführung subway)

der Taxistand [⁼e] taxi-rank

die U-Bahn-Station [-en]; der U-Bahnhof underground station

der Umzug [⁼e] procession; demonstration

der Verkehr traffic (die Verkehrsstockung [-en] traffic jam; die Verkehrsampel [-n] traffic-light; die Verkehrsinsel [-n] traffic island; das Verkehrszeichen [-]; das Straßenschild [-er] road sign; der Wegweiser [-] signpost)

der Wall [⁼e] rampart(s)

das Wartehäuschen [-] bus-shelter

der Zoo [-s] zoo

Stadtbauten Town buildings

die Abtei [-en] abbey

das Arbeitsamt [⁼er] job centre

der Bahnhof [⁼e] railway-station (der Hauptbahnhof main railway station; der Busbahnhof bus/coach station)

die Börse [-n] stock exchange

die Botschaft [-en] embassy

die Bücherei [-en] library (öffentlich public)

das Bürogebäude [-] office-block

der Dom [-e]; das Münster [-] cathedral

die Fabrik [-en] factory

die Feuerwache [-n] fire station (die Feuerwehr [-en] fire brigade)

das Gebäude [-]; der Bau [*pl* **Bauten**] building

das Gefängnis [-se] prison

der Gerichtshof law courts

das Haus [≈er] house; building (**das Hochhaus** high-rise building; tower block)

das Hotel [-s] hotel

das Jugendzentrum [*pl* **-zentren**] youth centre

die Kaserne [-n] barracks

das Kaufhaus [≈er] department store

das Kino [-s] cinema

der Kiosk [-e] kiosk

die Kirche [-n] church; [Nonconformist] chapel (**der Kirchturm [≈e]** tower; steeple)

das Konsulat [-e] consulate

die Konzerthalle [-n] concert hall

das Krankenhaus [≈er]; die Klinik [-en] hospital

die Kunstgalerie [-n] art gallery (**die Malerei** [art of] painting; **die Bildhauerei** [art of] sculpture)

die Moschee [-n] mosque

das Museum [*pl* **Museen**] museum

das Nonnenkloster [≈] convent (**die Nonne [-n]** nun; **das Kloster** monastery; **der Mönch [-e]** monk)

die Oper [-n]; das Opernhaus [≈er] opera-house

der Palast [≈e] palace

das Parkhaus [≈er] multi-storey car-park (**die Tiefgarage [-n]** underground car-park)

das Planetarium [*pl* **Planetarien**] planetarium

die Polizeiwache [-n]; das Polizeirevier [-e] police station (**das Polizeipräsidium** police headquarters)

die Post [-en]; das Postamt [≈er] post office

das Rathaus [≈er] town hall (**der Stadtrat [≈e]** town council(lor))

der Schlachthof [≈e] abattoir

das Schloß [≈sser] castle; mansion; palace (**die Burg [-en]** [fortified] castle)

der soziale Wohnungsbau council housing (**die Sozialwohnung [-en]** council flat)

die Spielhalle [-n] amusement arcade

das **Stadion** [pl **Stadien**] stadium
die **Synagoge** [-n] synagogue
das **Theater** [-] theatre (das **Theaterstück** [-e] play)
der **Turm** [¨e] tower
das **Verkehrsamt** [¨er]; das **(Fremden)verkehrsbüro** [-s] tourist
   information office
der **Wohnblock** [pl ¨e or -s] block of flats (der **Wohnkomplex** [-e]
   housing complex; die **Wohnsiedlung** [-en] housing estate)
der **Wolkenkratzer** [-] skyscraper

Die Einwohner The inhabitants

der/die **Autofahrer/in** [-/-nen] car-driver
der/die **Berliner/in** [-/-nen] etc. Berliner etc.
die **Bevölkerung** population
der/die **Bürger/in** [-/-nen] citizen (der/die **Staatsbürger/in** citizen
   of a country; national)
der/die **Bürgermeister/in** [-/-nen] mayor
der/die **Dorfbewohner/in** [-/-nen] villager
der/die **Einwohner/in** [-/-nen] inhabitant
der/die **Fußgänger/in** [-/-nen] pedestrian
der/die **Großstädter/in** [-/-nen] city-dweller
der/die **Kleinstädter/in** [-/-nen] small-town dweller
der/die **Passant/in** [-en/-nen] passer-by
der/die **Stadtbewohner/in** [-/-nen]; der/die **Städter/in** [-/-nen]
   town-/city-dweller
der/die **Stadtstreicher/in** [-/-nen] tramp; down-and-out
der/die **Tourist/in** [-en/-nen] tourist
der/die **Vorstädter/in** [-/-nen] suburbanite

Was man dort tut What you do there

als **Fremdenführer/in** dienen act as guide
beeindruckt *sein be impressed
be'suchen visit
bummeln stroll about (einen **Stadt-/Fensterbummel machen** take
   a stroll round town; go window-shopping)

die Sehenswürdigkeiten be'sichtigen see the sights
eine Stadtrundfahrt machen take a tour of the city
sich ver'irren; sich *ver'laufen [on foot]; sich *ver'fahren [in car]
  get lost
*vorbei|gehen an + D go past
über'queren cross
wohnen live
zeigen show

SEE ALSO: **Art and Architecture; Cooking and Eating; Places,
People, and Languages; Post and Telephone; Shops and
Shopping; Transport**

54. Transport Verkehrsmittel

der Fahrgast [¨e]; der Passagier [-e] passenger
die Fahrt [-en] trip; journey
das Fahrzeug [-e] vehicle (**das Motorfahrzeug; das Kraftfahrzeug** motor vehicle)
die Reise [-n] journey (**eine Reise machen** go on a journey)
der/die Reisende *adj n* traveller; passenger
das Reiseziel [-e] destination
das Verkehrsmittel [-] (means of) transport (**die öffentlichen Verkehrsmittel** public transport)

*fahren; reisen travel (**links/rechts fahren** drive on the left/right; **sich *ver'fahren** go the wrong way; **Schritt fahren!** dead slow!)

Verkehrsmittel der Straße Road transport

AUTOS CARS
der Anhänger [-] trailer
das Auto [-s]; der Wagen [-] car (**mit dem Auto** by car; **die Automarke [-n]** make of car; **der/die Autofahrer/in [-/-nen]** motorist)
der Campingbus [-se]; das Wohnmobil [-e] camper
der Firmenwagen [-] company car
der Führerschein [-e] driving-licence (**die Fahrprüfung [-en]** driving test; **die Fahrschule [-n]** driving school; **die Fahrstunde [-n]** driving lesson)
der Gebrauchtwagen [-] used car
das Kabrio [-s]; das Kabriolett [-s] convertible
die Klapperkiste [-n] banger
der Kombi [-s]; der Kombiwagen [-] estate car
die Limousine [-n] saloon car
der Miet-/Leihwagen [-] hire-car
das Modell [-e] model (**die Marke [-n]; das Fabrikat [-e]** make)

der Pkw; der PKW [G and *pl* - or **-s**] [= **Personenkraftwagen**] (private) car

der Rennwagen [-] racing car

der Sportwagen [-] sports car

das Taxi [-s]; **die Taxe** [-n] taxi

der Wohnwagen [-]; **der Wohnanhänger** [-]; **der Caravan** [-s] caravan

MOTOR- UND FAHRRÄDER
MOTOR CYCLES AND BICYCLES

der Beiwagen [-] side-car

das Fahrrad [⁼er]; **das Rad** [⁼er] bicycle (**mit dem Rad** by bike; **der/die Radfahrer/in** [-/-nen] cyclist)

das Mofa [-s] (low-powered) moped

das Moped [-s] moped

das Motorrad [⁼er] motor cycle (**der/die Motorradfahrer/in** [-/-nen] motor-cyclist; **der Beifahrer-/Soziussitz** [-e] pillion)

das Radfahren; der Radsport cycling

die Radtour [-en] cycle ride

der Radweg [-e] cycle-track

der Roller/Motorroller [-] (motor) scooter

auf das Rad *auf|steigen get on

auf|pumpen pump up

ein Loch flicken mend a puncture

im Freilauf *fahren freewheel

klingeln ring the bell

radeln; *rad|fahren cycle

vom Rad *ab|steigen get off

LASTWAGEN USW. LORRIES ETC.

der Abschleppwagen [-] breakdown lorry

der Anhänger [-] trailer

der Bulldozer [-]; **die Planierraupe** [-n] bulldozer

das Feuerwehrauto [-s] fire-engine

der Jeep® [-s] jeep®

der Karren [-] cart

der Kinderwagen [-] pram

der Krankenwagen [-] ambulance

der Lastwagen [-]; **der LKW**; **der Lkw** [G and *pl* - or -s]
[= **Lastkraftwagen**] lorry (**der Schwerlastwagen** heavy goods
vehicle; **der Lastzug** [≈e] lorry with trailer(s))

der Lieferwagen [-] van

der Möbelwagen [-] removal van

der Sattelschlepper [-] articulated lorry

der Tankwagen [-] tanker

der Traktor [G -s *pl* -en] tractor

der Transporter [-] goods vehicle

DIE TEILE EINES FAHRZEUGS
THE PARTS OF A VEHICLE

die Achse [-n] axle

der Anlasser [-]; **der Starter** [-] starter (***an|springen** start)

die Antenne [-n] aerial

das Armaturenbrett [-er] dashboard

der Auspuff *no pl* exhaust (**das Auspuffrohr** [-e] exhaust-pipe; **der
Auspufftopf** [≈e]; **der Schalldämpfer** [-] silencer)

der Außenspiegel [-] wing mirror

das Autoradio [-s] car radio

die Batterie [-n] battery (**leer** flat)

der Benzinkanister [-] petrol can

die Benzinuhr [-en] fuel gauge

die Birne/Glühbirne [-n] bulb

der Blinker [-]; **der Richtungsanzeiger** [-] indicator (**blinken**
indicate)

die Bremse [-n] brake (**die Scheibenbremse** disc brake; **die
Handbremse** handbrake; **der Bremsbelag** [≈e] brake lining; **die
Bremsflüssigkeit** brake fluid)

das Chassis [-]; **das Fahrgestell** [-e] chassis

der Choke [-s] choke

der Dachgepäckträger [-] roof-rack

das Ersatzteil [-e] spare (part)

die Federung suspension

das Fenster [-] window

der Feuerlöscher [-] fire-extinguisher

der Gang [≃e] gear (**einen Gang ein|legen** engage a gear; **der Rückwärtsgang** reverse; **der Leerlauf** neutral; **der Schalthebel** [-] gear-lever)

das Getriebe [-] transmission (**das Schalt-/Automatikgetriebe** manual/automatic transmission; **der Getriebekasten** [≃] gearbox)

das Heck [pl -e or -s] back (of the car) (**der Heckmotor** [G -s pl -en] rear engine; **die Heckscheibe** [-n] rear window; **die Heckklappe** [-n] hatchback)

die Heizung heating

die Hupe [-n] horn (**die Lichthupe** headlight flasher; **die Lichthupe be'tätigen** flash)

die Karosserie bodywork

der Keilriemen [-] fan-belt

der Kilometerzähler [-]; **der Wegmesser** [-] milometer

der Kofferraum [≃e] boot

der Kotflügel [-] wing

der Kühler [-] radiator (**leck** leaking)

die Kupplung [-en] clutch

das Lenk-/Steuerrad [≃er] steering-wheel

das Licht [-er] light (**ein-/aus|schalten** switch on/off)

die Lichtmaschine [-n] alternator

die Linkssteuerung left-hand drive (**die Rechtssteuerung** right-hand drive)

der Luftfilter [-] air filter (**der Ölfilter** oil filter)

der Meßstab [≃e] dip-stick

der Motor [G -s pl -en] engine (**der Motorraum** engine compartment; **die Motorhaube** [-n] bonnet; **der Motorlärm** engine noise; **der Motorschaden** engine trouble)

das Nummernschild [-er] number-plate

der Öl(stands)anzeiger [-] oil-gauge

das Pedal [-e] pedal (**das Gaspedal** accelerator)

das Rad [≃er] wheel (**das Vorder-/Hinter-/Ersatzrad** front/rear/spare wheel; **wechseln** change; **die Radkappe** [-n] hub-cap; **die Nabe** [-n] hub)

der Reifen [-] tyre (**der Reifenschaden** [≈]; *colloq* **der Platte** *adj n*
puncture; **platt** flat; **platzen** burst; **der Schlauch** [≈e] inner tube;
der Reifendruck tyre pressure; **prüfen** check; **das Reifenprofil**
tread)

das Rücklicht [-er] rear-light

der Rücksitz [-e] back seat

der Rückspiegel [-] rear mirror

der Schalthebel [-] gear-lever

der Scheinwerfer [-] headlight (**der Nebelscheinwerfer** fog-light;
der Rückfahrscheinwerfer reversing light)

das Schiebedach [≈er] sliding roof

das Schloß [≈sser] lock (**die Zentralverriegelung** central locking)

der Schmutzfänger [-] mud-flap

die Schneekette [-n] snow-chain

der Sicherheitsgurt [-e] seat-belt

die Sicherung [-en] fuse (*durch|brennen blow)

der Sitz [-e] seat (**der Vorder-/Hintersitz** front/rear seat)

das Standlicht [-er] sidelight(s) (**mit Standlicht *fahren** drive on
sidelights)

der Stoßdämpfer [-] shock absorber

die Stoßstange [-n] bumper

der/das Tachometer; der Geschwindigkeitsmesser speedometer

der Tank [*pl* -s *or* -e] tank (**das Benzin** petrol; **es ist mir
ausgegangen** I've run out)

der Tankanzeiger [-] fuel gauge

der Tankverschluß [≈e] petrol-cap

die Tür [-en] door

das Ventil [-e] valve

das Verdeck [-e] hood (**mit offenem Verdeck *fahren** drive with
the top down)

der Vergaser [-] carburettor

der Verteiler [-] distributor

der Vorderradantrieb front-wheel drive (**der Hinterradantrieb**
rear-wheel drive)

der Wagenheber [-] jack

der Warnblinker hazard warning lights

das Warndreieck [-e] hazard warning triangle

die **Warnlampe** [-n] warning light

die **Windschutzscheibe** [-n] windscreen (der **Scheibenwischer** [-] windscreen-wiper; die **Scheibenwaschanlage** screen wash)

die **Zündkerze** [-n] spark-plug

die **Zündung** ignition (der **Zündschlüssel** [-] ignition key; das **Zündschloß** [ʒsser] ignition lock)

der **Zündverteiler** [-] distributor (der **Kontakt** [-e] point)

DIE TEILE EINES RADES PARTS OF A CYCLE

der **Dynamo** [-s] dynamo

das **Flickzeug** [-e] repair kit

der **Gepäckträger** [-] luggage rack

die **Kette** [-n] chain

die **Klingel** [-n] bell

die **Lampe** [-n] lamp

die **Lenkstange** [-n] (pair of) handlebars

die **Motorradbrille** [-n] (pair of) goggles

das **Pedal** [-e] pedal

die **Pumpe** [-n] pump

das **Rad** [ʒer] cycle; wheel (der **Radkranz** [ʒe] wheel rim)

der **Rahmen** [-] frame

der **Rückstrahler** [-] reflector

der **Sattel** [ʒ] saddle (die **Satteltasche** [-n] saddle-bag)

das **Schutzblech** [-e] mudguard

die **Speiche** [-n] spoke

die **Stange** [-n] crossbar

das **Vorderlicht** [-er] front light (das **Rücklicht** rear light)

der **Zweitaktmotor** [G -s *pl* -en]; der **Zweitakter** [-] two-stroke (engine)

AUF DER STRASSE ON THE ROAD

der **Abschleppwagen** [-] breakdown vehicle

der **Abstand** [ʒe] distance (**Abstand** *halten keep one's distance)

die **Abzweigung** [-en] fork; turning

die **Ampel/Verkehrsampel**[-n] traffic light (das **Rot-/Gelb-/Grünlicht** [ʒer] red/amber/green light; *über'fahren shoot; go through; **bei Rot** on red; **die Bedarfsampel** pedestrian-controlled light)

der Anlieger [-] local resident (**Anlieger frei** access only)

die Autobahn [-en] motorway (**das Autobahnkreuz** [-e] motorway intersection; **die Anschlußstelle** [-n] junction; **die Ein-/Ausfahrt** [-en] entrance/exit)

die Auto-/Straßenkarte [-n] road map

die Autoschlange [-n] queue of cars

der Bahnübergang [ˁe] level crossing

das Bankett [-e]; **die Bankette** [-n] verge; shoulder (**Bankette nicht befahrbar** keep off verge)

die Bundesstraße [-n] = A road (**die Landstraße** = B road)

der Bürgersteig [-e] pavement

die Einbahnstraße [-n] one-way street

die Fahrschule [-n] driving school

die Fahrzeugpapiere *n pl* vehicle documents

der Führerschein [-e] driving-licence (**vor/zeigen** show)

der Fußgängerüberweg [-e] pedestrian crossing

die Garage [-n] garage (**die Tiefgarage** underground car-park)

die Gebühr/Straßengebühr [-en]; **die Maut** [-en] toll

die Geschwindigkeit [-en] speed (**das Tempolimit** [-s]; **die Geschwindigkeitsbeschränkung** [-en] speed limit; ***über'schreiten** exceed; break)

das Glatteis black ice

das Halteschild [-er] stop sign

die Hauptverkehrs-/Stoßzeit rush-hour

die Kreuzung [-en] crossroads

die Kurve [-n]; **die Biegung** [-en]; **die Windung** [-en] bend

der Mittelstreifen [-] central reservation

die Notbremsung [-en] emergency stop

die Notrufsäule [-n] emergency telephone point

die Panne [-n] breakdown (**die Reifenpanne** puncture; **eine Panne** ***haben** break down)

das Parkhaus [ˁer]; **die Hochgarage** [-n] multi-storey car-park

der Parkplatz [ˁe] car-park; parking-space

das Parkverbot ban on parking (**das Halteverbot** ban on stopping; **im Parkverbot** ***stehen** be parked illegally; **das Park-/**

Halteverbotsschild [-er] no-parking/no-stopping sign; **die Parkscheibe** [-n] parking-disc; **die Parkuhr** [-en] parking-meter)

die Querstraße [-n] junction; turning

der Rasthof [≃e] service area with motel

der Rastplatz [≃e] lay-by; rest area

die Raststätte [-n] service area

die Reiseroute [-n] route

die Reparaturwerkstatt [≃en] service garage (**der/die Mechaniker/in** [-/-nen] mechanic; **reparieren** repair)

die Ringstraße [-n] ring road

der Scheinwerfer [-] headlight (**ab|blenden** dip; **auf|blenden** switch to full beam; **mit Abblendlicht *fahren** drive on dipped headlights)

das Schlagloch [≃er] pot-hole

die Sichtweite visibility

die Spur [-en] lane (**die Stand-/Kriechspur** hard shoulder/crawler lane)

der Stau [pl -s or -e] traffic jam

die Steuerplakette [-n] tax disc

das Stoppschild [-er] stop sign

der Strafzettel [-] parking-/speeding-ticket

die Straße [-n] street; road (**die Hauptstraße** main road; **die Seiten-/Nebenstraße** side road)

die Straßenbauarbeiten f pl; [on sign] **Baustelle** f sing road-works

die Straßenkarte [-n] road-map

das Straßenschild [-er] road sign

die Straßenverkehrsordnung highway code

die Straßenwachthilfe recovery service

die Tankstelle [-n] petrol station (**der Tankwart** [-e] petrol pump attendant; **die (Zapf)säule** [-n] pump; **SB** [= **die Selbstbedienung**] self-service; **der Kraftstoff** fuel; **das Benzin** petrol; **das Super** four-star; **bleifrei** unleaded; **der Diesel** diesel; **das Öl** [-e] oil; **der Ölwechsel** oil-change; **die (Druck)luft** (compressed) air; **das Kühlwasser** radiator water; **das Gefrierschutz-/Frostschutzmittel** antifreeze; **kontrollieren** check)

die Überführung [-en]; **der Fly-over** [-s] fly-over

die Umgehungsstraße [-n] bypass

die Umleitung [-en] diversion
der Umweg [-e] detour
der Verkehr traffic (**der Durchgangs-/Gegenverkehr** through/oncoming traffic; **der Verkehrsunfall** [=e] traffic/road accident)
der Verkehrskreisel [-] roundabout
das Verkehrszeichen [-] road sign
die Vorfahrt no pl priority (**Vorfahrt *lassen** + D/***haben** give way to/have right of way; **Vorfahrt beachten!** give way!)
die Waschanlage [-n]; **die Waschstraße** [-n] car-wash
der Weg [-e] road; way (**unterwegs** on the way)
der Wegweiser [-] signpost
die Wende [-n] (**um 180°**) U-turn
die Zufahrtsstraße [-n] access road

erlaubt; gestattet permitted
gefährlich dangerous
gesperrt closed (**gesperrte Straße** road closed)
langsam slow
obligatorisch compulsory
verboten; untersagt prohibited

DIE LEUTE, DENEN MAN BEGEGNET
THE PEOPLE YOU MEET

der/die Anhalter/in [-/-nen]; **der/die Tramper/in** [-/-nen] hitch-hiker
der/die Autofahrer/in [-/-nen] motorist (**der/die Fahrer/in** driver)
der/die Chauffeur/in [-e/-nen] driver; chauffeur
der/die Fahrlehrer/in [-/-nen] driving instructor (**der/die Fahrschüler/in** [-/-nen] learner-driver)
der/die Fußgänger/in [-/-nen] pedestrian
der/die Kilometerfresser/in [-/-nen]; **der Verkehrsrowdy** [-s] road-hog
der/die Lkw-Fahrer/in [-/-nen] lorry driver
der Mechaniker [-] mechanic
der/die Mitfahrer/in [-/-nen] passenger
der/die Motorradfahrer/in [-/-nen] motor-cyclist

die Politesse [-n] traffic warden
der/die Polizist/in [-en/-nen] policeman/woman
der/die Radfahrer/in [-/-nen] cyclist
der/die Reisende *adj n* traveller
der/die Sonntagsfahrer/in [-/-nen] Sunday driver
der/die Verkehrspolizist/in [-en/-nen] traffic policeman/-woman

WAS MAN TUT WHAT YOU DO

*ab|biegen turn off
*ab|schließen lock
an|schalten switch on (**ab|schalten** switch off)
*an|schieben give a push
sich an|schnallen put on your seat belt
*an|springen start [of engine]
sich auf den Weg machen set off
*auf|fahren auf + A drive into the back of
auf|prallen auf + A collide with
be'schleunigen accelerate
bremsen brake
eine Panne *haben break down
sich ein|ordnen get in lane
*fahren in + A crash into
Gas *n* ***geben** put your foot down
*halten; *an|halten stop
*heiß|laufen run hot
hupen sound the horn
in Ordnung *f* ***bringen** fix
krachen crash
langsamer *fahren slow down
mieten hire
mit X Stundenkilometern *fahren drive at X kilometres an hour
motorisieren motorize
parken park
reparieren repair
rückwärts *fahren (in + A) reverse (into)
schalten change gear

schleppen; ab|schleppen tow
schleudern; schlittern skid
starten start (up); start the engine
*stehen|bleiben stall
stoppen stop
trampen; per Anhalter *fahren hitch-hike
über'holen overtake
über'prüfen check
über'queren cross
sich ver'irren get lost
voll|tanken fill up
warten service
wenden do a U-turn
*zusammen|fahren mit + D collide with

Andere Verkehrsmittel
Other means of transport

EISENBAHNEN RAILWAYS

die Abfahrt [-en] departure
die Ankunft [¨e] arrival
der Anschluß [¨sse] connection
die Anzeigetafel [-n] train indicator
die Auskunft information (office)
die Bahn railway; tram (mit der Bahn by rail; by tram)
der Bahndamm [¨e] (railway) embankment
der Bahnhof [¨e] station (auf dem Bahnhof at the station)
die Bahnhofsgaststätte [-n] station buffet
die Bahnhofshalle [-n] station concourse
der/die Bahnhofsvorsteher/in [-/-nen] station-master; station supervisor
der Bahnsteig [-e] platform (die Bahnsteigkarte [-n] platform ticket)
der Bahnübergang [¨e] level crossing
der Bahnwärter [-] signalman; level-crossing keeper (das Stellwerk [-e] signal-box)

die Brücke [-n] bridge

die Bundesbahn German Railways

der Einschnitt [-e] cutting

die Eisenbahn [-en] railway

der Eisenbahner [-] railwayman

die Fahrkarte [-n]; **der Fahrschein** [-e] ticket (**die einfache Fahrkarte** single; **die Rückfahrkarte** return; **die Wochen-/ Monatskarte** [-n] weekly/monthly season; **lösen** buy [ticket]; **zweimal einfach nach + D** two singles to . . . ; **nach + D** (**hin**) **und zurück** return to . . . ; (**un**)**gültig** (not) valid; **der Zuschlag** [-̈e] supplement; **zuschlagpflichtig** supplement payable; **zum halben Preis** half price)

der Fahrkartenautomat [-en] ticket machine

der/die Fahrkartenkontrolleur/in [-e/-nen] ticket collector; ticket inspector

der Fahrkartenschalter [-] ticket office

der Fahrplan [-̈e] timetable (**werktags** Monday to Saturday; **Sonn- und Feiertage** Sundays and public holidays; **über + A** via)

der Fahrpreis [-e] [price]; **das Fahrgeld** [money] fare (**der ermäßigte Fahrpreis** reduced rate)

der Fernverkehr main-line services (**der Vorortsverkehr** suburban services; **der Fern-/Vorortsbahnhof** main-line/suburban station)

das Fundbüro [-s] lost-property office

das Gepäck luggage (**die Gepäckaufbewahrung** left-luggage; **das Schließfach** [-̈er] left-luggage locker; **die Gepäckannahme** baggage check-in; **die Gepäckausgabe** baggage reclaim)

das Gleis [-e] track (**die Weiche** [-n] (set of) points; **die Schwelle** [-n] sleeper)

die Haltestelle [-n] stop

der Kofferkuli [-s] luggage trolley

die Reservierung [-en] reservation (**die Platzreservierung** seat-reservation (office))

die Richtung [-en] (**nach + D**) direction (of)

der Schaffner [-] guard; ticket inspector

der Schalter [-] ticket window

die Schiene [-n] rail

die Seilbahn/Drahtseilbahn [-en]; **die Schwebebahn [-en]** cable railway (**die Sesselbahn** chair-lift)

das Signal [-e] signal (**halt red**; **freie Fahrt** green)

die Sperre [-n] [on station]; **die Schranke** [of level crossing] barrier

die Strecke [-n] line; track (**das Streckennetz [-e]** network)

der Träger/Gepäckträger [-] porter

der Tunnel [-] tunnel

die Unterführung [-en] subway

die Verbindung [-en] connection

das/der Viadukt [-e] viaduct

der Wartesaal [-säle] waiting-room

der Zeitungsstand [¤e] news-stand

*ab|fahren depart [train]

*an|kommen arrive

*aus|steigen (aus + D) get out (of)

den Zug *nehmen take the train

einen Speisewagen führen have a dining-car

*ein|fahren pull in [to station]

*ein|steigen (in + A) get in(to)

ent'werten cancel; validate [ticket]

er'reichen catch

*halten stop

lochen; knipsen punch

mit dem Zug *fahren travel by train

reservieren *lassen reserve

*um|steigen change (trains)

ver'kehren run [of train etc.]

ver'passen miss [train etc.]

Verspätung *f* ***haben** be late

vom Bahnhof ab|holen meet at the station

zum Bahnhof *bringen take to the station

durchgehend through

planmäßig on schedule

pünktlich on time

verspätet late

LOKOMOTIVEN UND ZÜGE
ENGINES AND TRAINS

der Autoreisezug [≈e] motor-rail (train)

der EuroCity [-s] international fast train

der EuroCity-Express [*pl* -Expresszüge] international express

der Güterzug [≈e] goods train (**der Zug im Personenverkehr** passenger train)

der InterCity [-s] inter-city fast train

der InterCity-Express [*pl* -Expresszüge] inter-city express

die Lok [-s]; **die Lokomotive** [-n] engine (**der Lok(omotiv)führer** [-] engine-driver; **die Dampflok** steam engine; **der Dieseltriebwagen** [-] diesel locomotive)

die Standseilbahn [-en] funicular

der TEE [*pl* - or -s] [= **Trans-Europ-Express**] TEE

der Triebwagen [-] railcar

der Zug [≈e] train (**der Schnellzug** express; **der D-Zug** [= **Durchgangszug**] fast train; **der Eilzug** stopping train; **der Nahverkehrs-/Personenzug** slow train; local; **der Vorort(s)zug** suburban train; **der Zug mit Schiffsanschluß** boat-train)

IM ZUG IN THE TRAIN

das Abteil [-e] compartment (**das Dienstabteil** guard's compartment; **der Gang** [≈e] corridor)

der Dienstwagen [-] guard's van

das Gepäck luggage (**das Gepäcknetz** [-e] luggage rack)

der Güterwagen [-] goods wagon

die Klasse [-n] class (**erster/zweiter Klasse** first/second class)

der Kopf front (of train) (**das Ende** back)

der Kurswagen [-] through carriage

der Liegesitz [-e] couchette

die Notbremse [-n] emergency brake

der Platz [≈e] seat (**der Fensterplatz** window-seat; **reserviert** reserved)

der Schlafplatz [≈e] berth (**zurecht|machen** make up)

die Toilette [-n] toilet (**besetzt** occupied; **frei** vacant)

der Wagen carriage (**der (Nicht)raucherwagen** (non-)smoking carriage; **der Schlaf-/Liege-/Speisewagen** sleeping-/couchette-/dining-car; **der Gepäckwagen** luggage-van)

FLUGZEUGE PLANES

die Abfertigung check-in (**der Abfertigungsschalter** [-] check-in desk)

der Abflug [≃e] take-off

der Abstieg descent

die Ankunftshalle [-n] arrival lounge (**die Abflughalle** departure lounge; **die Ankunfts-/Abflugtafel** [-n] arrivals/departure board)

der Aufruf [-e] (boarding) call

die Besatzung [-en] crew

das Bodenpersonal ground staff

die Bordkarte [-n] boarding-card (**an Bord *gehen** board)

das Charterflugzeug [-e] charter aircraft (**chartern** charter)

der Duty-free-Shop [-s] duty-free shop (**zollfrei** duty-free)

das Fahrwerk landing-gear

der Fallschirm [-e] parachute

der Flug [≃e] flight; flying (**der Rück-/Charter-/Linien-/Direktflug** return/charter/scheduled/direct flight; **die Flugzeit** [-en] flying time)

der Flügel [-] wing

der Fluggast [≃e] passenger [male or female]

der Flughafen [≃] airport

die Flughöhe [-n] altitude (**in einer Flughöhe von** + D at an altitude of)

die Flugkarte [-n] ticket (**nicht termingebunden** open)

die Fluglinie [-n]; **die Fluggesellschaft** [-en] airline

der Fluglotse [-n] air-traffic controller (**die Flugsicherung** air traffic control)

der Flugplatz [≃e] airfield

der Flugpreis [-e] air fare

der Flugsteig [-e]; **das Gate** [-s] (boarding-)gate

das Flugzeug [-e]; **die Maschine** [-n] plane (**das Düsenflugzeug** jet plane; **der Jumbo-Jet** [-s] jumbo jet) der **Gangplatz** [≈e] aisle seat (**der Fensterplatz** window seat)

die **Geschwindigkeit** [-en] speed

das **Gepäck** baggage (**das Handgepäck** hand baggage; **die Gepäckausgabe** baggage claim)

der **Heißluftballon** [-s] hot-air balloon

der **Hijacker** [-] hijacker

die **Höhe** [-n] altitude

der **Hubschrauber** [-] helicopter

die **Kabine** [-n] cabin

der **Kontrollturm** [≈e] control tower

die **Landung** [-en] landing (**zur Landung an|setzen** come in to land; **die Landebahn** [-en] landing runway; **die Landebahnfeuer** *n pl* runway lights; **die Notlandung** emergency landing)

das **Luftkissenfahrzeug** [-e] hovercraft

die **Luftkrankheit** airsickness

das **Luftloch** [≈er] air pocket

der **Luftpirat** [-en] hijacker

das **Luftschiff** [-e] airship

die **Mannschaft** [-en] crew

der **Notausstieg** [-e] emergency exit

die **Paßkontrolle** passport check

der/die **Pilot/in** [-en/-nen] pilot

der **Propeller** [-] propeller

der **Radar** radar

die **Rakete** [-n] rocket (***ab|schießen** launch)

der **Raucherplatz** [≈e] smoking seat (**der Nichtraucherplatz** no-smoking seat)

das **Raumschiff** [-e] spaceship

die **Rollbahn** [-en] taxi-way

der **Rumpf** [≈e] fuselage

die **Schallmauer** sound barrier (***durch'brechen** go through)

die **Schalttafel** *sing* controls

das **Segelflugzeug** [-e] glider

der **Sicherheitsgurt** [-e] seat-belt (**an|legen** fasten)

der **Start** [-s] take-off (**beim Start** at take-off; **die Startbahn** [-en] take-off runway)

der **Steward** [-s] steward (**die Stewardeß** [-ssen] stewardess)

der/das Terminal/Air-Terminal [-s] air terminal
die Turbulenz turbulence
Überschall- supersonic
das UFO/Ufo [-s] [= unbekanntes fliegendes Objekt] UFO (**die fliegende Untertasse [-n]** flying saucer)
das Wasserflugzeug [-e] seaplane
der Windsack [ːe] windsock
der Zoll customs; duty (**der Zollbeamte [-n]/die Zollbeamtin [-nen]** customs officer; **der Paß [ːsse]** passport; **durch'suchen** search; **durch'leuchten** X-ray)
die Zwischenlandung [-en]; der Stopover [-s] stopover

ab|drehen turn
*ab|fliegen; starten take off
annulieren; stornieren cancel
sich an|schnallen fasten belts
be'stätigen confirm
ein|checken check in (**ab'fertigen** check [sb] in)
*fliegen fly
im Sturzflug *m* ***hinunter|gehen** nosedive
landen land (**im Bach landen** *colloq* ditch; **der Bach [ːe]** stream)
*über'fliegen fly over
um|buchen change [flights]
zwischen|landen stopover

SCHIFFE SHIPS

der Anker [-] anchor
der Anlegeplatz [ːe]; die Anlegestelle [-n] embarkation point
das Backbord port (**das Steuerbord** starboard; **nach Back-/Steuerbord** to port/starboard)
das Beiboot [-e] ship's boat
die Boje [-n] buoy
das Boot [-e] boat
die Boots-/Kreuzfahrt [-en] cruise (**die Flußfahrt** river cruise)
der Bug bow(s)
der Dampfer [-] steamer

das Deck [-s] deck (**an Deck** on deck; **das Bootsdeck** [-e] boat deck)

das Ding(h)i [-s] dinghy (**das Schlauchboot** [-e] inflatable dinghy)

das Dock [-s] dock

die Fähre [-n]; **das Fährboot** [-e] ferry (**die Autofähre** car ferry)

das Fahrgastschiff [-e] water-bus

die Flagge [-n] flag [on ship]

das Floß [ᵆe] raft

der Flugzeugträger [-] aircraft carrier

der Frachter [-]; **das Frachtschiff** [-e] freighter

die Gangway [-s] gangway

der Hafen [ᵆ] harbour; port (**die Hafenrundfahrt** [-en] trip around the harbour)

das Heck [pl -e or -s] stern

das Hovercraft [-s]; **das Luftkissenfahrzeug** [-e] hovercraft

die Jacht [-en] yacht

die Kabine [-n] cabin (**die Doppelkabine** two-berth cabin)

der Kahn; **der Fracht-/Lastkahn** [ᵆe] barge

der Kai [-s] quay(side)

das Kanu [-s]; **das Paddelboot** [-e] canoe

die Kommandobrücke [-n] bridge

die Landungsbrücke [-n] jetty

der Landungssteg [-e] landing-stage

das Lotsenboot [-e] pilot boat (**der Lotse** [-n] pilot)

der Mast [G -(e)s; pl -en or -e] mast

das Motorboot [-e] motor boat (**der Motor** [G -s pl -en] engine)

der Ozeandampfer [-]; **das Linienschiff** [-e]; **der (Ozean)liner** [-] liner

die Reling [pl -s or -e] rail(ing)

das Rettungsboot [-e] lifeboat (**der Rettungsring** [-e] lifebelt; **das Rettungsfloß** [ᵆe] life-raft)

das Ruder [-] rudder; helm; oar

das Ruderboot [-e] rowing-boat

das Schiff [-e] ship (**das Motorschiff** power vessel; **das Segelschiff** sailing-ship)

der Schiffsarzt [ᵆe] ship's doctor

der Schlepper [-] tug

der Schornstein [-e] funnel
die Schwimmweste [-n] life-jacket
der Seemann [*pl* -leute]; [navy] der Matrose [-n] seaman
das Segelboot [-e] sailing-boat (das Segel [-] sail)
der Tanker [-] tanker
das Tragflügelboot [-e] hydrofoil
das Tretboot [-e] pedalo
die Überfahrt [-en] crossing
das U-Boot [= Unterseeboot] [-e] submarine

an Bord *gehen embark (von Bord gehen disembark)
an|legen berth
*aus|laufen; in See *gehen put to sea
aus|schiffen put ashore
aus|setzen; zu Wasser *lassen launch
ein|docken dock
eine Bootsfahrt machen go boating
ein|schiffen take on board
gelöscht *werden unload [ship]
*laden load
mit dem Schiff *fahren (nach + D) sail (to)
paddeln canoe
rudern row
segeln sail [a sailing-boat]
über|setzen ferry across
vor Anker *m *gehen drop anchor (den Anker lichten weigh
  anchor)

BUSSE, STRASSEN- UND U-BAHN
BUSES, TRAMS, AND THE UNDERGROUND

die Bahn *colloq*/Straßenbahn [-en] tram
der Bus/Autobus [*pl* -busse] bus (der Reisebus coach; mit dem Bus
  *fahren go by bus)
der Busbahnhof [¨e] bus station
der Busfahrer [-] bus driver (der Straßenbahnfahrer tram driver)
die Bushaltestelle [-n] bus-stop (die Straßenbahnhaltestelle tram-
  stop; die Bedarfshaltestelle request stop)

die Dauer-/Zeitkarte [-n] season ticket (**die Monats-/Wochen-karte** monthly/weekly season; **die Netz-/Streifenkarte** rover/multiple ticket)

der Einstieg [-e] entrance (**der Ausstieg** exit)

die Endstation [-en] terminus

der Fahrgast [ˌe] passenger [male or female]

der Fahrschein [-e] ticket (**gültig bis** + A valid as far as/until; **der Nachtzuschlag [ˌe]** night-time supplement; **die Zone [-n]** zone)

der Fahrscheinautomat [-en] ticket machine

das Fahrscheinheft [-e] book of tickets

die Häufigkeit frequency

der/die Kontrolleur/in [-e/-nen] inspector

die Linie [-n] line (**die Richtung [-en]** direction; **in Richtung Flughafen** to the airport)

die Rolltreppe [-n] escalator

die S-Bahn [-en] [= **Stadt-Bahn**] local train/network

der/die Schaffner/in [-/-nen] conductor; inspector

der/die Schwarzfahrer/in [-/-nen] fare-dodger

der Sitzplatz [ˌe] seat (**der Stehplatz** standing place)

der Tarif [-e] (scale of) fares (**die Ermäßigung [-en]** reduction)

die Teilstrecke [-n]; die Zahlgrenze [-n] fare-stage

der Tunnel [pl - or **-s]** tunnel

die U-Bahn [-en] [= **Untergrundbahn**] underground; underground train

die U-Bahnstation [-en] underground station

die Verbindung [-en] connection

das Wartehäuschen [-] bus-shelter

*an|halten stop

ent'werten cancel; validate [ticket, in machine]

*schwarz|fahren travel without paying

ver'passen miss

vorne/hinten *sitzen sit at the front/back

TAXIS TAXIS

die Droschke [-n] cab (**die Pferdedroschke** horse-drawn cab)

der Fahrpreis [-e] fare

das Taxi [-s]; die Taxe [-n] taxi (**mit dem Taxi** by taxi)
der/die Taxifahrer/in [-/-nen] taxi-driver
die Taxifahrt [-en] taxi ride
der Taxistand [-e] taxi-rank
das Trinkgeld [-er] tip

*bringen zu + D take (sb) to
frei *sein be free (**besetzt *sein** be taken)
*nehmen take
*rufen call
warten wait

SEE ALSO: **Accidents; Directions; Holidays; Towns; War, Peace, and the Armed Services**

55. War, Peace, and the Armed Services
Krieg, Frieden und die Streit-kräfte

Krieg War

der Abzug [ᵉe] evacuation; withdrawal

der Angriff [-e] attack (**durch|führen** launch; **der Gegenangriff** counter-attack; **der Bombenangriff** bombing raid)

die Anwerbung enlistment

die Aufklärung; die Erkundung reconnaissance

die Belagerung [-en] siege

die Besatzung occupation

der Beschuß bombardment

die Blockade [-n] blockade

die Bombardierung [-en] bombing

die Burg [-en] castle (**die Zinne** [-n] battlement)

der Deserteur [-e]; **der/die Fahnenflüchtige** *adj n* deserter

die Disziplin discipline

die Ehre honour

die Eroberung [-en] conquest

die Fahne [-n] flag

der/die Feind/in [-e/-nen] enemy

der Feldzug [ᵉe] campaign

die Festung [-en] fortress

der Flüchtling [-e] refugee

die Folter [-n] torture

die Front [-en] front (**an die Front schicken** send to the front; **die Ostfront** the Eastern Front; **der Rücken** the rear)

das Gas [-e] gas (**das Tränen-/Giftgas** tear-/poison gas; **die Gasmaske** [-n] gas-mask)

der/die Gefangene *adj n* prisoner (**der/die Kriegsgefangene** prisoner of war; **das Gefangenenlager** [-] prisoner of war camp)

die Geisel [-n] [*always f*] hostage (***nehmen** take; **das Lösegeld** ransom)

die Grausamkeit cruelty

der/die Held/in [-en/-nen] hero (**das Heldentum** heroism; **die Heldentat** [-en] exploit)

die Invasion [-en] invasion

der Kampf [⸚e] combat; fight (**der Zweikampf** duel)

die Kapitulation capitulation; surrender

das Kommando [-s] command; commando

das Konzentrationslager [-]; **das KZ** [*pl -* or *-s*] concentration camp

der Krieg [-e] war (**der erste/zweite Weltkrieg** the First/Second World War; **Krieg führen/er\klären** make/declare war)

das Kriegsgericht [-e] court martial

das Kriegsmaterial munitions

der Luftangriff [-e] air raid

der Luftschutz air-raid precautions (**der Luftschutzwart** [-e] air-raid warden; **der Luftschutzbunker** [-]; **der Luftschutzraum** [⸚e] air-raid shelter; **der Atombunker** [-] nuclear shelter)

der Marsch [⸚e] march (**der Vorbeimarsch** march-past)

das Massaker [-] massacre

der Militärdienst military service (**ab\leisten** do)

die Mobilmachung mobilization

die Moral morale (**gut** high; **schlecht** low)

die Munition ammunition (**die Muni** ammo)

der Nachschub supplies

die NATO NATO

die Niederlage [-n] defeat

der Niederschlag [⸚e] fall-out (**radioaktiv** radioactive)

die Offensive [-n] offensive

das Opfer [-] victim; sacrifice

die Plünderung pillage

der Rückzug [⸚e] retreat (**den Rückzug *an\treten** beat a retreat)

der Ruhm fame; glory

das Scheitern failure

das Schießen; die Schießerei fire; firing (**unter Beschuß** *m* ***ge'raten** come under fire)

die Schlacht [-en] (bei/von + D) battle (of)

das Schlachtfeld [-er] battlefield

die Schußweite range (**in/außer Schußweite** within/out of range)

der Schützengraben [¨] trench

der Sieg [-e] victory (**den Sieg *davon|tragen** be victorious; **der/ die Sieger/in [-/-nen]** victor; **die Besiegten** *pl adj n* the conquered)

der/die Spion/in [-e/-nen] spy

der Stacheldraht barbed wire

die Strategie [-n] strategy

die Taktik [-en] tactic(s)

die Tarnung camouflage

der Tod [-e] death

der/die Verbündete *adj n* ally (**die Alliierten** the Allies)

das Verhör [-e] interrogation (**beim Verhör** under interrogation)

der/die Verräter/in [-/-nen] traitor (**das Exekutionskommando [-s]** firing-squad)

die Verstärkung *sing* reinforcements

der Wachtposten [-]; [group] die Wache [-n] guard (**Wache *haben** be on guard; **die Wache [-n]** [also] sentry)

der Widerstand resistance (**Widerstand leisten** resist)

die Wunde [-n] wound (**die Verwundeten** *pl adj n* the wounded)

der Zivilist [-en] civilian (**Zivil-** civilian *adj*)

*ab|schießen [plane]; ***nieder|schießen** [person] shoot down

*an|greifen attack

be'festigen fortify

be'waffnen arm

blockieren blockade

desertieren desert

Dienst *m* ***haben** be on duty

*ein|fallen in + A invade

*ein|nehmen [town]; ***fest|nehmen** [person] capture

*er'schießen shoot (dead)

er'sticken suffocate

explodieren explode
flüchten flee
kämpfen fight; give battle
kapitulieren capitulate; surrender
*****laden** load
*****leiden** suffer
marschieren march
massakrieren massacre
mobil machen mobilize
plündern pillage; plunder
scheitern fail
*****schießen** shoot
*****schlagen** beat
schützen protect
sprengen blow up
tarnen camouflage
torpedieren torpedo
töten kill
um'ringen surround
*****ver'brennen** burn
ver'folgen pursue
ver'gasen gas [kill by gassing] (**mit Gas vergiftet** gassed [on battlefield])
ver'sorgen mit + D provide with
ver'stärken reinforce
ver'teidigen defend
ver'wüsten lay waste
zer'stören destroy
zielen/an|legen auf + A aim at (**richten/anlegen/zielen auf** + A aim [weapon] at)
sich *zurück|ziehen retreat

blutig bloody
heroisch heroic
kriegerisch warlike
tödlich deadly
tot dead

unversehrt unscathed
vermißt missing
verwundet wounded
wehrlos defenceless

Frieden Peace

die Abrüstung disarmament (**die Atomabrüstung** nuclear disarmament)
die Durchsetzung enforcement
die Freiheit freedom
der Frieden [-] peace; peace settlement (**Frieden *schließen** make peace)
die Konferenz [-en] conference
die Menschenrechte *n pl* human rights
die Neutralität neutrality
der Pakt [-e] pact (***(ab)schließen** make; conclude)
der Pazifismus pacifism
die Reparationen *f pl* reparations
die Verhandlung [-en] negotiation
der Vertrag [ːe] treaty (**der Friedensvertrag** peace treaty)
die Waffenruhe [-n] (short) truce
der Waffenstillstand [ːe] truce; armistice

sich einigen über + A agree about
er'setzen compensate for
garantieren guarantee
ge'währen grant
ratifizieren ratify
***unter'schreiben** sign

Die Wehrmacht und die Luftwaffe
The army and the air force

Achtung! attention! (***still**|-/**stramm**|**stehen** stand to attention)
die Armee [-n] army; the armed forces (**die Bundeswehr** Federal Armed Forces; **die reguläre Armee** regular army)

die Artillerie artillery

die Beförderung promotion (**zum . . . befördert *werden** be promoted to the rank of . . .)

der Dienstgrad [-e]; der Rang [≈e] rank

das Feldlager [-] camp

der Feldposten [-] picket

das Hauptquartier [-e] headquarters

die Infanterie infantry

die Kantine [-n] mess; canteen (**das Kasino [-s]** officers' mess)

die Kaserne [-n] barracks (**der Kasernenhof [≈e]** barrack square)

die Kavallerie cavalry

das Kommando [-s] command; order (**der Befehl [-e]** written order; **be'fehligen** be in command of)

die Luftwaffe [-n] air force

der Luftwaffenstützpunkt [≈e] air base

das Manöver [-] manœuvre (**im Manöver *sein** be on manœuvres)

die Militärakademie [-n] military academy

die Militärkapelle [-n] military band

die motorisierten Streitkräfte motorized troops

die Patrouille [-n] patrol

der Pionier [-e] engineer (**die Pioniere** the engineers)

die Truppe [-n]; die Einheit [-en] unit (**die Truppen** the troops; **das Trüppchen [-]** detachment)

der Urlaub leave

die volle Stärke full strength

die Wachtstube [-n] guardroom

das Wecksignal [-e] reveille

ANGEHÖRIGE PERSONNEL

der Befehlshaber [-] commander (**der Oberbefehlshaber** Commander-in-Chief)

der/die Berufssoldat/in [-en/-nen] regular

der Brigadegeneral [pl -e or **≈e]; der Brigadier [-s]** brigadier/air commodore

der/die Einberufene adj n conscript

der Feldmarschall [≈e] field marshal/marshal of the air force

der Feldwebel [-] sergeant
der Gefreite *adj n* lance-corporal/aircraftman first class
der General [*pl* -e or ⁼e] general/air chief marshal
der Generalleutnant [-s] lieutenant-general/air marshal
der Generalmajor [-e] major-general/air vice-marshal
der Hauptfeldwebel [-] staff sergeant/flight sergeant
der Hauptgefreite *adj n* corporal/leading aircraftman
der Hauptmann [*pl* -leute] captain/flight lieutenant
der Kaplan [⁼e] chaplain
der Kommandant [-en] commandant
der Leutnant [-s] second lieutenant/pilot officer
der Oberleutnant [-s] lieutenant/flying officer
der Oberst [G -en or -s; *pl* -en or -e] colonel/group captain
der Oberstleutnant [-s] lieutenant-colonel/wing commander
der Offizier [-e] officer
der Major [-e] major/squadron leader
der Rekrut [-en] recruit
der/die Soldat/in [-en/-nen] soldier (**der einfache Soldat** private/
  aircraftman second class; **Soldat Schmidt** Private Schmidt/
  AC 2 Schmidt; **der Unbekannte Soldat** the Unknown Soldier)
der Träger [-] stretcher-bearer
der Unteroffizier [-e] non-commissioned officer; corporal

EINHEITEN UNITS

das Bataillon [-e] battalion
die Brigade [-n] brigade
die Division [-en] division
die Gruppe [-n] squadron (**die Schwadron** [-en] cavalry squadron)
die Kompanie [-n] company
das Korps [-] corps
das Regiment [*pl* -e or -er] regiment
die Staffel [-n] flight
der Trupp [-s] squad; detachment

KRIEGSGERÄT ARMAMENTS

das Bajonett [-e] bayonet (**auf|pflanzen** fix)

die Bombe [-n] bomb (**die Atom-/Brand-/Napalmbombe** atom/
incendiary/napalm bomb; **die H-Bombe** H-bomb; ***ab|werfen**
drop)

der Bomber [-] bomber (**das Ziel [-e]** target; ***treffen** hit)

die Flugabwehr anti-aircraft defence (**die Flak [-]** [= **Flugab-
wehrkanone**] anti-aircraft gun)

das Flugzeug [-e] aircraft (**das Kampf-/Aufklärungsflugzeug**
combat/reconnaissance aircraft)

das Gewehr [-e] gun; rifle

die Granate [-n] shell (**die Handgranate** hand-grenade)

die Haubitze [-n] howitzer

der Jäger [-] fighter (**der Jagdflieger [-]** fighter pilot; **der
Abfangjäger** interceptor aircraft)

der Kampfhubschrauber [-] helicopter gunship

die Kanone [-n] cannon

die Kugel [-n] bullet (**die Patrone [-n]** cartridge)

die Landmine [-n] land-mine

das Maschinengewehr [-e]; das MG [-s] machine-gun

der Minenwerfer [-]; der Mörser [-] mortar

der Panzer [-] tank (**der Panzerwagen [-]** armoured car; **die
Panzerfahrzeuge** *n pl* armour)

die Pistole [-n] pistol (**die Maschinenpistole** sub-machine-gun)

das/der Radar radar

die Rakete [-n]; das Missile [-s] rocket; missile

der Revolver [-] revolver

das Schwert [-er] sword (***ziehen** draw; **die Scheide [-n]** scabbard)

die Waffe [-n] weapon (**die Schnellfeuerwaffe** automatic weapon)

Die Kriegsmarine The navy

das Boot [-e] boat

der Geschützturm [⁼e] gun turret

die Hängematte [-n] hammock

der Kompaß [-e] compass

die Marine [-n]; die Flotte [-n] fleet (**die Kriegsmarine** navy; **der
Flottenstützpunkt [-e]** naval base; **die Marineschule [-n]** naval
academy; **die Marineuniform [-en]** naval uniform)

die Offiziersmesse [-n] wardroom

das Schiff [-e] ship (das Kriegsschiff warship)

der Torpedo [-s] torpedo

die Wache watch [-n] (der wachhabende Offizier [-e] officer of the watch)

ANGEHÖRIGE PERSONNEL

der Admiral [pl -e or ⸚e] admiral (der Konter-/Vize-/Großadmiral rear-admiral/vice-admiral/admiral of the fleet)

der Gefreite adj n able seaman

der Kapitän [-e] captain (der Korvettenkapitän; der Kapitänleutnant [-s] lieutenant-commander)

der Leutnant zur See sub-lieutenant

der Maat [G -s; pl -e or -en] mate; petty officer (der Obermaat chief petty officer)

der Marineflieger [-] naval airman

der Marineoffizier [-e] naval officer

der Marinesoldat [-en] marine

der Matrose [-n] seaman (der Leichtmatrose ordinary seaman)

der Oberleutnant zur See lieutenant

der Seeoffiziersanwärter [-] naval cadet

SCHIFFE SHIPS

das Flaggschiff [-e] flagship

der Flugzeugträger [-] aircraft-carrier

die Fregatte [-n] frigate

das Kanonenboot [-e] gunboat

die Korvette [-n] corvette

der Kreuzer [-] cruiser

der Minenleger [-] minelayer (das Minensuchboot [-e] minesweeper; die Mine [-n] mine)

das Patrouillenboot [-e] patrol boat

das Schlachtschiff [-e] battleship

das U-boot [= Unterseeboot] [-e] submarine

der Zerstörer [-] destroyer

SEE ALSO: **Accidents; History; Politics; Science; Transport**

56. The Weather Das Wetter

die Änderung [-en] change
die Atmosphäre atmosphere
das Barometer [-] barometer
die Besserung [-en] improvement
die Dürre [-n] drought (die Dürreperiode [-n] period of drought)
die Feuchtigkeit humidity (die Luftfeuchtigkeit atmospheric
  humidity)
der Himmel [-] sky (am Himmel in the sky)
die Kälte cold (bitter bitter)
das Klima [pl -s or Klimate] climate
die Luft [ːe] air (in der Luft in the air; der Luftdruck air pressure;
  der Luftzug [ːe] draught)
die Meteorologie meteorology
die Sichtweite visibility
die Temperatur [-en] temperature (die Höchst-/Tiefsttemperatur
  maximum/minimum temperature; das Thermometer [-] thermometer; der Grad [-e] degree; zwanzig Grad twenty degrees)
die Wärme; die Hitze heat
das Wetter weather (der Wetterbericht [-e] weather report; die
  Wettervorhersage [-n] weather forecast; laut Wettervorhersage
  according to the forecast)

Wie ist das Wetter? What's the weather like?

es ist . . .
  angenehm pleasant
  drückend oppressive
  eisig icy
  feucht damp
  frostig frosty
  gut good
  heiß hot
  heiter bright; fine

kalt cold
kühl cool
mies foul
mild mild
neb(e)lig foggy; misty
rauh harsh; raw
regnerisch rainy; wet
scheußlich ghastly
schlecht bad
schön nice; fine
schrecklich; furchtbar dreadful; terrible
schwül close
sonnig sunny
stickig stifling
stürmisch stormy
trocken dry
ungünstig heavy
veränderlich changeable
warm warm
windig windy
winterlich wintry

der Himmel ist . . .
  bedeckt overcast
  bewölkt; wolkig cloudy
  dunkel dark
  klar clear
  trüb dull

sich ändern change
sich auf|hellen brighten up
auf|hören stop
auf|klaren clear (up)
***aus|sehen nach** + D look like (**es sieht nach Sturm aus** it looks stormy)
sich bessern improve
blitzen flash [lightning]
donnern thunder

drohen threaten
dunkeln grow dark
*frieren freeze (**es wird Frost geben** it'll freeze)
*gießen pour
hageln hail
sich legen die down; blow over
nieseln drizzle
prasseln pelt down
regnen rain (**stark/Bindfäden** *m pl* **regnen** rain hard/cats and dogs [literally: *strings*]; **schütten/in Strömen** *m pl* ***gießen** pour with rain)
*scheinen shine
*schmelzen melt
schneien snow
stürmen blow a gale
tauen [get warmer]; **auf|tauen** [melt] thaw
sich ver'schlechtern get worse
vorher|sagen forecast
wehen blow [wind]

bei gutem/schlechtem Wetter in good/bad weather
bei Regen/Schnee/Kälte in the rain/in snow/in cold weather
im Schatten *m* in the shade
in der Sonne in the sun
in der Wärme in the warm

Wettererscheinungen Weather phenomena

die Aufheiterung [-en] bright period/interval
der Blitz [-e] (flash of) lightning (***(ein|)schlagen in** + A strike; **der Blitzableiter** [-] lightning-conductor)
die Bö(e) [*pl* **Böen**] squall
die Brise [-n] breeze
die Dämmerung; das Zwielicht twilight (**die Morgendämmerung** dawn; **die Abenddämmerung** dusk)
der Donner thunder (**der Donnerschlag** [¨e] clap of thunder)
der Dunst haze
das Eis ice (**das Glatteis** black ice; **der Eiszapfen** [-] icicle)

das Erdbeben [-] earthquake

die Flutwelle [-n] tidal wave

der Frost [ˑe] frost (**hart; streng** hard)

das Gewitter [-] thunderstorm

der Hagel hail (**das Hagelkorn** [ˑer] hailstone)

die Hitzwelle [-n] heatwave (**die Hundetage** *m pl* dog days)

die Lawine [-n] avalanche

das Mondlicht; der Mondschein moonlight (**der Mond** [-e] moon)

der Nebel fog; mist

der Niederschlag [ˑe] precipitation; shower

der Orkan [-e] hurricane

der Regen rain (**der Regentropfen** [-] raindrop; **der Platz-/ Schnee-/Niesel-/Dauerregen** cloudburst/sleet/drizzle/continuous rain; **der Regenbogen** [-] rainbow; **der Regenguß** [ˑsse] downpour)

der Reif/Rauhreif hoar frost (**bereift** frost-covered)

der Schatten [-] shade; shadow (**die Finsternis** darkness)

der Schauer [-] shower

der Schnee snow (**die Schneeflocke** [-n] snowflake; **der Schneefall** [ˑe] snowfall; **der Schneesturm** [ˑe] snowstorm; blizzard **das (Schnee)gestöber** [-]; **der Schneeschauer** [-] snow flurry; wintry shower; **der Papp-/Pulverschnee** sticky/powdery snow; **die Schneewehe** [-n] snowdrift; **der Schneematsch** slush; **der Schneeball** [ˑe] snowball; **der Schneemann** [ˑer] snowman)

der Smog smog

die Sonne [-n] sun (**der Sonnenschein** sunshine; **der Sonnenstrahl** [G -(e)s *pl* -en] ray of sunshine; sunbeam)

der Sonnenaufgang [ˑe] sunrise (**der Sonnenuntergang** sunset; **bei Sonnenaufgang/Sonnenuntergang** at sunrise/sunset; ***auf-/ *unter|gehen** rise/set)

der Staub dust (**die Staubwolke** [-n] cloud of dust)

das Sternenlicht starlight (**der Stern** [-e] star)

der Sturm [ˑe] storm; gale

der Tagesanbruch daybreak (**bei Tagesanbruch** at daybreak)

der Tau dew

das Tauwetter thaw

der Tornado [-s] tornado

die Überschwemmung [-en] flood

das Unwetter [-] violent storm; tempest

der Wind [-e] wind (**der Windstoß** [⁼e] gust of wind; **der Nord-/ Süd-/Ost-/Westwind** north/south/east/west wind)

der Wirbelwind [-e] whirlwind (**der Wirbelsturm** [⁼e] cyclone)

die Wolke [-n] cloud (**die Wolkenschicht** [-en] cloud layer; **der Wolkenbruch** [⁼e] cloudburst; downpour)

SEE ALSO: **Accidents; Clothing; Disasters; Holidays; Nature**